Chapter opening introduces topics to be discussed

Numbered headings identify chapter and section

Action headings show what to do.

Examples illustrate point being made.

Three of the most common problems with sentences are sentence fragments, comma splices, and run-on sentences. This chapter will suggest ways to avoid such problems.

10a Sentence Fragments

Incomplete sentences, or fragments, can distract readers and sometimes make you look like a careless writer. These suggestions will help you get rid of unwanted fragments.

• 10a-1 Check that you have not tried to make a dependent clause stand alone as a sentence. Dependent clauses—clauses that start with words such as *although, because, if, since, unless, when, while*—don't work as sentences by themselves even though they have a subject and a verb. Fragments can usually be fixed by linking them to another sentence.

Fragment: If the invoice comes by Friday

Sentence: If the invoice comes by Friday, the sale will go through.

Fragment: Although I have never seen their credentials

Sentence: Although I have never seen their credentials, they come well recommended.

• 10a-2 Check that you haven't made a relative clause or appositive stand alone as a sentence. Words such as *who, which, where,* and *that* often signal the beginning of a clause that must be attached to the main part of the sentence.

Roberto was the son of immigrants. ~~Who~~ who had never aspired to public office.

An appositive is a word or group of words that explains another noun or pronoun. An appositive that gets separated from the word it goes with can become a fragment.

Paragraph explains term.

Link ties boxed items to discussion.

Box highlights useful information.

Checklist: Subordinating Words

Whenever you write a clause that begins with a subordinating word, check for a fragment. Subordinating words include the following.

after	in order that	until
although	once	when
as	rather than	whenever
as soon as	since	where
because	so	whether
before	so that	which
even though	sooner than	while
for	that	who
how	though	whose
if	unless	why

Symbol identifies section of book.

Running foot shows chapter content.

How to Use This Handbook

Consult this index to locate the correct bibliography and parenthetical note forms for the following systems of scholarly documentation.

Modern Language Association (**MLA**)
Alliance for Computers and Writing (**ACW**)

Chicago Manual of Style Humanities-Notes (**CMS**)
American Psychological Association (**APA**)

MLA

Books/Dissertations

Articles and Magazine Pieces

Newspapers

Reference Works/Electronic Sources

Documentation Index

The Writing Process

 Style

 Grammar

 Punctuation and Mechanics

 Research and Writing

Designing Documents

Front Matter, Glossary

Gives practical advice to make composing easier

Alerts you to a potential trouble spot

What the Page Symbols Mean

[CoreText]

[**CoreText**]
a handbook for writers

Maxine Hairston
University of Texas at Austin

John J. Ruszkiewicz
University of Texas at Austin

Daniel E. Seward

LONGMAN

An Imprint of Addison Wesley Longman, Inc.

New York • Reading, Massachusetts • Menlo Park, California • Harlow, England
Don Mills, Ontario • Sydney • Mexico City • Madrid • Amsterdam

Publishing Partner: Anne Elizabeth Smith
Developmental Editor: Leslie Taggart
Supplements Editor: Lily Eng
Project Editor: Bob Ginsberg
Design Manager: Sandra Watanabe
Text and Cover Designer: Sandra Watanabe
Cover Photo: Tatsuhiko Sawada/Photonica
Art Studio: Academy ArtWorks, Inc
Production Manager: Valerie A. Sawyer
Desktop Administrator: Jim Sullivan
Manufacturing Manager: Helene G. Landers
Electronic Page Makeup: Carole Desnoes and Sandra Watanabe
Printer and Binder: RR Donnelley & Sons Company
Cover Printer: The Lehigh Press, Inc.

For permission to use copyrighted material, grateful acknowledgment is made to the copyright holders on pp. x-xi, which are hereby made part of this copyright page.

Library of Congress Cataloging-in-Publication Data

Hairston, Maxine.
CoreText : a handbook for writers / Maxine Hairston, John J.
   Ruszkiewicz, Daniel E. Seward.
   p. cm.
Based on the 4th ed. of The Scott, Foresman handbook for writers.
Includes index.
ISBN 0-673-98121-5 (alk. paper)
1. English language—Rhetoric—Handbooks, manuals, etc.
   2. English language—Grammar—Handbooks, manuals, etc.
   I. Ruszkiewicz, John J. date. II. Seward, Daniel E.
   III. Hairston, Maxine. Scott, Foresman handbook for writers.
IV. Title.
PE1408.H2963 1996   96-23003
808'.42—dc20   CIP

ISBN 0-673-98121-5
ISBN 0-673-97801-X CoreText Online (Windows)
ISBN 0-673-98535-0 CoreText Online (Macintosh)

12345678910—DOC—99989796

Dedication

To all the graduate instructors with whom we have worked and from whom we have learned so much over the past two decades. We admire your commitment, envy your creativity, and cherish your friendship.

M.H. and J.R.

credits

Illustrations:

p. 18: Copyright © by Bridgman/Art Resource, NY.

p. 273: Copyright © & ® 1994 Microsoft Corporation. All rights reserved.

pp. 277, 279: Copyright © Corel Corporation 1994.

Text:

Elijah Anderson. "The Code of the Streets." *The Atlantic Monthly*, May 1994, p. 81.

Natalie Angier. "Chasing Cheetahs." *The Beauty of the Beastly*. Boston: Houghton Mifflin, 1995, p. 157.

Natalie Angier. "Admirers of the Scorpion." *The Beauty of the Beastly*. Boston: Houghton Mifflin, 1995, p. 97.

Natalie Angier. "Please Say It Isn't So, Simba: The Noble Lion Can Be a Coward." *The New York Times*, September 5, 1995, p. B1.

Wendell Berry. "Conservation Is Good Work."*Sex, Economy, Freedom and Community*. New York: Pantheon Books, 1993, p. 27.

Robert Blake et al. *Theories of Scientific Method*. New York: Gordon and Breach Science Publishers, 1989, p. 22.

Dennis Bloodworth. *The Chinese Looking Glass*. New York: Farrar, Straus & Giroux, 1980, p. 155.

Robert H. Bork. "Give Me a Bowl of Texas." *Forbes*, September 1985, p. 184.

Ernest L. Boyer. "Creating the New American College." *The Chronicle of Higher Education*, 1994.

Robert Draper. "The Real Buddy Holly." *Texas Monthly*, October 1995, p. 108.

Nikki Giovanni. "Campus Racism, 101." *Racism 101*. New York: Morrow, 1994, p. 106.

Carey Goldberg. "The Simple Life Lures Refugees from Stress." *The New York Times*, September 21, 1995, p. B1.

Daniel Goleman. *Emotional Intelligence*. New York: Bantam Books, 1995, p. 28.

Stephen Jay Gould. "The Power of Narrative." *The Urchin in the Storm*. New York: Norton, 1987, p. 77.

Donald J. Grout. *A History of Western Music*. New York: Norton, 1980, p. 540.

Barry Hoberman. "Translating the Bible," as originally published in the February 1985 issue of *The Atlantic Monthly*, Vol. 255, No. 2. Copyright © 1985 Barry Hoberman. Reprinted by permission of the author.

Robert Hughes. *The Culture of Complaint*. New York: Oxford University Press, 1993, pp. 38–39, 74, 75.

Paul Johnson. *Intellectuals*. Harper & Row, 1988, p. 73.

Michiko Kakutani. "Egos and Outlaws: Like Attracts Like." *The New York Times*, September 29, 1995, p. B1.

Martin Luther King, Jr. "I Have a Dream." Reprinted in *The Riverside Reader*, 5th ed., eds. Joseph Trimmer and Maxine Hairston. Boston: Houghton Mifflin, 1996, p. 467.

Ted Kleine. "Living the Lansing Dream." *NEXT: Young American Writers on the New Generation.*, ed. Eric Liu. New York: Norton, 1994, p. 95.

David McCullough. *Truman*. New York: Touchstone Books, 1992, p. 324.

Lori S. McWilliams. "Acupuncture: Energy or Nerves?" Copyright © 1989 by Lori S. McWilliams. Reprinted by permission of the author.

Tom and Ray Magliozzi. "Inside the Engine." *Car Talk*. New York: Dell, 1991. Reprinted in *The Riverside Reader*, 5th ed., eds. Joseph Trimmer and Maxine Hairston. Boston: Houghton Mifflin, 1996.

Brock N. Meeks, "Fueling the Net Porn Hysteria." *Wired*, September 1995, p. 80.

From *MLA Style Manual*. Copyright © 1995 Modern Language Association of America. Reprinted by permission.

Nicholas Negroponte. "Get a Life?" *Wired*, September 1995, p. 206.

Kathleen Norris. "Status." *Dakota: A Spiritual Biography*. Boston: Ticknor and Fields, 1993, p. 136.

Sherwin B. Nuland. "Medical Fads: Bran, Midwives, and Leeches. *The New York Times*, June 25, 1995, p. E16.

Letty Cottin Pogrebin. *Among Friends*. New York: McGraw-Hill, 1987.

Richard Preston. *The Hot Zone*. New York: Random House, 1994, p. 34.

Thomas T. Samaras, "Let's Get Small."*Harper's*, January 1995, p. 32. Reprinted from *The Truth About Your Height: Exploring the Myths and Realities of Human Size and Its Effects on Performance, Health, Pollution, and Survival*. San Diego: Telecote Publications.

Chiori Santiago. "The Fine and Friendly Art of Luis Jimenez." *Smithsonian*, 1993.

Barbara Lang Stern. "Tears Can Be Crucial to Your Physical and Emotional Health." *Vogue*, June 1979, Condé Nast Publications.

William K. Stevens. "Prairie Dog Colonies Bolster Life in the Plains." *The New York Times*, July 11, 1995, p. B5.

Doug Stewart. "To Buy or Not to Buy, That Is the Question at *Consumer Report*." *Smithsonian*, September 1993, p. 35.

Scott Turow. "Doomed." *Austin American Statesman*, October 5, 1995, p. A15.

Brian Urquhart. *Ralph Bunche: An American Life*. New York: Norton, 1993, p. 435.

Rob van der Plas. *The Mountain Bike Book*. San Francisco: Bicycle Books, 1993, p. 106.

Robert Westbrook. *John Dewey and American Democracy*. Ithaca, NY: Cornell University Press, 1991, p. 30.

Ted Williams. "Only You Can Postpone Forest Fires." *Sierra*, July/August 1995, p. 42.

Gary Wills. *Lincoln at Gettysburg*. New York: Touchstone Books, 1992, p. 177.

William Julius Wilson. *The Truly Disadvantaged*. Chicago: University of Chicago Press, 1987, p. 156.

Daniel Yankelovitch. "The Work Ethic Is Underemployed." *Psychology Today*, May 1982, Ziff-Davis.

Cathy Young. "Keeping Women Weak." *NEXT*, ed. Eric Liu. New York: Norton, 1994, p. 218.

aids
at a glance

contents

[5] *Revising, Editing, and Proofreading 33*

[6] *Critical Thinking and Persuasive Writing 39*

II Style 45

[7] Language Choices 47

[8] Effective Sentences 55

[9] Stylish Sentences 63

III Grammar 71

[10] Sentence Fragments, Comma Splices, and Run-ons 73

[11] Modifiers 79

[20] Capitalization, Apostrophes, Abbreviations, and Numbers 143

[23] The Research Project 175

[24] MLA Documentation 189

[25] ACW Documentation 225

preface

CoreText is the first of a new generation of short handbooks conceived from the beginning as a work that would appear simultaneously in print and electronic versions. The authors and software designer worked closely together from the first to ensure that the two versions would be tightly linked and complementary.

CoreText has its origins in the fourth edition of *The Scott, Foresman Handbook for Writers*. It offers succinct but thorough answers to writers' questions about style, usage, and research strategies. As does the fourth edition, *CoreText* also offers up-to-date information essential for writers working in electronic environments. Specifically, it provides comprehensive information about doing research online; about documenting electronic sources; and about using the design capabilities of computers to produce attractive documents for today's visually minded and impatient readers. As always, we have worked to produce a readable and friendly book in which users can find information easily and quickly.

An Overview of CoreText

Part I, **The Writing Process,** begins with a discussion of the psychology of writing situations and ends with guidelines for thinking critically and writing persuasively.

Part II, **Style,** focuses on language, particularly on the choices writers can make to adapt their writing to an audience and to produce clear, graceful, and effective sentences.

Part III, **Grammar,** and Part IV, **Punctuation and Mechanics,** provide brief yet comprehensive coverage of all those nuts-and-bolts matters that writers need to check when revising and editing their work.

Part V, **Research and Writing,** covers writing a research paper from start to finish. This comprehensive section benefits from the cycles of refinement and attention to detail that culminated in the research section of the fourth edition of *The Scott, Foresman Handbook for Writers*. Part V includes a special section on navigating electronic resources and provides guidelines for four standards of documentation, those of the Modern Language Association (MLA), the Alliance for Computers and Writing (ACW), *The Chicago Manual of Style* (CMS), and the American Psychological Association (APA).

Part VI, **Producing Handsome Documents,** brings a new dimension to the short handbook. It discusses document design, including guidelines for layouts and for the selection of typefaces. It also provides models of eight kinds of documents, including the newsletters and brochures that many students find relevant to their work or avocations.

What's Special in This Book?

- An innovative, four-color design that brings the book fully into the electronic information age and enhances its appeal to writers. The design itself exemplifies current theories of graphic design.
- A fresh format that displays checklists, tips, and summaries in easy-to-find boxes and presents information in accessible lists.
- A section on critical thinking and persuasion.
- A style section that advises students about how to avoid biased language and how to craft and polish sentences.
- A chapter covering key issues for ESL writers.
- A complete chapter on document design that includes but goes beyond traditional academic papers. A second chapter provides colorful models for slide presentations, newsletters, brochures, e-mail, and even World Wide Web pages.
- A strong and comprehensive research section with up-to-date information about using and documenting electronic resources.
- Thorough documentation guides for four systems: MLA, ACW, CMS, and APA.
- The inside covers and pages i to iv feature these aids: (1) an index for all four documentation standards, (2) a key word index that allows writers to find help quickly, (3) a revision guide, and (4) a model page showing how to use the handbook.
- A comprehensive index.

Finally, as we have done through four editions of *The Scott, Foresman Handbook for Writers,* we have designed *CoreText* as a highly accessible, do-it-yourself manual that will help students become confident and competent writers who can work with each other to solve problems and produce writing attuned to an electronic age.

Indeed, *CoreText* is likely the first writing handbook designed as a product for both conventional and electronic environments. Its software version—known as *CoreText Online* and available in both Windows and Macintosh versions—contains all the material in the conventional book, as well as a "drag and drop" portfolio feature which includes exercises, worksheets, and templates; it can be linked to *The Scott, Foresman Handbook's Rhetoric Online* (1996) to provide a complete writing course. More than just a book transferred to the screen, *CoreText Online* takes advantage of its electronic interface to present conventional material in innovative ways. *CoreText Online* is, of course, easy to use, fully compatible with major word processors, and cross-referenced via hypertextual links. Since the architecture of *CoreText Online* so greatly influenced the contents, organization, and look of the entire *CoreText* project, software designer Daniel E. Seward is listed as a co-author. We believe this is an important precedent, reflecting the way textbooks will be written in the future.

Acknowledgments

We thank the fine editorial team at Addison Wesley Longman, which has worked closely with us to bring this new kind of handbook to completion. We owe special thanks to Anne Smith, who initiated the project and enthusiastically encouraged us while we wrote it, and we thank Marcus Boggs for believing in the project and supporting it. We also thank our developmental editor, Leslie Taggart, for her commitment to the book and for working so closely with us to refine and strengthen the manuscript. We are grateful to Patricia Rossi for giving us the benefit of her handbook experience, and once more we appreciate Bob Ginsberg's meticulous and patient supervision of the production process. We are also grateful to Sean Casey for helping to develop *CoreText Online*.

We give special thanks to Sandra Watanabe for creating *CoreText*'s distinctive design. David Cooper also deserves thanks for giving his expert advice on the chapter on English as a Second Language and for his good disposition and patience.

For helping us to improve this first edition of *CoreText,* we would like to thank the following instructors: Bret Benjamin, University of Texas at Austin; Susan-Marie Birkenstock, University of Florida at Gainesville; Ed Block, Marquette University; Robert Canter, Virginia Technological University; Adam Collins, Grambling State University; Dan Damerville, Tallahassee Community College; Joanne Gates, Jacksonville State University; Julia Gergits, Youngstown State University; Jan Hall, Louisiana Technical University; Regan Hicks-Goldstein, Delaware Technical and Community College; Michael Hogan, Southeast Missouri State University; Michael Keller, South Dakota State University; Judith Kohl, Dutchess Community College; Douglas Krienke, Sam Houston State University; Susan Lang, Southern Illinois University; Sarah Liggett, Louisiana State University; Anne Maxham-Kastrinos, Washington State University; Alan Merickel, Tallahassee Community College; Alexis Nelson, Spokane Falls Community College; Jane Peterson, Richland College; Ed Reynolds, Spokane Falls Community College; William Testerman, Castleton State College; Janet Wingeroth, Spokane Falls Community College Library; and Mark Withrow, Columbia College.

MAXINE HAIRSTON
JOHN J. RUSZKIEWICZ

[CoreText]

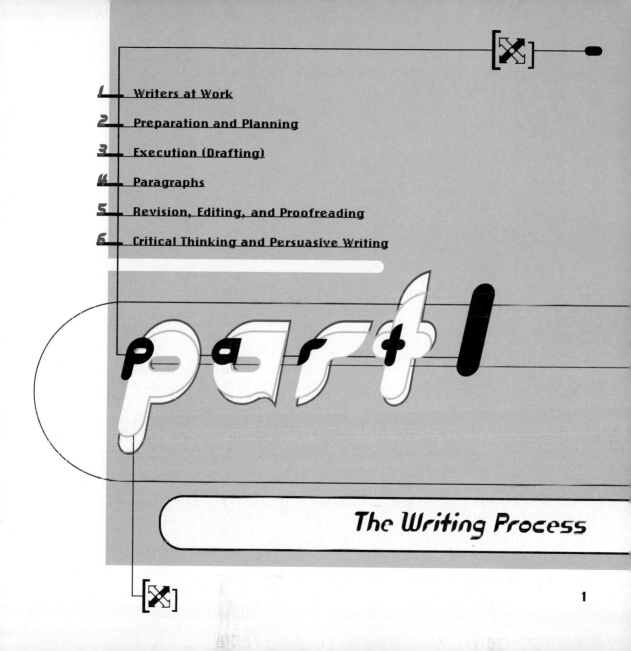

part 1

The Writing Process

1

chapter [1]

Writers at Work

*M*any people feel intimidated at the prospect of writing because they think it's some mysterious activity at which only a few people can succeed. It's not. Writing is a craft that can be learned by almost any literate person willing to invest time and energy.

1a Myths About Good Writers

It may bolster your confidence to look at some myths about good writers. ¶ When you're feeling unsure about beginning a new piece of writing, you might review these myths to help you start. You'll realize you're more capable than you might have thought.

1b The Process of Writing

In the past decade, researchers have learned a lot about how people write. We know there's no one process; nevertheless, writers, like other craftspeople, seem to go through distinct stages in producing their work. For writers these stages include preparation, planning, execution (drafting), incubation, revision, and editing and proofreading. ¶ We say more about all these operations in the next chapters.

1c The Writing Situation

Every time you write anything other than a personal journal, you're engaged in a writing situation that involves other people; that is, you're writing to

- Say *something*
- To *somebody*
- For *some purpose*

It's a good idea to begin every writing task by asking yourself this question:

What do I want to say to *whom* and *why?*

Probably no other single habit will do more to help you become an effective writer than learning to think about each writing situation in these terms. We even recommend that when you start an especially important piece of writing, you write out the answers to these prompts: *What? To Whom? Why?*

Don't underestimate your ability to write something other people will enjoy reading. If you choose a topic that you know well or care about—even something as simple as observations about people on the subway or in the grocery store—other people are likely to find your essay worth reading.

Writers don't always have a choice about their topic or their audience. Even when this is the case, working through the suggestions that follow in Sections 1c-1 through 1c-3 will help you clarify what you're writing about and why.

Myths About Good Writers

Myth: Good writers are born, not made. They're inspired.

Fact: Good writers develop through study and practice.

Myth: Good writers work in isolation.

Fact: Good writers often work with others.

Myth: Good writers know in advance what they're going to say.

Fact: Many good writers generate their ideas as they work.

Myth: Good writers always outline before they write.

Fact: Some good writers outline; others don't.

Myth: Good writers get it right the first time.

Fact: Most good writers write several drafts.

Myth: Good writers have to know all the rules of grammar in order to write.

Fact: Knowing the rules of grammar won't make anyone a good writer, but learning the conventions is important.

Myth: Good writers have found the correct way to write.

Fact: Good writers have different ways of writing; there is no "correct" way.

CAUTION

Our analysis of the Stages of Writing below makes composing seem more linear than it typically is. In reality, it's often a messy process that involves moving back and forth among the various stages.

Stages of Writing

- *Preparation.* You read and do research about your topic and talk to others to generate ideas.
- *Planning.* You take notes, develop points, and organize material you're going to use.
- *Execution.* You start writing. You may write one or more drafts, perhaps rethinking your goals and strategies as you work.
- *Incubation.* You relax or switch your attention to something else while your subconscious "cooks" and solves problems.
- *Revision.* You reread what you've written and revise it, perhaps two or three times.
- *Editing and proofreading.* You edit to polish your revised draft. Finally, you proofread to correct spelling, typos, and mechanical errors.

• 1c-1 Decide what you're going to write about. Examine your tentative topic and decide whether it has enough potential to warrant your time and your readers' time. Is the topic important? Definitely. For both economic and environmental reasons, car-buying trends in the United States are worth thinking and writing about. The topic is also likely to generate interest since most Americans like cars and enjoy reading about new automotive trends.

• 1c-2 Decide for whom you want to write. Can you identify an audience that wants or needs to know more about the topic? Are these readers worth trying to reach? Yes. They want to be informed about car-buying trends, and their responses to what you write may influence those trends.

• 1c-3 Decide why you want to write. What do you want to accomplish? Is this a useful purpose? Yes. Such a change in car buyers' priorities is important because it affects the environment and could also affect oil imports.

These preliminary analyses leave many questions unanswered, but you have a good start on your plan and can begin to work on a draft.

The summary raises many questions, and you'll certainly need to narrow your focus as you work, but you have a good start on your paper.

1d Audience

To write an effective paper or report, you have to know for whom you are writing, what they already know, and what interests them. A checklist can help. Making such an analysis is only a start, of course. As you work, you need constantly to remind yourself—*Think about the audience!* If you can develop that habit and practice it consistently, you're on your way to becoming a successful writer!

 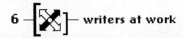

1e Purpose

When you're planning a paper, think in advance about your specific goals. Whom do you want to do what? If you can't answer that question in some detail, you may need to clarify your purpose by working through the purpose checklist below. Remember too that purpose and audience are always tightly interrelated. For example, if you're writing an article for your church newsletter in which you ask members to contribute money for new playground equipment for the church school, you need to write to those groups in the church that are most likely to respond to your request and consider what kinds of arguments and appeals they will find effective. ●

Summary: *Your Writing Situation*

I want to convince my readers that the surge in the sales of sport utility vehicles and minivans in the last ten years has significant implications.

TIP Use the audience and purpose checklists below as prompts for writing rather than as fill-in-the-blanks lists. By doing so, you can generate substantial material that will help you develop an essay.

Checklist: *Purpose*

✔ What kind of paper am I writing? Do I want to inform, entertain, persuade, provoke thought, or stimulate action? (You may have more than one goal.)
✔ How do I want my audience to respond? Rationally? Emotionally? Both?
✔ What change, if any, do I want to bring about in my readers? Do I want to change their opinions? Do I want them to take action? Do I want simply to enlighten them?
✔ How might I achieve my purpose?

Checklist: *Audience*

✔ Who is my audience? Is it a small, specific group or a more generalized one?
✔ What are members of this audience interested in? What is important to them? How much do they already know about my topic? What new information do they need?
✔ What questions about my topic will they have?
✔ What kinds of evidence and examples should I provide? What details will they want?
✔ Where might this article be published? In what specific newspaper, magazine, or letter might it appear?

7

chapter [2]

Preparation and Planning

*W*riters vary greatly in the amount of planning they usually do. Writing projects differ, too. Some require considerable preparation and planning; others can be carried out with only a modest amount of preliminary work. Most writers, however, find that they have to plan before they write. This chapter explores the different stages of such preparation and planning.

2a Topics

Sometimes you're given a writing assignment or project. When that happens, suggestions in this chapter and the next will help you to focus, organize, and develop it. At other times you're able to choose your own topic. When that's the case, the strategies in this section will help you select a topic you enjoy and work with it successfully.

• **2a-1 Assess your interests.** Ask yourself these questions.

• What subjects do I read and talk about most?
• What are my strengths? What do I know a good deal about?
• What would I like to learn more about?

Put your answers into a list. For example, such a list might include the following interests.

Fly-fishing
Prehistoric art
Urban blight
Chinese art
Moorish architecture
Russian history
Women's suffrage

You'd probably decide quickly that urban blight, Chinese art, and Russian history are too ambitious for one paper.

• **2a-2 Brainstorm.** Choose something from your list that you think you'd enjoy writing about and that's limited enough to be doable. Start spinning off ideas, making notes as you go. For instance, you might have recently seen an article on unusual paintings in a newly discovered cave in southeastern France. If that sparks your interest in prehistoric art and you choose it as a subject, a brainstorming session could generate material such as this.

animal figures	famous caves—Altamira, Lascaux
handprints, symbols	recent discovery of Chauvet cave
details of paintings	locations—Europe vs. Southwest U.S.
theories about origins	age of paintings

The key to brainstorming is to put down everything you think of—there's no right and wrong.

• **2a-3 Freewrite.** Choose two items from the list that you brainstormed, and freewrite on each

one for fifteen or twenty minutes. When you freewrite, put down every thought on your topic that comes to you without trying to organize or screen your ideas. Don't stop to correct anything. Just allow associations to flow. Think of the process as harvesting ideas off the top of your head so more will surface.

• 2a-4 Get ideas from other writers.

Work in a group with other writers so you can talk over your topic and ask for information or ideas. Often someone will know about a resource you can use or will raise a question that will take you in the right direction.

• 2a-5 Use computer assists.

If you have access to a computer invention program such as Writer's Workshop, use its questions and prompts to generate material on your subject. You can also use a computer search program such as Proquest or Enigma in your library, getting help from the staff if necessary. Make a key word search in a library catalog to find out what's available. You can also explore topics on the Internet. For example, you might find a Usenet group or a World Wide Web page on the topic so you could communicate with others interested in your topic. (See Chapter 22 for more information on electronic sources.)

• 2a-6 Browse and read.

Look through books in the appropriate section of the library or the local bookstore, and check out the specialized magazines you'll find in most large bookstores. For example, if you chose the prehistoric art topic, you could check out some archaeology magazines.

Summary: *Preparation*

Assess your interests.
Brainstorm.
Freewrite.
Get ideas from other writers.
Use computer assists.
Browse and read.

2b Focus

Even experienced writers often start with a topic that's too broad. They have to narrow it substantially to produce a piece of writing that's specific enough to interest readers.

Think about narrowing your topic in the same way you might focus down a beam of light to concentrate it on one small area so you could see particular details. It's those details that interest your readers. For example, if you write about the pros and cons of affirmative action in general, you're not likely to engage many readers. But if you write about some of the specific effects of a 1996 Supreme Court decision involving the University of Texas, you'll catch their attention.

or *Periodicals Abstract*. If your topic were prehistoric art, you could look in the *Art Index* or the *Humanities Index*. (For more information, see Sections 22b and 22c.)

• 2b-1 Start by "treeing down" your topic into its components.

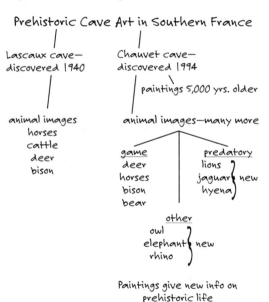

Prehistoric Cave Art in Southern France

Lascaux cave— discovered 1940

Chauvet cave— discovered 1994

paintings 5,000 yrs. older

animal images
horses
cattle
deer
bison

animal images—many more

game
deer
horses
bison
bear

predatory
lions
jaguar } new
hyena

other
owl
elephant } new
rhino

Paintings give new info on prehistoric life

• 2b-2 Look up your topic in an index related to the field you're researching.

For instance, check one of the multidisciplinary indexes in your library, such as the *Academic Index*

2c Thesis Sentences

While not all experienced writers construct thesis sentences when they begin writing, drafting a tentative thesis when you begin can provide focus and give you a solid base from which to work.

• 2c-1 Make a strong point.

A good thesis sentence is more than a statement; it's an assertion that sparks interest.

Weak Thesis: The prehistoric wall paintings in the newly discovered Chauvet cave in southeastern France raise intriguing questions.

Strong Thesis: Archaeologists are calling the wall paintings in the newly discovered Chauvet cave in southeastern France a prehistoric bombshell; the paintings surprise not only because they are executed with a beauty and precision not seen in later cave art, but also because they show a Stone Age that is different from the one we have previously understood, one in which ferocious and predatory animals far outnumber game animals.

The first thesis is vague; the second is specific and previews an entire paper.

• 2c-2 Position the thesis sentence early in your paper, and be sure it forecasts the content. A thesis sentence doesn't have to be the opening sentence, but usually readers of academic papers expect it to be in the first paragraph. For other types of essays, particularly arguments, you have more leeway in working up to the thesis. (For more information about shaping a thesis, see Section 23a.)

2d Organization

While not everyone wants to work from an outline, you do need a plan. There are several possibilities.

• 2d-1 Use a straightforward introduction/body/conclusion pattern. Compose an introductory paragraph based on your thesis sentence, follow it with evidence and explanations, and close with a summary paragraph. This is similar to the claim-and-support pattern discussed in Section 6b-2.

• 2d-2 Choose one of the common patterns of development. (For more on how to develop these patterns, see the examples in Section 4b.)

• 2d-3 Use an evidence/conclusion pattern. Present your findings in a series of paragraphs, and draw a concluding inference. (For more on this pattern, see Section 6b-1.)

2e Outlines

Writers who like to work from outlines have several options.

• 2e-1 Make a working list. Start by jotting down key points, leaving lots of space after each. As you think of specific subpoints and examples, enter them under the main points.

• 2e-2 Create a scratch outline. Begin with a tentative thesis sentence. Decide on three or four major points you want to make, and write them

down as brief sentences rather than single words. Jot down some specific points under the sentences. If you use the outlining tool on a computer, the process is easy and convenient.

• 2e-3 Make a formal sentence outline. Some professionals recommend a formal, or full, sentence outline because they believe it forces the writer to think a topic through before starting to write. In such an outline, statements are expressed in parallel sentences, with points and subpoints broken out and carefully arranged. Here's an example. •

2f Titles

Titles are important. A good title reflects the commitment the writer makes to his or her readers and gives readers a strong signal of what to expect.

• 2f-1 Work with a tentative title. Choosing a working title early in the drafting

13

Thesis: Experts regard recently discovered wall paintings in the Chauvet cave as significant because the paintings revise the history of European art and reveal a surprising natural environment.

I. Chauvet cave art revises the history of early European art.

   A. Chauvet art is bolder than later work at Lascaux.

      1. Chauvet paintings are 30,000 years old.

      2. Paintings at Lascaux are 14,000 years old.

   B. Chauvet drawings show greater depth and perspective.

II. Chauvet art reveals a surprising natural environment.

   A. Chauvet includes more images than later sites.

   B. Chauvet shows animals not previously seen in Europe.

      1. Cave art shows rhinos, elephants, owls.

      2. Art includes an unknown human/bison figure.

   C. Chauvet portrays different types of animals.

      1. At Chauvet, predatory animals dominate.

      2. At Lascaux, game animals are featured.

• **2f-2 Keep your readers in mind.** Include some details to catch your readers' interest. For example, "Ancient Cave Drawings of Southeastern France" is clear but ordinary. In contrast, "The Glorious Cave Art of an Ancient People" suggests an interesting story.

• **2f-3 Make sure your title accurately reflects the content of your paper.** A title should catch the eye of someone interested in the subject. It should also include key words that identify the topic for anyone making a computer search. In the revised title above, *cave art* and *ancient* would lead a researcher to your article.

Titles are surprisingly important. Readers want and expect them; in fact, readers are annoyed when a title doesn't give them a good signal about what to anticipate.

process helps you focus your writing. After you've polished the final piece to your satisfaction, you can revise your title if you need to do so. For now, it should serve as a guide.

chapter [3]

Execution [Drafting]

*A*n important writing assignment may bring on a touch of panic, especially if you are a perfectionist. Such anxiety is normal, but don't let panic become paralysis. Take a deep breath and say, "I'm writing a draft; it doesn't have to be perfect." Then get started.

3a Getting Started

Even professional writers agree that getting those first words down on paper may be the hardest part of any writing project. So recognize that if you have trouble getting started, it's not because you're a bad writer or because you don't have anything to say. You just need to break through the inertia barrier and begin writing. This section offers suggestions on ways to do that.

• 3a-1 Choose a place to write, and get organized. Find a spot away from distractions. Then gather your tools (computer materials, a tablet for notes, pencils, books, and so on), and adjust your chair and light. Try to establish a writing place that you use every time you work on a paper.

• 3a-2 Don't agonize over your opening. That first paragraph is tough to get down, no doubt about it. But you can waste a big chunk of your available working time trying to get it right when there really isn't any "right." If you don't like your opening, lower your standards and go on. You can revise it later.

• 3a-3 Don't criticize your work as you go along. Telling yourself "I hate this" or "This is awful" makes you feel bad and accomplishes nothing. Congratulate yourself that you've made a start.

• 3a-4 Avoid editing your writing prematurely. In an early draft, don't stop to correct your grammar and polish your sentence structure. That's for the editing stage, and if you bog down in such details too early, you may lose momentum in getting ideas down on paper.

• 3a-5 Create incentives to keep yourself working. If you're a procrastinator (and who isn't at times?), make a deal with yourself. For example, vow that you won't leave the house until you get two pages written, or promise yourself a movie if you finish the first draft by 5:00.

• 3a-6 Draft on a computer when you can. Most writers work faster and write more easily when they use a computer because it's so easy to make changes and try different versions.

3b Developing a Draft

As you write your first draft, refer back to your preparatory notes or scratch outline, check your plan of organization, and identify your audience, at least tentatively.

• 3b-1 Decide whether you're writing a discovery draft that's primarily for yourself or a solid first draft in which you keep audience and purpose in mind. A discovery draft can help you generate ideas, but it requires two or three revisions.

• 3b-2 Write according to a plan of organization. You can develop your main idea by telling stories, by laying out a cause-and-effect argument, by making comparisons, or by using some other method or a combination of methods. Try looking at your topic from a variety of perspectives, such as the following.

- Description
- Cause and effect
- Process
- Classification
- Definition
- Narration
- Comparison and contrast
- Persuasion

If your topic were cave paintings, description, narration, and comparison would be good possibilities. (For more on using these patterns, see Section 4b.)

• 3b-3 Use a journalist's questions.

Who?	Why?
What?	When?
Where?	How?

You could phrase these into one provocative question: *Who* is (or was) doing *what* to *whom, when, where, why,* and *how?*

• 3b-4 Read. Once you have chosen your topic, go back to the library, either on foot or via modem. If your topic were cave paintings, you could look for archaeology magazines or do a key word search with terms such as *prehistoric art, cave paintings,* or *Chauvet cave.* See whether there's a Usenet group on your topic on the Internet.

• 3b-5 Keep track of new ideas as they surface. Because writing often acts as a stimulus that generates new ideas, be sure to take notes and capture the ideas for future use. If you're working on a computer, you can use the annotation feature of your program or just start a separate file for notes.

• 3b-6 Keep your audience in mind as you work. Unless you're writing a discovery draft and haven't yet decided on your audience, keep checking with yourself: "Is this what my audience wants and needs to know?"

• 3b-7 Develop your points with specific examples. In writing, as with other crafts, good work comes from attention to details. Look for anecdotes, pictures, or graphs you could use to

3c Taking a Break

When you're working on a writing project, it's important to take a break for incubation, a period when you stop and let your subconscious cook for a while. Such periods are productive for most writers, particularly when they seem to be stuck.

• **3c-1 Plan to take both short and long incubation periods.** When you're stuck for a phrase or an example, get up and get a snack or run a short errand. A solution may surface while you're away from your desk. Also take longer breaks between drafts—several hours will give your subconscious time to work on what you've written.

• **3c-2 Don't allow incubation periods to turn into procrastination.** Downtime is important, but if your brain continues to stall, get back to work anyway. Reread what you've done, and just start writing. Something will come.

3d Evaluating a Draft

How do you know when you have a satisfactory first draft, one that reflects a good faith effort on your part? When you can answer "Yes" to the following three questions, you probably have a draft that's good enough to let others look at and to start revising.

Paintings at Lascaux cave

strengthen your paper. Here's an illustration from *Encarta* encyclopedia that could be used to enhance a paper on cave art.

• **3b-8 Allow time to write a strong conclusion.** Because your conclusion is what readers are most likely to remember, don't neglect it in a last-minute rush. (See Section 4f for details on how to write closing paragraphs.)

- **3d-1 Does the draft reflect a substantial investment of time and effort?** A solid first draft should have a clear main idea, relevant supporting examples, an organization that can be followed, and a clear conclusion. Don't expect other writers, an instructor, or a supervisor to spend time responding to a sketchy effort.

- **3d-2 Is the draft fairly complete?** A solid first draft should have an introduction, a body that develops several points, and at least a tentative conclusion. An outline with a few paragraphs doesn't qualify; neither does a polished opening followed by a description of what will follow. Even a discovery draft should explore the topic fully, although it does not have to do so in a well-organized way.

- **3d-3 Is the draft readable?** Whether you're showing your draft to an instructor, a boss, or a group of other writers, be sure all copies are neat and dark enough to read. You probably shouldn't ask anyone outside your family to read a handwritten draft.

3e Working Collaboratively

When you've finished a solid first draft, if possible you should get some outside response to it before you begin to revise. Fortunately, both in classes and in business, it's common these days for writers to work on drafts collaboratively. Keep in mind, however, that neither giving nor receiving comments on drafts is easy; writers have to remain open-minded and objective and try to work together.

- **3e-1 Read the draft straight through once.** Do you understand everything? What is your first response? Make a note of it.

- **3e-2 Read the draft a second time.** Working with the checklist at the end of this section, write down your responses. Note strong points and specific examples that work well, and also indicate where the draft needs more development. Focus more on broad issues than on specific problems, which can be corrected later during the editing process.

- **3e-3 Keep your comments on someone else's writing constructive.** Make suggestions rather than judgments. Sometimes the best comments are questions, such as "Could you elaborate on this?" or "What's the background for this claim?"

- **3e-4 When you receive comments on your own writing, try to be receptive, not defensive.** If a reader doesn't understand something you've written, trying to explain your point orally won't help. The point needs to be clear in what you have written. Remember, you're fortunate to have interested readers give you feedback early in the writing process.

• 3e-5 Make editing and proofreading comments only if you are reading second or third drafts. When your fellow writers ask for editing help on those drafts, give it if you can. Wait to be asked, though.

It takes skill and tact to be an honest and helpful responder to other people's writing. Remind yourself that you're not "correcting" their drafts; you're acting as an editor, not a grader. You can help a fellow writer most by showing an interest in what he or she has written, asking questions, giving encouragement, and making constructive suggestions for future drafts.

chapter

[4]

Paragraphs

*B*ecause a piece of writing is constructed from individual paragraphs, the decisions you make about paragraphs affect the way your readers will respond to your report or essay.

4a Unified Paragraphs

A paragraph is a collection of sentences that work together to develop a point. A paragraph shouldn't sprawl, with individual sentences going off in different directions. Rather, it should have unity; each sentence should be connected with the others to form a chain or a web that keeps the reader focused on the central idea.

Here is an example of a sprawling paragraph.

No longer do college graduates automatically plan on moving behind a desk as soon as they get their diplomas. Some are going into mills and factories. As technological expertise becomes increasingly important in today's factories and production plants, a high school education is no longer sufficient for many entry-level jobs. In the 1990s, the jobs are no longer there for all college graduates to count on starting on the executive ladder at a corporation or industry. Beginning salaries in many white-collar jobs come as a shock to new college graduates, who often leave college owing tens of thousands of dollars for school loans.

While a reader senses some kind of connection running through this collection of sentences, the central point isn't at all clear. In this revised version, the opening sentence is supported with specific details that unify the paragraph.

A surprising number of today's college graduates are heading for mills and factories where they are finding well-paid jobs that require sophisticated, high-tech knowledge. For instance, with bonuses and incentive pay, an engineer starting on the factory floor at Gallatin Steel in Kentucky can now earn close to $50,000 in a good year, considerably more than the pay in a white-collar management trainee program. Such jobs are especially attractive to young graduates who leave school with debts of tens of thousands of dollars for school loans. Says one engineer starting at Gallatin, "I'm getting exposure to the management of new technology, and that has to help wherever I go."

Here are three strategies for unifying your paragraphs.

• **4a-1 Use topic sentences.** A topic sentence that states your main idea doesn't have to be the first sentence in a paragraph, although it often is. The next two examples are from professional writers; the topic sentences are shown in bold-face type.

 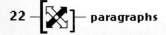

The [Soviet] society in which I had grown up was one that officially proclaimed sexual equality and made it a point of great pride, yet stereotyped men and women in ways reminiscent of the American fifties. At school, we had mandatory home economics for girls and shop for boys, a practice no one thought of challenging. At the music school where my mother taught, to say that someone played "like a girl"—pleasantly, neatly, and without substance—was a commonly used put-down; in literary reviews, the highest compliment to be paid a woman writer or poet was that she wrote like a man.

> —Cathy Young, "Keeping Women Weak"

This next paragraph builds toward the topic sentence that carries the main idea.

It is tempting to think that Lincoln went too far when he cleansed the morally infected air of Gettysburg. By turning all the blood and waste into a hygienic testing of an abstract proposition, he may have ennobled war, the last thing he wanted to do in other contexts. Slavery was not mentioned, because he wanted to lift his ideal of America as the Declaration's nation above divisive particulars. But the war was not just an intellectual affair, and the burden of slavery could not be ignored. **That is why the Gettysburg Address, weighty as it is with Lincoln's political philosophy, fails to express the whole of Lincoln's mind.** It must be supplemented with his other most significant address, the Second Inaugural, where *sin* is added to the picture.

> —Gary Wills, *Lincoln at Gettysburg*

Not all paragraphs have topic sentences, nor do they need them. There are many other good ways to structure paragraphs. Nevertheless, building a paragraph from a topic sentence helps to keep it focused. The strategy works especially well to organize reports and analyses.

• 4a-2 Pose a question and answer it.

This strategy is a common and reliable way to anchor a paragraph.

What is it about the cave paintings discovered in the south of France late in 1994 that has so excited archaeologists? One extraordinary feature is the variety of animal images. Horses, reindeer, bison—these are familiar to European cave experts. But elephants, rhinos, panthers, hyenas, and lions? Such figures are unique to this newly discovered cave at Chauvet. These beautifully executed images, more than 30,000 years old, have prompted France's foremost expert on cave art to say, "The paintings in this cave will force us to change how we interpret Stone Age art."

• 4a-3 Make a claim and illustrate it.

Prairie dogs have long been viewed, particularly by urban dwellers, as the epit-

ome of cute. The scene here a few days ago was typical. When the animals emerged from their dens, some touched teeth in "kisses" of recognition. They romped, rolled, wrestled, and chased each other around. They assiduously tended their burrows, dirt flying from their busy paws, bundles of grass for lining underground nests drooping from their mouths. —William K. Stevens, "Prairie Dog Colonies Bolster Life in the Plains"

The paragraph begins with a general statement or claim and all following sentences give specific details to illustrate that statement.

4b Paragraph Development

Writers use several other paragraph patterns that correspond closely to the methods of development mentioned in Section 3b-2.

• 4b-1 Cause and effect. In this kind of paragraph, you can state the effect and then give the causes, or you can list the causes first and then describe the effect. Here the author begins with the effect, which is framed as a question.

Summary: *Common Paragraph Patterns*

Cause and effect	Classification
Definition	Narration/process
Analogy	Comparison and contrast

Why do so many of the citizens of the world's oldest democracy not vote when they can, at a time when the struggle for democracy in Europe and throughout the rest of the world has reached its most crucial and inspiring level since 1848? Partly, it's an administrative problem—the disappearance of the old party-machine and ward system, whose last vestige was Mayor Daley. Whatever its abuses, it got people street by street, household by household, to the ballot-boxes. Its patronage system did help tie American people, especially blue-collar and lower middle-class ones, to the belief that they as citizens had some role to play in the running of their country from the bottom up, ward by ward. It reinforced the sense of participatory democracy. —Robert Hughes, *The Culture of Complaint*

• 4b-2 Definition. A paragraph of definition often works well to introduce or limit a concept that's important to the writer's thesis. For example:

In a sense we have two brains, two minds—and two different kinds of intelligence: rational and emotional. How we do in life is determined by both—it is not just IQ, but emotional intelligence that matters. Indeed, intellect cannot work at its best without emotional intelligence. Ordinarily . . . each is a full partner in mental life. When these partners

 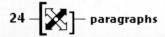

interact well, emotional intelligence rises—as does intellectual ability.

—Daniel Goleman, *Emotional Intelligence*

• 4b-3 Analogy. Writers often employ analogies—that is, extended comparisons—to make their writing more vivid and powerful. For instance:

The cheetah may be a gorgeous Maserati among mammals, able to sprint at speeds approaching seventy miles an hour, yet it has not been able to run away from its many miseries. Once, the cat ranged through the African continent, the Near East, and into southern India; now it is extinct almost everywhere but in scattered patches of the sub-Sahara. Farmers and ranchers in Namibia shoot them as vermin. On reserves, where cheetahs are often forced into unnatural proximity with other predators, they are at the bottom of the meat eaters' grim hierarchy; lions will go out of their way to destroy cheetah cubs, while hyenas, leopards, and even vultures can easily chase a cheetah away from its hard-caught prey. —Natalie Angier, "Chasing Cheetahs"

• 4b-4 Classification. Writers often start with a classification paragraph that establishes a pattern to follow. For example:

There are, as nearly as I can make out, three kinds of conservation currently oper-ating. The first is the preservation of places that are grandly wild or "scenic" or in some way spectacular. The second is what is called "conservation of natural resources"—that is, of the things of nature we intend to use: soil, water, timber, and minerals. The third is what you might call industrial troubleshooting: the attempt to limit or stop or remedy the most flagrant abuses of the industrial system. All three kinds of conservation are inadequate, both separately and together.

—Wendell Berry, "Conservation Is Good Work"

• 4b-5 Narration/process. A narration/process paragraph, which relates events in chronological order, is probably the simplest of all patterns because it tells a story about what happens. It can get an article or report off to a good start.

In a grimy and very wet warehouse, David Tallman and Bob Solomon are testing lawn sprinklers. To make their test more precise, they've dispensed with using a lawn. Instead they've covered the pitted concrete floor with 229 graduated cylinders. Glued to the top of each is a wide plastic funnel. Just laying out the grid with a tape measure, string, and white paint, they tell me, took several days. Now, having let a cheap rotary sprinkler operate for exactly 30 minutes, Tallman and Solomon are working their way down the rows,

Summary: *Terms Used for Transitions*

Relationship Adverbs:
although, consequently, however, likewise, moreover, nevertheless, similarly, yet

Similarity and Contrast Terms:
although, likewise, moreover, similarly, yet

Sequence Adverbs:
after, before, finally, first, henceforth, later, next, now, subsequently, then

Causation Adverbs:
as a result, because, for, since, therefore, thus

Relative Pronouns:
who, whom, which, where, that

Demonstrative Pronouns:
that, this, these, those

ucation, the social position he had known since childhood were everything Harry Truman never had. Life and customs on the Roosevelt estate on the upper Hudson River were as far removed from Jackson County, Missouri, as some foreign land. Roosevelt fancied himself a farmer. To Truman, Roosevelt was the kind of farmer who had never pulled a weed, never known debt, or crop failure, or a father's call to roll out of bed at 5:30 on a bitter cold morning.
—David McCullough, *Truman*

4c Transitions, Repetition, Parallelism, and Linking Pronouns

Writers frequently work without consciously thinking about paragraph patterns and depend on internal devices such as transitional terms, repetition, and parallelism to unify their writing. The adverbs and pronouns that introduce clauses and phrases also act as unifiers.

• **4c-1 Transitional terms.** All words that show connections are transitional terms. The following paragraphs illustrate just a few ways to use transitions.

picking up cylinders, recording the water levels, and dumping them out.
—Doug Stewart, "To Buy or Not to Buy, That Is the Question at *Consumer Reports*"

• **4b-6 Comparison and contrast.** This paragraph pattern is also useful for organizing a whole piece of writing.

[Roosevelt and Truman] could not have been more dissimilar. Roosevelt was now in his twelfth year in office. . . . His wealth, ed-

One can hardly open a newspaper these days without reading prescriptions for health. **First** on the list is "Don't smoke!" **Second** is "Eat a low-fat, high-fiber diet." **Next** is "Exercise, exercise, exercise." **Finally,** and probably the most difficult to carry out, is "Avoid stress."

 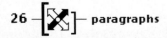

If one lives in an affluent suburb or around a large university, it's easy to get the impression that the American population is healthy. In **such** places, walkers, joggers, and bicycle riders abound, and restaurants feature vegetables and low-fat entrées. The truth is, **however,** that many Americans are not healthy. Thirty percent of Americans are seriously overweight, alcoholism is a chronic problem, and an increasing number of teenagers are smoking. **Moreover,** obesity among children is increasing.

• 4c-2 Repetition.
A key word or phrase repeated throughout a paragraph is a powerful unifier.

It's hard to talk about western Dakota without mentioning **Jell-o.** A salad, in local parlance, is a dish made with **Jell-o:** lime **Jell-o** with Cool-Whip and sliced bananas; cherry **Jell-o** with fruit cocktail and miniature marshmallows; lemon **Jell-o** with grated carrots, celery, sliced green olives, and walnuts for a fancy touch. —Kathleen Norris, "Status"

• 4c-3 Parallelism.
Parallelism, which establishes repeated patterns, is a forceful device for achieving unity. (See Section 8d.)

To the ancient Chinese, snakes embodied both good and evil, but **scorpions** symbolized pure wickedness. **To the Persians, scorpions** were the devil's minions, sent to destroy all life

by attacking the testicles of the sacred bull, whose blood should have fertilized the universe. **In the Old Testament,** the Hebrew King Rehoboam threatened to chastise his people, not with ordinary whips, but with **scorpions**— dread scourges that sting like a **scorpion's** tail. The Greeks blamed **scorpions** for killing Orion, a lusty giant and celebrated hunter.
—Natalie Angier, "Admirers of the Scorpion"

• 4c-4 Linking pronouns.
A series of pronouns can work well to tie a paragraph together.

She and her husband, Wolcott Gibbs, Jr., a writer, decided to simplify. **She** gave up real estate. **They** threw away masses of stuff. **They** moved from their sprawling 3,000-square-foot house into a 600-square-foot condominium. **They** stopped their junk mail and gave up their newspapers. Ms. St. James cropped her hair to save the time needed for blow-drying. **She** distilled her wardrobe to its current limited palette of black, gray and white. **She** reduced her purse to a credit card, library card, license and money. **She** even stopped making the bed.
—Carey Goldberg, "The Simple Life Lures Refugees from Stress"

4d Paragraph Appearance

When you're drafting a series of paragraphs, don't stop to worry about how long or short they are. When you start to edit, however, it's time to pay attention to paragraph length. Because the purpose of paragraphing is to chunk print into manageable units for the reader, the length of your paragraphs becomes an audience issue.

To many readers, long stretches of print un-broken by subheadings or paragraph breaks give a strong message: **I am hard to read.** Your own experience probably confirms that impression. Such a style may be fine when one is writing for a serious and patient audience, but for the most part, readers appreciate short paragraphs that give them minuscule breaks as the writer moves along.

• 4d-1 Break up long paragraphs when you can.

You shouldn't chop up paragraphs arbitrarily, but when a paragraph runs half of a printed page or more, it's time to look for places to break it up.

• 4d-2 Reconsider short paragraphs.

A paragraph is supposed to develop a point, and that's hard to do in one or two sentences. So use one-sentence paragraphs very sparingly, but don't be afraid of them either. Professional writers often use them to good effect, especially as a transitional statement to a new idea.

• 4d-3 Adapt paragraph length to your audience.

Since there are no rules about paragraph length, you have to use your intuition. These guidelines may help.

4e Opening Paragraphs

Good opening paragraphs vary greatly, but they're always important. An effective opening paragraph should accomplish the following.

 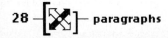

- Get your readers' attention.
- Lead them into your main idea.
- Set the tone of your writing.

The purpose of your document will partially control the kind of opening paragraph you write, but there are some useful patterns you can try.

· 4e-1 Start with a direct statement that announces your topic to the reader. This kind of opening works especially well for arguments and reports.

Any significant social phenomenon creates a backlash. The Net is no exception. It is odd, however, that the loudest complaints are shouts of "Get a life"—suggesting that online living will dehumanize us, insulate us, and create a world of people who won't smell flowers, watch sunsets, or engage in face-to-face experiences. Out of this backlash comes a warning to parents that their children will "cocoon" and metamorphose into social invalids. —Nicholas Negroponte, "Get a Life?"

Note that this author repeats ideas from his opening paragraph in the last paragraph. See 4f-3.

· 4e-2 Use an attention-getting narrative or anecdote that catches the reader's attention and rouses his or her curiosity. Such openings work especially well as leads for personal essays, magazine articles, and human-interest stories in newspapers.

Summary: Deciding on Paragraph Length

If . . .	Then . . .
readers are experienced and skillful,	they will probably tolerate long paragraphs.
readers are patient and want information,	they'll put up with long paragraphs.
readers are impatient and looking for diversion,	paragraphs of 75 to 150 words are about right.
readers are skimming for content,	they want short paragraphs.
readers are quite young or inexperienced,	paragraphs of around 100 words or less work best.

A customer of ours had an old Thunderbird that he used to drive back and forth to New York every other weekend. And every time he made the trip he'd be in the shop the following Monday needing to get something fixed because the car was such a hopeless piece of trash. One Monday he failed to show up and Tom said, "Gee, that's kind of unusual." I said jokingly, "Maybe he blew the car up."

—Tom and Ray Magliozzi,
"Inside the Engine"

• 4e-3 Ask a question. Questions often provide a tantalizing lead-in to an essay, raising the reader's expectations about what is to come.

What draws us to one person as opposed to another? Those who study behavior seem to agree that friendship thrives on familiarity. Thus, although "opposites attract" (heterophily) some of the time, "birds of a feather flock together" (homophily) most of the time.

—Letty Cottin Pogrebin,
Among Friends

• 4e-4 State the key facts. In this kind of opening paragraph, the writer lays out the key facts as the takeoff point for the essay or report.

Of all the problems besetting the poor inner-city black community, none is more pressing than that of interpersonal violence and aggression. It wreaks havoc daily with the lives of community residents and increasingly spills over into downtown and residential middle-class areas. Muggings, burglaries, carjackings, and drug-related shootings, all of which may leave their victims or innocent bystanders dead, are now common enough to concern all urban and many suburban residents. The inclination to violence springs from the circumstances of life among the ghetto poor—the lack of jobs that pay a living wage, the stigma of race, and the resulting alienation and lack of hope for the future.

—Elijah Anderson,
"The Code of the Streets"

4f Closing Paragraphs

There are no simple prescriptions for writing those difficult last paragraphs, but three patterns can work well.

• 4f-1 Make a recommendation. Making a recommendation will bring the issue you've been discussing to closure. For example:

But even if you are an athlete who wants quick results, you should not go to extremes in trying to improve your overall nutrition. When you decide to change your eating habits, your motto should be "Eat better," not "Eat perfectly." By increasing carbohydrates and reducing fat in the diet—that is, by eating more fruits, vegetables, and whole grains and less whole milk and red meat—you can improve your energy level rather quickly. You will also feel better, play better, and look better than you ever imagined.

• 4f-2 Summarize the main points you have made.
You can conclude with a paragraph that sums up your argument. Poet and professor Nikki Giovanni does so in an essay of advice directed to African-American college students.

It's really very simple. Educational progress is a national concern; education is a private one. Your job is not to educate white people; it is to obtain an education. If you take the racial world on your shoulders, you will not get the job done. Deal with yourself as an individual worthy of respect, and make everyone else deal with you the same way. College is a little like playing grown-up. Practice what you want to be. You've been telling your parents you were grown. Now is your chance to act like it.　　—Nikki Giovanni, "Campus Racism, 101"

• 4f-3 Link the closing paragraph to the opening paragraph.
This is one of the most elegant strategies, since it gives your writing a frame. In Section 4e-1 you read the first paragraph of an essay about living with "the Net"; here is the last paragraph of the same essay.

But the current sweep of digital living is doing exactly the opposite. Parents of young children find exciting self-employment in the home. The "virtual corporation" is an opportunity for tiny companies (with employees spread across the world) to work together in a global market and set up base wherever they choose. If you don't like centralist thinking, big companies, or job automation, what better place to go than the Net? Work for yourself *and* get a life.　　—Nicholas Negroponte, "Get a Life?"

4g Electronic Paragraphs

You may have to shape paragraphs somewhat differently when working in electronic environments such as e-mail or the World Wide Web.

• 4g-1 In e-mail, use paragraphs to chunk information.
When sending e-mail, you don't have many options for highlighting information. Most programs restrict you to a single plain font—without boldfacing, underscoring, or italics. You may not even be able to indent para-

graphs. Yet uninterrupted blocks of prose on a computer are difficult to read, especially when a screen is also displaying the clutter typical of most e-mail messages.

To highlight information under these difficult conditions, break long, uninterrupted messages into block paragraphs simply by skipping lines whenever you introduce a new thought. Keep your messages brief and put important ideas in the opening sentences of block paragraphs. E-mail is usually more readable when paragraphs run no longer than a few sentences (two to five). Avoid presenting dense blocks of prose on screen.

Within paragraphs, you can highlight items by using the tab key to create indented and bulleted lists. Items in any list should be short, usually less than a full line. When you need a strong boundary between ideas in an e-mail message, consider typing a line of hyphens or underscores across approximately three-quarters of the page. Leave some space so your page will look handsome even if persons receiving it are using larger fonts for their screen presentations: a line set at 10 points that runs all the way to your right margin will turn over to a second line if the machine reading it is set for 12 or 14 points.

• 4g-2 On the World Wide Web, create paragraphs that suit the design of a page. You'll find paragraphs of every shape on the WWW, from dense blocks of prose to sentences that flow around thumbnail photographs. Web sites also make extensive use of block paragraphs and bulleted lists, which (in some cases) replace more conventional sentence groupings.

In a Web site, the home page typically outlines or maps the project, directing readers to specific information deeper in the structure. That's why you need to plan any site you create fully and why you should examine other sites to determine what works visually and what does not. Generally, opening pages work best if they deliver information in outline form, using simple headings and clear graphics; later pages may use a denser, more traditional arrangement. But as is true with e-mail, most dense blocks of uninterrupted type on the World Wide Web just aren't readable or attractive.

Fortunately, the Web offers many devices for highlighting ideas, including color, boldfacing, and even sound. Use these elements strategically; if you highlight too much on a given page, nothing will stand out.

If your paragraphs include links to other pages or sites, consider how to place these links for the appropriate impact. Would a given page be easier to use, for example, if important links appear immediately within paragraphs or later in bulleted lists? The answer will depend on the overall purpose and design of your page.

chapter [5]

Revising, Editing, and Proofreading

_W_hen writers revise, edit, and proofread, they are engaged in separate stages of the writing process, each essential and each qualitatively different from the others.

Definition of Terms

REVISE:
To make large-scale changes that involve focus, purpose, concerns about audience, organization, and content

EDIT:
To make small-scale changes that involve style, word choice, tone, choice of examples, and arrangement

PROOFREAD:
To check for punctuation, omissions, mistakes in spelling, and lapses in standard grammatical usage

5a Revising a Draft

When you revise a draft, you are not "correcting" it. Rather you are making significant changes so that clearer meaning and direction will emerge. At this stage, THINK BIG—try not to tinker with sentences and words. Concentrate on larger concerns such as those discussed in this section.

• 5a-1 Read your draft thoughtfully. Ask yourself whether, on the whole, you like it and feel it has potential. If you really dislike the draft, consider abandoning it and starting over from scratch. If you do that, you haven't wasted your time. Often a discarded first draft helps a writer find a focus and produce a stronger new draft.

• 5a-2 Rethink your focus. Ask yourself these questions.

- Is my thesis narrow enough? Does it make specific points that I can support with examples?
- Is my topic limited enough to develop adequately in the space I have available?

If you realize your thesis is too broad, select a subtopic from the thesis instead.

Example

ORIGINAL THESIS:
Sport utility vehicles are taking over the American road and causing problems.

FOCUSED THESIS:
With light trucks and sport utility vehicles accounting for four out of ten new automotive purchases in the 1990s, the American Automobile Manufacturers Association is pitted against the Environmental Protection Agency in a battle over fuel-economy standards for such vehicles.

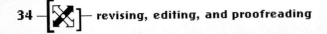

• 5a-3 Review your purpose. Someone reading your draft should quickly understand the key points you want to make. Ask yourself these questions.

- For an argument or a cause-and-effect essay, did I state my main points early in the paper? In a narrative or descriptive piece, is my intent easy to infer?
- Am I clear about what I want to accomplish?

You can't revise your draft effectively until you know clearly what you want to accomplish.

• 5a-4 Think about your audience. You may have written your first draft primarily for yourself, concentrating on getting down your ideas. If so, you now need to revise it with your readers in mind. Ask yourself these questions.

- Am I clear about whom I want to reach with this essay? Why would they want to read it?
- What do I know about my readers that affects the kind of examples and arguments I will use?
- How much do I know my readers already know about my subject? What new information can I give them?
- Is my language and writing style suitable for my audience?

An acute sense of your audience is your most important tool for effective revision.

• 5a-5 Review the organization of your draft. Friends and fellow writers can often help

---

Example

ORIGINAL PURPOSE:
To show that the increased number of sport utility vehicles on the road today is increasing gasoline consumption

CLARIFIED PURPOSE:
To explain the issues involved in the conflict between manufacturers who want to sell the versatile sport utility vehicles consumers want in the 1990s and government officials and environmentalists who are concerned about the environmental impact of increased gasoline consumption by such vehicles

---

Example

ORIGINAL AUDIENCE ANALYSIS:
General readers who are interested in car-buying trends in the United States

REVISED AUDIENCE ANALYSIS:
Readers of *The New York Times* or *The Wall Street Journal*. They know sport utility vehicles are increasingly popular with Americans but haven't thought much about the environmental ramifications of this trend. They'll be interested in reading about both sides of the issue and how the conflict might be resolved.

Summary: Editing Strategies

- Make your language more vivid and concrete.
- Review your word choices.
- Get rid of excess words.
- Check your transitions.
- Review your paragraphing.
- Reconsider your introduction, conclusion, and title.

you spot organizational problems. Ask them whether they can follow your piece easily. If they say they got lost, have them show you where. Ask yourself these questions.

- Does my paper have a clear pattern that is easy to discern and follow? What is the progression of ideas?
- What expectations did I raise in my readers at the beginning of the paper? Did I meet those expectations?
- Are my points arranged to work toward a strong conclusion, or should I move them around?
- If the paper is more than three or four pages, have I used headings and subheadings to guide the readers?

• 5a-6 Review the content of your draft. You may need to add information to your essay to give it the "weight of facts." Ask yourself these questions.

- Have I answered the questions *who, what, where, when, how,* and *why?*
- Do I need more details and concrete examples to develop my points and add interest?
- Have I supported my claims with evidence and arguments? (See Section 6a for questions you can ask yourself to check the quality of your evidence.)

5b Editing a Draft

When you're satisfied with the focus, organization, and content of your writing, you're ready to edit—that is, to make the small-scale changes that will give you a tighter, clearer, and more polished essay.

• 5b-1 Look for ways to make your language more concrete and vivid. (See Chapter 9 on stylish sentences.) Ask yourself the following questions.

- Are there places where I need to make an abstract point concrete by giving an example or detail?
- Where can I improve the paper by adding a metaphor or vivid image?
- How can I rewrite some sentences to focus on people doing things?

• 5b-2 Review your word choices. You may want to change the tone of your writing, making it less formal or more direct. You may also want to make it livelier and more readable. Ask yourself these questions.

- Is my writing overloaded with abstract, noun-heavy language, often called gobbledygook or jargon?
- Is my language too colloquial and informal for my audience and purpose?
- Have I used specialized terms that my audience may not understand?
- Have I used strong, active verbs most of the time?

(See Chapters 7 and 9 for suggestions about word choice.)

• 5b-3 Get rid of excess words.

First drafts can bog down in sprawling sentences and unnecessary explanation. Ask yourself these questions.

- Is the draft heavy with strung-out verb phrases and double constructions? (See Section 9b for help in using words economically.)
- Am I telling my readers things they already know?
- Have I given more examples than readers need?
- Are there frequent generalizations that say little?

• 5b-4 Check your transitions.

Smooth transitions help hold your paper together and move your reader along from point to point. (See Section 4c for a list of transitional terms.) Ask yourself the following questions.

- Are there clear links between paragraphs, either through the use of connecting words or through repeated patterns or terms?

- Have I used enough transitional terms such as *however, in addition to, first, next, in that case,* and *consequently* to help readers understand how ideas are related to one another?

• 5b-5 Review your paragraphing.

A series of short paragraphs makes a piece of writing resemble a newspaper column more than an essay or a report. Very long paragraphs, on the other hand, can be tedious and can turn readers off. To review paragraph length, ask yourself these questions.

- Do I have several paragraphs of one or two sentences? If so, should I combine some of them?
- Do several of my paragraphs run from eight to ten sentences or more? If so, where can I find places to break them apart?

(See Chapter 4 for information and suggestions on how to use paragraphs effectively.)

• 5b-6 Reconsider your introduction, conclusion, and title.

When you have a revised draft, it's time to see how well your introduction, conclusion, and title fit the finished product. Ask yourself these questions.

- Does the introduction catch my readers' attention and provide a strong lead into the paper? (See Section 4e on opening paragraphs.)
- Does my conclusion tie up loose ends and leave the reader satisfied that I've covered the subject? (See Section 4f on closing paragraphs.)

- Does my title accurately reflect the content, and will it attract readers? (See Section 2f on picking a good title.)

5c Proofreading a Draft

When you've typed or printed out your revised and edited essay, give it a final careful inspection to correct errors.

• 5c-1 Check your weakest area. If you're a poor speller, highlight any words about which you're in doubt. If commas are your nemesis, check all of them. If you typically confuse *affect* and *effect* or stumble over other troublesome pairs such as *infer* and *imply* or *lie* and *lay,* check to see you've made the right choices.

• 5c-2 Check punctuation. Look over places where you've used semicolons and colons, check for incomplete sentences, and be sure quotation marks and parentheses come in pairs. Also check for missing apostrophes in contractions and possessives.

• 5c-3 Check spelling throughout. If you can, use a computer spelling checker but remember that such programs are most useful for catching typographical errors. They don't catch important misspellings such as *"there"* for *"they're,"* *"ruff"* for *"rough,"* or *"no"* for *"know"* because all these words are acceptable in their dictionaries. Remember to check the spelling and capitalization of proper nouns and adjectives (for example, *France* and *African*).

• 5c-4 Check the format of your paper. Be sure you've left margins of at least one inch all around and that pages are numbered. Review page breaks, and check headings and subheadings. Be sure titles are italicized and quotations indented when appropriate.

• 5c-5 Review the "body language" of your document. See Chapters 28 and 29 for design tips and examples of ways to make your paper look good in print.

• 5c-6 Get help from your friends and fellow writers. Proofreading is tedious, and when you're reading something over for the second or third time, it's easy to miss errors. Enlist a fresh eye if you can.

Checklist: Proofreading

✔ Check grammar and mechanics.
✔ Check punctuation.
✔ Check for correct spelling and typographical errors.
✔ Check the format of your paper.
✔ Review the "body language" of your document.
✔ Get help from your friends and fellow writers.

[6]

chapter

Critical Thinking and Persuasive Writing

*I*f you want to participate in a democratic society, you need to sharpen your abilities to think critically and to argue persuasively. Without these skills, you'll have trouble evaluating information so that you can make intelligent decisions, and you won't be able to present your own point of view forcefully and effectively. Critical thinking and persuasive writing are not innate skills; they need to be learned and practiced. This chapter gives an overview of both skills and outlines the basics of presenting arguments in college papers.

6a Critical Thinking

Although much of the information you acquire today may be obsolete ten or twenty years from now, the critical-thinking skills you acquire will serve you for a lifetime.

• 6a-1 Cultivate the habit of inquiry.
Never accept arguments at face value. Always ask questions regarding the source, the motivation, and the evidence.

- What are the writer's or speaker's credentials?
- Whose interests does the proposal serve?
- How good is the evidence being presented?

• 6a-2 Know who the writer or presenter is and where he or she is coming from.
Ask yourself these kinds of questions.

- For whom does the speaker or writer work?
- What interests may be concealed behind a fine-sounding organizational name?

• 6a-3 Evaluate the evidence. Ask yourself these questions.

- Is there sufficient evidence to prove a case?
- What is the source of the evidence? Is it reliable?

- Has significant evidence been omitted?
- Is the evidence factual, anecdotal, or hearsay?

• 6a-4 Understand what constitutes good evidence. Appropriate evidence for college papers or business reports includes, but is not limited to, sources such as these.

Historical documents	Eyewitness accounts
Expert testimony	Articles from major newspapers
Statistics	Interviews with authorities
Case studies	Data from reliable documents

• 6a-5 Consider whether the writer's claims go beyond what the evidence warrants. Try to determine whether conclusions rest on insufficient or biased data.

• 6a-6 Look for the unstated assumptions that underlie an argument. Be alert to situations in which writers take for granted that they and their audience share common knowledge or beliefs when in fact they do not.

• 6a-7 Check for biased language and loaded metaphors. Most writers use some biased language—it's difficult to write without it.

critical thinking and persuasive writing

However, you should be skeptical about speech or writing that is overloaded with "god terms"—words like *democratic, natural,* or *family*—or "devil terms"—*destructive, irresponsible,* or *fascist.*

• 6a-8 Avoid stereotypes and scapegoating. Be alert for stereotyping, which makes broad generalizations about how people of different races, gender, or geographic areas look and act. (See Section 7c for ways to avoid using stereotypes in your own writing.) Also be critical of writers or speakers who look for a scapegoat to take the blame for problems.

• 6a-9 Be suspicious of simple solutions to complex problems, and avoid black-and-white thinking. Critical thinkers realize that the most serious problems in our society are extremely complex and won't yield to slogans or easy answers. Casting those involved in a dispute as "good guys" or "bad guys" shows simplistic thinking and makes it harder to solve problems.

6b Structures for Arguments

Your ability to persuade people depends, to a great extent, on your ability to understand people—their needs, their desires, their fears, and their hopes. When presenting an argument in writing, you must also be able to write connected, well-supported, logical arguments, particularly when you're writing college papers. This chapter gives an overview of two ways to construct

Summary: *Data-to-Conclusion Arguments*

1. *Formulate a thesis.* Write a tentative thesis, and decide what evidence is needed to test it.
2. *Gather sufficient evidence.* Remember that the larger the population you're writing about, the larger your sample must be.
3. *Gather random evidence.* Make sure your evidence represents a cross section of the population you're generalizing about.
4. *Make sure your evidence is accurate.* Verify your evidence. Check its source, and allow for possible bias in that source.
5. *Make sure your evidence is relevant.* Take care to show a legitimate connection between your evidence and the conclusion you draw.

such arguments. The bottom line, however, is that no amount of logic and evidence will convince people to adopt your point of view if you threaten them or put them on the defensive. Thus the first rule in presenting an argument is to think about your audience. (For more on this topic, see Sections 1d and 5a-4.)

• 6b-1 Use data-to-conclusion arguments. One way to construct an argument is to present data and work toward a conclusion. This method involves gathering evidence, analyzing it, and drawing a conclusion from it. This pattern is sometimes called "the scientific method," or inductive argument. In its basic form, it involves the five steps summarized in the box.

Example: Data-to-Conclusion Argument About Children's Health

1994 DATA FROM AMERICAN HEALTH FOUNDATION

- Increase in measles and rubella among children
- Increase in high school children who smoke
- Increase in high school children who use drugs
- U.S. infant mortality higher than thirteen other industrialized nations
- Increase in obesity among children

CONCLUSION: CHILDREN'S HEALTH IS DECLINING IN THE UNITED STATES.

Inductive argument appeals to audiences who consider themselves rational and logical. Thus, when you construct such arguments, lean heavily on facts and authorities, letting them carry the weight of persuasion. Avoid overheated language or obvious emotional appeals.

• 6b-2 Use claim-and-support arguments. A second way to construct an argument is to make your claim first and then gather evidence to support it. Lawyers most often choose this kind of argument when they're presenting a case in court. It's the kind most of us turn to almost intuitively when we try to persuade others. While such arguments aren't usually as neat as data-to-conclusion arguments, there is a pattern to them. Here are six steps to take in making claim-and-support arguments.

As with trial lawyers, people making this kind of argument are likely to present their views in persuasive language, colorful imagery, apt analogies, and illustrative stories. They must still use restraint, however, or they risk alienating their audience. That's a special risk when writing academic papers and reports.

Here is an example of a claim-and-support argument used by Robert Hughes, a cultural critic. He uses two strategies. He narrates the past failures of Marxism, and he defines the American character as incompatible with Marxist theory and practice. Although he relies more on observation and common knowledge than on hard facts, he presents a strong argument.

• 6b-3 Keep your arguments civil. Writers, like everyone else, have their biases—they like this and dislike that, they strongly favor one program or politician and strongly oppose others. It's almost impossible to suppress such biases

Summary: *Claim-and-Support Arguments*

1. *Decide on your audience and your purpose.* To construct a good argument, you must know for whom you're writing and why.
2. *Decide what your claim will be and state it.* Keep your claim reasonable; the writer who claims more than the evidence supports looks naive.
3. *Consider what counterarguments might be offered.* You need to show that you know there's another side to the issue.
4. *Gather the evidence to support your claim.* Focus on facts and statements from authorities; use anecdotes and opinions sparingly.
5. *Analyze your audience to decide how you can present your evidence most effectively.* The possibilities correspond to the patterns suggested for paragraph development in Section 4b—cause and effect, narration, comparison, and so forth.
6. *Explain how and why your evidence leads to your conclusion.*

Example: *Claim-and-Support Argument, Based on an Argument in* The Culture of Complaint *by Robert Hughes*

CLAIM: MARXISM HOLDS NO PROMISE IN AMERICA.

SUPPORT: MARXISM HAS FAILED EVERYWHERE IT WAS TRIED.

- It produced misery, tyranny, and mediocrity.
- It wrongly assumed that people would divide by class.
- Americans are too diverse to accept a dominant ideology.
- Americans reject the model of central planning for all.

CONCLUSION:
Americans value individuality too much to embrace a system that emphasizes control and penalizes self-expression.

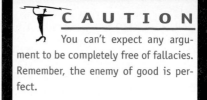

CAUTION
You can't expect any argument to be completely free of fallacies. Remember, the enemy of good is perfect.

when you're writing arguments, nor should you necessarily try. If, however, you want your arguments to be taken seriously by people who may not share your biases, it's important to choose your language carefully—to keep a civil tongue in your head, so to speak. (For more on this issue of using civil language, see Section 7c.)

6c Fallacies in Arguments

Fallacies in arguments invite an audience to bypass critical thinking and accept faulty claims and dubious generalizations. Once you learn to identify the most common fallacies, you'll not only be able to spot them in the arguments of others, but you'll also strengthen

43

Summary: *Common Fallacies*

1. *Argument against the person* (ad hominem). Making a personal attack on an opponent rather than addressing the issue under debate
2. *Begging the question.* Assuming that readers share important assumptions and beliefs with the arguer when, in fact, they don't
3. *Hasty generalization.* Drawing broad conclusions from too little evidence
4. *False cause* (post hoc, ergo propter hoc). Assuming falsely that because *A* follows *B*, *B* caused *A*
5. *False dilemma or the fallacy of insufficient options.* Stating an argument in terms that imply that one must choose between only two options when, in fact, several exist
6. *Red herring.* Diverting the audience's attention from the main issue by bringing in an irrelevant point
7. *Special pleading.* Presenting a biased statement that is based on partial facts and suggesting it is supported by all the facts
8. *False analogy.* Creating a comparison between two things that won't hold up under scrutiny; for example, suggesting that the U.S. president's job is like that of a football coach
9. *Non sequitur.* Suggesting a cause-and-effect link between two events or conditions that aren't necessarily connected
10. *Bandwagon.* Claiming that widespread popularity makes an idea or an object valuable

your own arguments by avoiding them. Here are ten fallacies you're likely to encounter.

6d Guidelines for College Papers

College instructors have special requirements in mind when they evaluate students' papers. It's helpful to keep these guidelines in mind.

Summary: *Guidelines for College Papers*

- *Keep your topic narrow enough so that you can develop it with specific details and illustrations.* Train yourself to write more about less.
- *Limit your claims to those you can support.* Don't put yourself in an indefensible position by overstating your case.
- *Support any claim you make with reasons and evidence.*
- *Keep in mind what constitutes good evidence in college writing.* See Section 6a-4.
- *Document your sources carefully.* Your readers should be able to track down references.

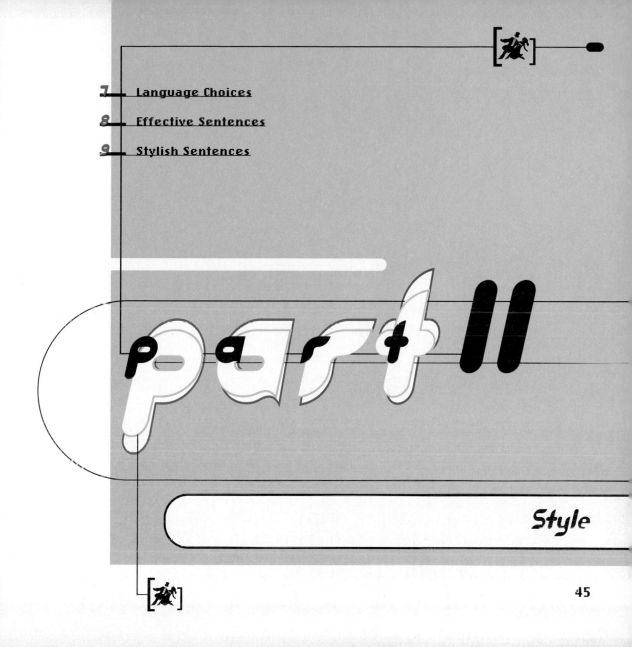

part II

Style

chapter [7]

A   Levels of Language
B   Denotation and Connotation
C   Civil Language

Language Choices

*G*ood writers work at adapting their language to the various writing situations in which they work. This chapter explains some of the choices available to you.

7a Levels of Language

One can think of levels of language as being on a continuum from very formal at one end to casual and colloquial on the other. Documents that use stiff, technical language, such as legal briefs and scientific reports, lie at the formal end of the scale, while breezy writing and slang fall at the other, informal end. In the broad middle range comes the informal language of essays, reports, academic papers, newspaper columns, and newsletters.

Two questions will help you identify the level of language you should choose when you write.

1. Who is my audience, and what relationship do I want to have with it?
2. What is my purpose? How do I want to present myself?

• **7a-1 Recognize when formal language is appropriate.** When you're writing for an audience that seems distant and you want that audience to perceive you as competent and worthy of respect, a formal tone and style is appropriate. Here is an example from a scholarly biography of John Dewey.

Dewey was not disposed to the public revelation of personal feelings, but it is clear from his early work . . . that he clung to idealism because it seemed to him the only persuasive alternative to philosophies that left the universe utterly bereft of purpose.

—Robert Westbrook, *John Dewey and American Democracy*

The sentence is clear, but the language and tone is detached and rather formal. You can use this kind of style for writing speeches, reports, or letters to people whom you don't know but want to think well of you.

• **7a-2 Recognize when informal language is appropriate.** A broad range of writing is informal in tone: the work of authors and columnists such as Anna Quindlen and Thomas

> **Checklist:** *Characteristics of Formal Style*
>
> ✔ Long sentences and paragraphs
> ✔ Abstract language
> ✔ Impersonal tone—few personal references
> ✔ No use of *I* or *you*
> ✔ Few contractions
> ✔ Few active verbs
> ✔ Serious subject and tone
> ✔ Feeling of distance between reader and writer

 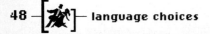

Friedman; the articles in popular magazines such as *Time, Rolling Stone, Sports Illustrated,* and *Vanity Fair;* the writing in books such as David McCullough's *Truman* and Richard Preston's *The Hot Zone;* and most college undergraduate papers. Here are two examples of informal language.

> Inside Lubbock's pancake house on Q Street, it's breakfast all day long, and the patrons who file in at all hours fall heavily into wooden chairs as if to take root there.
> —Robert Draper, "The Real Buddy Holly"

> In the kitchen of a Victorian house near the edge of town, Major Nancy Jaax, a veterinarian in the United States Army, stood at the counter making dinner for her children.
> —Richard Preston, *The Hot Zone*

Checklist: *Characteristics of Informal Style*

- ✔ Variety of sentence lengths
- ✔ Short- to medium-length paragraphs
- ✔ Mixture of abstract and concrete language
- ✔ Occasional use of *I* and *you*
- ✔ Occasional use of contractions
- ✔ Frequent use of active verbs
- ✔ Variety of topics, from casual to serious
- ✔ Little distance between writer and reader

You'll probably use some variation of this informal style for most pieces you write. You can choose to use contractions, *I* and *you,* personal references, or anecdotes, depending on how close you want to come to your audience.

7a-3 Recognize when casual, colloquial style is appropriate. For a few writing situations—perhaps a humorous article for the college paper or a folksy newspaper column—a colloquial style may work well. Here's an example.

> Yep, that's your bullshit detector hitting the red light.
> —Brock N. Meeks, "Fueling the Net Porn Hysteria"

Checklist: *Characteristics of Casual, Colloquial Style*

- ✔ Short- to medium-length sentences; short paragraphs
- ✔ High proportion of active verbs and vivid language
- ✔ Many personal pronouns, with frequent use of *I* and *you*
- ✔ Frequent use of contractions
- ✔ Slang terms and colloquial language
- ✔ Light topics or satire
- ✔ Very little distance between reader and writer

College and business writers have few occasions to use such a breezy, slang-loaded style, but it can work well for a writer trying to project a jazzy, hip image for an audience with whom he or she feels very connected.

7b Denotation and Connotation

Denotative language describes events, ideas, and people in straightforward, objective terms. *Connotative language* is messier but more interesting; it describes events, ideas, and people in language that is colored by emotions and associations.

Whether you want to emphasize denotation or connotation depends on who your audience is and why you're writing. If you want to sound impersonal and detached, you can use denotation; if you want to sway your readers' opinions and get their sympathy, you can use connotation. But be careful—readers are apt to respond poorly to extremes of either kind.

• 7b-1 Know when to choose denotative language.
When you are writing reports, scientific analyses, legal or business documents, or papers for most college courses, keep your language neutral and objective. Your readers expect a direct statement, uncolored by slanted language. Still, don't make your writing so dry that it sounds like an insurance policy. Here is an example of clear, objective writing from a science writer.

> Aristotle adopted the system of Eudoxus with some modification in detail. But instead of being satisfied with the purely mathematical combinations of Eudoxus, he gave the system a realistic interpretation. In his view the various heavenly bodies were carried around by a machinery of solid, though hollow, corporeal spheres.
> —Robert Blake et al.,
> *Theories of Scientific Method*

• 7b-2 Know when to choose connotative language.
When you are writing book or movie reviews, fundraising appeals, promotional pamphlets, ads, or campaign speeches, it's appropriate to use more emotional and vivid language. Here's the first paragraph of a book review that uses connotative language.

> It's easy to understand why Norman Mailer would want to write a biography of Picasso. The painter, after all, can be seen as a kind of artistic role model for Mr. Mailer, which explains much of what is wrong with this ham-handed, derivative, and highly subjective biography.
> —Michiko Kakutani,
> "Egos and Outlaws:
> Like Attracts Like"

You'll find even more connotative language in ceremonial addresses such as Martin Luther King, Jr.'s great "I Have a Dream" speech.

> There will be neither rest nor tranquillity in America until the Negro is granted his citizenship rights. The whirlwinds of revolt will continue to shake the foundations of our nation until the bright day of justice returns.
> —Martin Luther King, Jr.,
> "I Have a Dream"

TIP Don't think of denotative and connotative language in either/or terms. Denotation isn't always good just because it seems to be objective, and connotation isn't always bad because it appeals to the emotions. Each has its appropriate uses.

and the heavy connotation of propaganda and campaign oratory on the other.

7c Civil Language

All of us see the world through our own unique lenses, lenses that have been shaped by background, reading, and experiences. Accordingly, all of us have our biases, but we should recognize them and try to control them. This section suggests ways to control bias and maintain civility when we write.

• **7b-3 Choose denotative or connotative language according to your writing situation.** The examples given in Sections 7b-1 and 7b-2 can't begin to cover the range of situations for which denotative and connotative language is used—from technical journals to scare pieces sent out by political organizations. The range shown here suggests where various kinds of writing might fall on a continuum that has the pure denotation of legal documents at one end

• **7c-1 Control your language to eliminate gender bias.** The women's movement has made most of us aware of how profoundly language shapes attitudes and reinforces stereotyped gender roles. Here are some guidelines for avoiding sexist language.

1. Avoid using *he* and *him* as all-purpose pronouns to refer to people in general. Either use *he* and *she* or *him* and *her*. Using plurals will often solve the problem of a sexist pronoun.

Why Write . . .	When You Could Write . . .
Everyone should exercise **his** right to vote.	**All** people should exercise **their** right to vote.
Each secretary may bring **her** husband.	**Each** secretary may bring **his** or **her** spouse.
Everybody can bring **his** favorite record.	Everybody can bring **a** favorite record.

2. Avoid using the term *man* as a catchall term to refer to all people or members of a group.

Why Write . . .	When You Could Write . . .
the **man** who wants to be an astronaut	**anyone** who wants to be an astronaut
men who do their own car repairs	**car owners** who do their own repairs

3. Avoid implying that professions or roles are primarily for men or for women.

Why Write . . .	When You Could Write . . .
young **men** who hope to get basketball scholarships	young **people** who hope to get basketball scholarships
women who like to cook	**anyone** who likes to cook
police**man**	police **officer**
business**men**	business **executives**

4. When possible, find out what name a married woman wants to go by, and honor that choice. The possibilities are shown here.

Husband's name	**Mrs. Robert Collins**
First name + husband's last name	**Rosita Collins**
First name + maiden name + husband's last name	**Rosita Perez Collins**
First name + hyphenated last name	**Rosita Perez-Collins**
Maiden name	**Rosita Perez**

Many women, single and married, prefer the title *Ms.* to either *Miss* or *Mrs.* If you're not sure, *Ms.* is the best choice.

5. Avoid between-the-line implications that men and women behave in stereotypical ways. For example, don't suggest that men are poor housekeepers and love sports or that women are generally talkative and love to shop.

• 7c-2 Control your language to eliminate racial and ethnic bias. Avoid racial and ethnic designations if they're not relevant to the point you're making.

1. Make your description accurate. *Asian* is too broad; *Filipino, Chinese, Japanese, East Indian,* and so on are more accurate. For those whose forebears come from another country but who are American born, combine the term with *American,* —for example, *Japanese American.* Likewise, rather than use *Hispanic,* be specific and use *Cuban, Puerto Rican, Mexican, Bolivian,* and so on if you can. *American Indian* and *Native American* are both acceptable. *Inuit* is now preferred to *Eskimo.*

2. Use the terminology preferred by the people you're writing about, insofar as you know their preferences. If you're not sure of your subject's preference, follow the usage of major newspapers or magazines. The term currently favored by individuals whose ancestors came from Africa seems to be shifting from *black* to *African American.* The term *people of color* seems too vague to be useful for identifying specific ethnic groups.

3. In editing, see that you have not let hints of ethnic or national stereotypes sneak into your writing. Might one infer from your language that you think of Jews as rich financiers? Is there a hint that someone with an Italian name has Mafia connections? Run your bias monitor to check.

• 7c-3 Control your language to avoid bias toward age, physical condition, and sexual orientation. The writer who strives to treat people fairly does not demean or patronize them because of traits over which they may have no control.

1. For people in their sixties or older, use specific designations such as *middle sixties* or *early seventies* rather than *elderly* or *old people.* Avoid patronizing comments such as, "For a seventy-year-old, he's very astute."

2. Reserve the terms *boys, girls,* and *kids* for people under the age of twelve. *Teens* and *youths* are fine for high school students. *College kids* is patronizing as well as inaccurate; almost half of the college students in the United States today are older than twenty-five.

3. Be as specific as possible when referring to people with disabilities or illnesses; avoid the term *crippled.* In general, it works well to mention the individual first and his or her handicap or illness second—for example, "my cousin who is autistic" or "my hairdresser who has multiple sclerosis." The terms *disabled* and *hearing impaired* are both acceptable.

4. Mention a person's sexual orientation only when it is relevant to the discussion, and use specific, nonjudgmental terminology when doing so. Many people seem comfortable with the designation *homosexual* to refer to both men and women whose sexual orientation is toward those of their own gender. However, you may choose the term *gay* or *lesbian* if you want to be more specific.

5. Avoid using language that suggests derisive attitudes about some professions or implies unflattering class distinctions. In serious writing, don't use *shrink* for *psychiatrist, prof* for *professor,* or *cop* for *police officer.* Avoid terms that have negative class connotations, such as *Junior Leaguer, country club set, welfare mother, redneck,* or *dropout.*

6. Use good judgment and keep your sense of humor when you edit for bias. Every day you read columnists and magazine writers who use biased language to spoof, praise, persuade, or criticize and do it effectively and in good taste. Just keep your audience in mind. When you do, you can have fun with language and still be civil and respectful.

• *7c-4 Maintain a civil tone when presenting an argument.* Avoid name calling and demonizing those with whom you disagree.

Because a healthy democracy depends on *civil discourse* and on negotiation and compromise among groups that have competing interests, thoughtful people object to a "take no prisoners" approach to discussion of social issues.

People who use terms such as *environmental wacko, fascist, terrorist, welfare queen,* and *cry baby* are engaging in verbal violence. Such invective only alienates an audience who isn't already partisan, and it shuts down discussion. Moreover, if you lapse into such language when you're writing a proposal, a report, or an academic paper, you'll lose your credibility because you'll be dismissed as too biased to be reliable.

The effects of verbal violence linger after the occasion itself passes, so before you try to win your point by attacking and demeaning others, consider this: If someday you were to meet the person you're vilifying, would you be ashamed to face him or her?

chapter

[8]

Effective Sentences

When writing a draft, don't worry too much about the shape of your sentences. But as you begin to revise, consider these suggestions for producing clear and lively prose.

8a Agent/Action Sentences

You can build readable sentences by using an agent/action pattern. In agent/action sentences, clear subjects perform strong actions.

agent/**action**	*agent*/**action**
The *pilot* **ejected.**	An *accountant* **calculated** our debt.

Agent/action sentences are highly readable because they answer two important questions:

- What's happening?
- Who's doing it (and to whom)?

8a-1 Whenever you can, make persons or things the subjects of your sentences and dependent clauses. Put people in your writing, making them the agents that are performing the actions.

Abstract Agent: Knowledge about women's health is inadequate worldwide because in some non-Western cultures, most women live isolated and sheltered lives that make it difficult to obtain data about them.

People as Agents: In much of the world, **medical researchers** know too little about women's health because in many non-Western cultures **the women** live isolated and sheltered lives that make it difficult to obtain data about them.

Agent/action sentences that show people doing things can also improve your writing.

Impersonal Subject: Bicycles are one of the most common modes of transportation in China. A **bicycle** with several passengers is not an uncommon sight.

Personal Agent Acting: Millions of Chinese ride bicycles in cities as well as in villages. The **astonished visitor** can often see two or three people on one bike, sometimes even carrying an animal.

Your readers will take more interest in your writing if people are involved. And they usually are—most issues touch on human lives, one way or another.

Without People: Although the federally funded **student-loan program** has made education accessible to a low-income population, the **default rate** among that population has had a significant effect on the future of the program.

With People: Hundreds of thousands of **young people** have been able to go to college because of federally funded student loans, but now **students** who have defaulted on their loans may be jeopardizing the program for **others.**

• 8a-2 Don't overload the subjects of sentences. Readers will get lost if you bury subjects under abstract words and phrases. Instead, make people or things your agents.

Overloaded Subject: The inability of intelligence tests, whether IQ tests or SATs, to predict people's behavior poses a longstanding dilemma for social scientists.

People as Subject: Social scientists have long wondered why intelligence tests, whether IQ tests or SATs, predict behavior so poorly.

• 8a-3 Make sure verbs convey real actions. Not only will the use of action verbs make your writing more lively, but identifying the action may also help you spot the real agent in a sentence, as in this example.

Dull Verb: American society **has** long **had** a fascination with celebrities.

Stronger Verb: Celebrities **have** long **fascinated** Americans.

Don't clutter action verbs with expressions such as *start to, manage to,* or *proceed to.*

Malls and markets ~~always manage to~~ irritate me when they ~~start to~~ display Christmas paraphernalia immediately after Halloween.

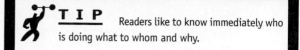

• 8a-4 Avoid "to be" verbs whenever possible. Though the verbs *is, are,* and their variants are often unavoidable, they're not as interesting as verbs that do things.

Dull Verbs: It **is** the tendency of adolescents **to be more concerned** about the opinion of others in their age group than they **are** about the values their parents are trying to instill in them.

Action Verbs: Adolescents **crave** the approval of their peers and often **resist** their parents' values.

8b Coordination

To show relationships between sentences of *equal* importance, link them with coordinating conjunctions or semicolons. Coordination can smooth choppy passages that have too many short sentences. The seven coordinating conjunctions are *and, or, nor, for, so, but,* and *yet.*

• 8b-1 Join only independent clauses of equal importance with coordinating conjunctions or semicolons. A semicolon used in this way is often followed by a word such as *therefore* or *however.*

The auditor couldn't pinpoint the problem, **so** she recalculated her figures.

Most architects love to design residences, **but** they solicit commissions for offices and schools to survive financially.

Rain fell in torrent(s;) however, the cheering fans hardly noticed.

• 8b-2 Don't use the conjunction and when a more precise conjunction is available.

The bill was past due, ~~and~~ but the bank hadn't charged a penalty.

8c Subordination

To emphasize one idea over another in a sentence, use subordination. Subordinating conjunctions provide the link between main ideas (independent clauses) and secondary ones (dependent clauses). Among the many subordinating conjunctions are words such as the following.

after	before	unless	which
although	if	when	while
because	since	where	who

A subordinating conjunction turns an independent clause into a dependent clause that cannot stand alone as a sentence:

Independent: Ramon started his car.

Dependent: When Ramon started his car, the dog barked

Independent: I wrote the paper quickly.

Dependent: Although I wrote the paper quickly, I had carefully read all the required sources and gathered data.

• 8c-1 Use subordination to clarify vague relationships between clauses.

Many people go into debt/ ~~Credit~~ when credit is easy to get.

• 8c-2 Use subordination to shift the emphasis of sentences.
Generally, readers will focus on ideas in your independent clauses. Compare the following sentences, both equally good, but with different emphases.

Although *most senators now campaign for a balanced budget,* they often lobby hard for federal projects in their home states.

Although *they often lobby hard for federal projects in their home states,* most senators now campaign for balanced budgets.

• 8c-3 Use subordination to expand your sentences.
You can use subordination to combine simple clauses into more graceful or powerful sentences, as in this example.

Despite
~~The~~ running back had an ankle injury/ and ~~He had~~
a two-month layoff too. ~~Still, he~~ the running back chalked up
a hundred-yard afternoon.

• 8c-4 Use dependent clauses sensibly.

If you pile more than two or three dependent clauses into one sentence, you may confuse readers.

Too Much Subordination: Although his book *Politically Correct Bedtime Stories,* which has been a best-seller for more than a year, was turned down by thirty publishers while he struggled at two jobs while he wrote the book, James Finn Garner isn't resentful, **which suggests the importance of persistence.**

Revised: Persistence counts. James Finn Garner isn't resentful, **even though his *Politically Correct Bedtime Stories,* a best-seller for more than a year, was turned down by thirty publishers.** He struggled at two jobs **while he wrote the book.**

8d Parallelism

Sentences are especially easy to read when related ideas follow similar language patterns. These sentences with similar patterns demonstrate parallelism. When an item doesn't follow a pattern of language already established in a sentence, it lacks parallelism. Review how these two examples have been reworded to achieve parallelism.

> The job requires good computer skills, original
>   *dedication*
> thinking, and ^the ~~hours are long~~.

>   *in the air*
> Over the land, on the sea, or ^~~if they fly~~, the
> Marines move troops fast.

• 8d-1 Recognize sentence patterns that require parallel construction.

When words or phrases comes in pairs or triplets, they usually need to be parallel. That is, each element must follow the same form: a noun or noun phrase, an adjective or adjective phrase, or an adverb or adverbial phrase.

Noun Phrases: Optimism in outlook and **egotism in behavior**—those are essential qualities for a leader.

Adjectives: The best physicians are **patient, thorough,** and **compassionate.**

Adverbs: The lawyers presented their case **passionately** and **persuasively.**

Items in a list should also be parallel.

> The school board's objectives are clear: **to hire** the best teachers, **to create** successful classrooms, **to serve** the needs of all families, and **to prepare** the students for the twenty-first century.

• 8d-2 Use parallelism in comparisons.

This is especially important in expressions following *as* or *than.*

The city council is **as** likely *to adopt* the measure **as** ~~vetoing~~ it.
_{to veto}

Smiling takes fewer muscles **than** ~~to frown~~.
^{frowning}

•8d-3 Recognize expressions that signal the need for parallel structure. These include the following constructions: *not only . . . but also; either . . . or; neither . . . nor; but . . . and; on the one hand . . . on the other hand.*

> We spoke **not only** *to the President* **but also** *to the Speaker of the House.*

> **On the one hand,** *interest rates might be tightened;* **on the other hand,** *prices might be increased.*

•8d-4 Use parallelism to show a progression of ideas. You can set up parallel structures within sentences or within entire paragraphs.

> Jane Brody, *The New York Times* health writer, says, "Regular exercise comes closer to being a fountain of youth than anything modern medicine can offer." **Exercise halves** the risk of heart disease and stroke, **lowers** the chance of cancer colon, and **reduces** the likelihood of osteoporosis. **It lessens** the chances of developing diabetes and **strengthens** the immune system. **Exercise** even **helps** people overcome depression.

8e Sentence Problems

When readers have trouble figuring out what your sentences mean, there's little point in trying to explain them. Just fix the problems.

•8e-1 Make sure your subjects, verbs, and complements work together logically. You can sometimes lose the connection between subjects and predicates, creating a problem called faulty predication.

Faulty Predication: Prejudice is unacceptable behavior in this club. ("Prejudice" is not behavior; it's an attitude.)

Revised: Prejudiced behavior is unacceptable in this club.

Faulty Predication: The narrative **structure** of Peggy Lee's song "Is That All There Is?" **begins** as a child and continues through her adult life. (Can narrative structures begin as children? That's unlikely.)

Revised: Peggy Lee's song "Is That All There Is?" follows the life of a character from childhood to adult.

•8e-2 Watch for places where sentences derail. Quite often a modifying phrase or clause can throw writers off, making them lose the connection between various components of their sentence.

It is a fact that ^{two-thirds of} juveniles, ~~when~~ sent to *adult prisons* rather than *juvenile facilities,* ~~two-thirds of them~~ go on to commit more serious crimes.

Sentences also commonly derail when subordinate clauses pile up and the writer leaves out a main clause.

Talks with North Korea will create a situation ~~in which~~ ^{favorable to} the emergence of a middle class that will push for democratization.

• 8e-3 Reorganize overloaded sentences.

If your readers are impatient—and many are—you will lose them if your sentences are jammed with too much information. For example, when the long sentence in the following example is split, the passage becomes more readable.

Too Long: And when the Fourth Amendment and other constitutional rights restricting police behavior are violated, it necessarily carries with it a strong message to our political minorities—including members of racial minori-

ties, who are more likely to have contact with the police than are whites—that the legal system is a joker, one which says, "We make the rules, and we'll follow the ones we like."
—Scott Turow, "Doomed"

Revised: When the Fourth Amendment and other constitutional rights restricting police behavior are violated, it necessarily carries with it a strong message to our political minorities, who are more likely to have contact with the police than are whites. To blacks and Hispanics especially, the legal system is often a joker, one which says, "We make the rules, and we'll follow the ones we like."

chapter

[9]

Stylish Sentences

*A*writer's first job is to write clearly, but just as there's more to cooking than preparing wholesome meals, there's more to writing than crafting clear, effective sentences. As you revise, you can make your sentences varied, rhythmic, and rich in detail.

9a Clarity

When something is well written, a careful reader should be able to move along steadily without backtracking to puzzle about meaning. Writers can work toward that goal using a number of strategies.

• **9a-1 Use specific details.** Abstract terms such as *health-care provider system, positive learning environment,* and *two-wheeled vehicle* are usually harder to understand than concrete terms such as *hospital, classroom,* and *Harley.* Of course, you have to use abstract words sometimes; it's impossible to discuss ideas without them. However, the more you use specific details, the clearer your sentences will be. For example, specialists might understand the following abstract sentence from a scholarly book, but stating the ideas more concretely gives it broader appeal.

Abstract: It is also important to recognize that just as we can learn from knowledge about the efficacy of alternative bargaining structures, we can also benefit from knowledge of alternative approaches to welfare and employment policies. —William Julius Wilson, *The Truly Disadvantaged*

Revised: We should recognize that just as it helps us to learn more about how groups bargain in other countries, it would also help us to learn more about how they handle welfare and unemployment.

An especially effective way to add texture to sentences is to downshift—that is, to state a general idea and then to provide more and more details. The resulting sentences will be both clear and interesting.

Toi Soldier was a magnificent black Arabian stallion, **a sculpture in ebony, his eyes large and dark, his graceful head held high on an arched neck.** He was a competitor in any Arabian horse show, **equally poised in equitation classes or under harness.**

• **9a-2 Use examples to illustrate general statements.** Readers like to understand exactly what an idea means, as in the following example.

We live in a society that is convinced of the benefits of taller stature. Conventional wisdom has it that taller, larger people are more powerful, effective, and intelligent. Men, especially, are often obsessed with height, hoping to reach the magical six-foot mark.

—Thomas T. Samaras,
"Let's Get Small"

• 9a-3 State ideas positively. Negative statements can be surprisingly hard to read. When you can, turn negative statements into positive ones, as shown in this example.

Do we have the right ~~not~~ to be ~~victims of~~ safe from street crime?

• 9a-4 "Chunk" your writing. Break lengthy paragraphs into manageable bits, and present unusually complex information in lists. An example follows.

To get started with your new computer,

- Unpack it, saving the Styrofoam packing;
- Position your computer away from sources of heat;
- Plug the keyboard, mouse, monitor, and printer into the designated ports on the back of the computer;
- Check that the outlet you are using is grounded;
- Attach the power cord to the computer, and plug it in.

Notice that all the items in the list are parallel. (See Section 8d.)

• 9a-5 Use charts and graphs to present quantitative information. Readers grasp numbers and statistics much more quickly when they can see them presented visually rather than in words. Fortunately, these days writers can create such displays with word processing programs. See Chapter 28, Producing Handsome Documents, for more on this topic.

9b Economy

For those who aspire to be good writers, the war against what writer and editor William Zinsser calls "clutter" never ends. Such clutter consists of those clichés, strung-out phrases, pointless repetitions, and overstuffed descriptions that keep writing from being sharp.

• 9b-1 Condense sprawling lead-in phrases.

Why Write . . .	When You Could Write . . .
in the event that	if
in light of the fact that	since
on the grounds that	because
regardless of the fact that	although
on the occasion of	when
at this point in time	now
it is obvious that	obviously

• 9b-2 Condense long verb phrases to focus on the action.

Why Write . . .	When You Could Write . . .
give consideration to	consider
make acknowledgment of	acknowledge
they have doubts about	they doubt
is reflective of	reflects
have an understanding of	understand
put the emphasis on	emphasize

• 9b-3 Eliminate doublings and redundancies.
Doublings are expressions in which two words are used to say exactly the same thing. One word can usually be deleted.

trim and slim	proper and fitting
icy and cold	eager and willing

Redundancies are words or concepts unnecessarily repeated. They can be hard to spot.

> Bumper stickers help to classify drivers ~~into certain classes.~~

Don't repeat major words in a sentence unless there's a good reason. Such repetitions make sentences tedious.

> When a large group of sorority **women come** together, you'll inevitably find some ~~women who come~~ from the same background.

• 9b-4 Eliminate surplus intensifiers.

Why Write . . .	When You Could Write . . .
We're **completely** finished.	We're finished.
I'm **totally** exhausted.	I'm exhausted.
That's **absolutely** pointless.	That's pointless.
The work is **basically** done.	The work is done.

• 9b-5 Get rid of "it is . . ." and "there are . . ." openings.

Why Write . . .	When You Could Write . . .
there is a desire for	we want
there are reasons for	for several reasons
there was an expectation	they expected
it is clear that	clearly
it is to be hoped	we hope

• 9b-6 Cut the number of prepositional phrases.
Although you must often use prepositional phrases, they clog up sentences when combined with abstract nouns. In the example that follows, the abstract nouns are in boldface type and the prepositional phrases are in italics.

Wordy: The **proliferation** *of credit cards among college students* is the result *of extensive **marketing*** *by banking **institutions*** who see college students *in terms of future **profits**.*

Tighter: Banks market credit cards to college students because they see them as promising future customers.

• 9b-7 Condense sentences into dependent clauses and dependent clauses into phrases or words. Often one forceful word can do the work of several. Say more with less.

~~Queen Elizabeth I was a~~ complex and sensuous ^Queen Elizabeth I ~~woman. She~~ seemed to love ~~many~~ men, yet she never came close to marrying ~~any of her suitors.~~

Thanksgiving is a time for ~~all of~~ us to be together, ~~for the simple purpose of~~ enjoying each other's company.

9c Variety

Your readers will quickly be bored if all your sentences are of the same type and pattern. You'll also want to tailor sentence length to the needs of your audience—for example, experienced readers are usually more comfortable with long sentences than are children. But, audience aside, you'll want to vary sentence lengths in most paragraphs just to keep readers interested.

Chart: Sentence Types

Simple Sentence
independent clause
Windows rattled.

Compound Sentence
independent clause + independent clause
Windows rattled and doors shook.

Complex
dependent clause(s) + one independent clause
As the storm blew, windows rattled.

Compound-Complex
dependent clause(s) + two or more independent clauses
As the storm blew, windows rattled and doors shook.

• 9c-1 Vary sentence types. The familiar sentence types are all built from independent clauses (a subject and predicate that can stand alone) and subordinate clauses (a subject and predicate that cannot stand alone). Simple sentences attract the attention of readers with their clarity and punch.

Every charity is a special interest.
—P. J. O'Rourke, "Among the Compassion Fascists"

I belong to a Clan of One-Breasted Women.
—Terry Tempest Williams, "The Clan
of One-Breasted Women"

Compound sentences put ideas of equal weight side by side, sometimes to make a specific point (see Section 8b).

Small children and babies were perched on every lap available and men leaned on the shelves or on each other.
—Maya Angelou, "Champion of the World"

Complex and compound-complex sentences give you means to state ideas subtly, richly, and fully.

Error of opinion may be tolerated where reason is left free to combat it.
—Thomas Jefferson

The blue-collar Negroes I grew up among took a liking to the Kennedys because they thought the Eisenhowers were dull and that Ike was on the golf course too much when he should have been doing his presidential job.
—Stanley Crouch, "Blues for Jackie"

The old man is a widower whose seven children are long since gone from Hog Wallow, and he is as expansively talkative and worldly as the young one is withdrawn and wild.
—John McPhee, "The Pines"

Varying sentence types in a paragraph or essay will keep readers engaged. But understand that there is no one-to-one relationship between sentence type and length. Simple sentences with compound subjects, verbs, or objects can be quite lengthy; complex sentences can be short, if the subordinated elements are brief.

• 9c-2 Vary sentence patterns. The standard sentence patterns in English are reliable but sometimes dull if repeated over and over.

Subject + verb + object
Subject + verb + complement/object

A few changes can add style. For example, consider inverting the usual word order.

Gone is the opportunity to win this month's lottery.

Intelligent, cultured, and politically shrewd was Eleanor of Aquitaine, a twelfth-century liberated woman.

Alternatively, you can put interesting details into modifying clauses or phrases that can be moved to different points in a sentence.

At the Beginning: Convinced that he could not master rhetoric until he knew Greek, Thomas began studying the language when he was 40.

In the Middle: Li Po, **one of the greatest of the Chinese poets,** drowned when he fell out of a boat while trying to kiss the reflection of the moon in the water.

At the End: Sixteenth-century Aztec youths played a complex game called ollamlitzli, **which some anthropologists believe to have been the forerunner of modern basketball.**

9d Figurative Language

Writers who make an impact on their readers are often the ones with the gift for finding the image that lasts, the metaphor that makes a concept come alive, the analogy that clarifies. Probably no writer learns directly how to use figurative language effectively. The best you can do is to stay alert for the way authors use metaphor and analogy and have the courage to experiment yourself.

• 9d-1 Look for fresh images that will strike your readers' imaginations.

I went to high school at J. W. Sexton in Lansing, Michigan, a Depression-era brick fortress that sat across the street from a Fisher Body auto assembly plant. The plant was blocks long on each side and wrapped in a skin of corrugated steel painted a shade of green somewhere between the Statue of Liberty and mold. It loomed so near the high school that on football Fridays, when the Big Reds butted heads in Memorial Stadium, night-shift workers stood on balconies and watched the game.
—Ted Kleine,
"Living the Lansing Dream"

T I P   **Don't mix metaphors.** What's a mixed metaphor? It is a comparison that is either inconsistent or illogical. The following passage contains a mixed metaphor, because it's hard to move from *melting pot* to *backbone.*

The United States is a **melting pot,** blending diverse substances into a uniform mass. This is the **backbone** of my argument against multiculturalism.

To create such powerful images, sometimes all you have to do is turn general terms into more specific ones.

While striking ~~athletes~~ baseball players drove off in their ~~fancy sports cars,~~ Porsches and BMWs, ground crews and peanut ~~ployed~~ vendors the newly created unemployed at the parks struggled to find work.

• 9d-2 Use similes and metaphors to dramatize ideas. Similes are comparisons that use *as* or *like.* Here are two examples.

As another fire season approaches, anxiety about fires in the West is building **as inexorably as piles of dead wood on the forest floor.**
—Ted Williams, "Only You Can Postpone Forest Fires"

Life in China was for millennia **like a lethal board game in which a blind destiny threw the dice, and to land on the wrong square**

69

at the wrong moment could mean sudden ruin and repulsive death.

—Dennis Bloodworth,
The Chinese Looking Glass

Metaphors are direct comparisons, without the use of *as* or *like,* as in these two examples.

Better watch out or **the pendulum of medical dogma** will bash your head in. **It swings back and forth** far more often than most people realize, and with far more velocity.

—Sherwin B. Nuland, "Medical
Fads: Bran, Midwives, and Leeches"

The **geological time scale is a layer cake** of odd names, learned by generations of grumbling students with mnemonics either too insipid or too salacious for publication: Cambrian, Ordovician, Silurian, Devonian.

—Stephen Jay Gould,
"The Power of Narrative"

• 9d-3 Use analogies to explain concepts. Analogies are extended comparisons. Here is an elegant opening paragraph that draws an analogy between cowardly lions and fallen heroes.

The spectacle is becoming all too familiar. One by one heroes are being knocked from their pedestals, their veils of nobility, bravery, and omnipotence stripped away to reveal a selfish, cowering heart. Now, to the legion of fallen sports stars, artists, politicians, and religious leaders must be added the cream of cats, the universal symbol of courage and royalty, a beast powerful enough to match Mickey as one of Disney's biggest money machines: the lion.

—Natalie Angier, "Please Say It
Isn't So, Simba: The Noble
Lion Can Be a Coward"

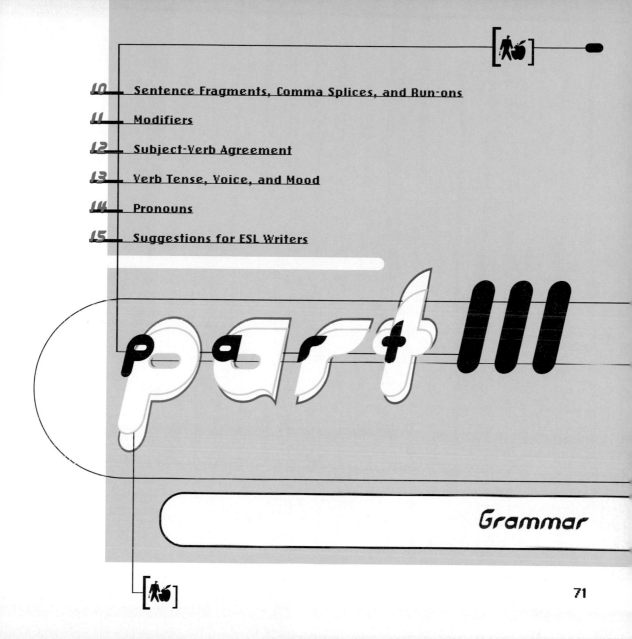

part III

Grammar

chapter [10]

A — Sentence Fragments
B — Intentional Fragments
C — Comma Splices
D — Run-on Sentences

Sentence Fragments, Comma Splices, and Run-ons

*T*hree of the most common problems with sentences are sentence fragments, comma splices, and run-on sentences. This chapter will suggest ways to avoid such problems.

10a Sentence Fragments

Incomplete sentences, or fragments, can distract readers and sometimes make you look like a careless writer. These suggestions will help you get rid of unwanted fragments.

• 10a-1 Check that you have not tried to make a dependent clause stand alone as a sentence.

Dependent clauses—clauses that start with words such as *although, because, if, since, unless, when, while*—don't work as sentences by themselves even though they have a subject and a verb. Fragments can usually be fixed by linking them to another sentence.

Fragment: If the invoice comes by Friday

Sentence: If the invoice comes by Friday, the sale will go through.

Fragment: Although I have never seen their credentials

Sentence: Although I have never seen their credentials, they come well recommended.

• 10a-2 Check that you haven't made a relative clause or appositive stand alone as a sentence.

Words such as *who, which, where,* and *that* often signal the beginning of a clause that must be attached to the main part of the sentence.

Roberto was the son of immigrants, ~~Who had~~ who never aspired to public office.

An appositive is a word or group of words that explains another noun or pronoun. An appositive that gets separated from the word it goes with can become a fragment.

Checklist: *Subordinating Words*

Whenever you write a clause that begins with a subordinating word, check for a fragment. Subordinating words include the following.

after	in order that	until
although	once	when
as	rather than	whenever
as soon as	since	where
because	so	whether
before	so that	which
even though	sooner than	while
for	that	who
how	though	whose
if	unless	why

Marcia cringed when she saw Mr. Bonaven-
ture, ⌃a **A man she thought had been dead for
twenty years.**

•10a-3 Check that you have not mistaken a verbal for the verb in a sentence.
Verbals are tricky constructions because they look like verbs but act as nouns, adjectives, or adverbs.

- Verbals that act as nouns are called gerunds: **Voting** is important, **Flying** is exciting.
- Verbals that modify nouns are called participles: the **running** team, the **dancing** children.
- Infinitives—the to form of verbs—are also verbals: **to go, to see, to participate.**

To eliminate fragments caused by verbals, it helps to remember the following.

- An -ing word by itself can never act as the verb of a sentence. It must have an auxiliary verb such as have, is, or were.
- An infinitive such as to run, to go, and so on can never act as the verb in a sentence.

Here are examples of how to edit sentence fragments caused by verbals.

When Glaxco bought his company, Phil decided to retire, ⌃s **Suspecting there would be no
place for him in the new office.**

To hold out until her opponents collapsed,
~~That~~ was Hannah's strategy.

•10a-4 Check that you have not treated a list as an independent sentence.
Sometimes a list gets detached from its introduction, and a fragment results.

Bucking a Hollywood stereotype, some stars have had marriages lasting more than fifty
years, ⌃among them **Robert Mitchum, Bob Hope, Jane Wyatt, Danny Thomas, and Charlton Heston** ⌃
~~among them.~~

10b Intentional Fragments

From time to time you probably notice sentence fragments in magazines and newspapers and wonder what's going on. Are sentence fragments wrong in some situations but not in others? The answer is "Yes." It depends on the context.

Some constructions can be called intentional fragments. These are phrases or words that don't have all the components of a sentence but effectively convey a complete idea. You'll often find them in advertisements or in newspaper and magazine articles written in a very casual tone. Look at the following magazine ad from the September 1995 issue of *Wired* magazine for a miniature phone that AT&T plans to offer soon.

Miniature. Wireless. Small enough to wear on your wrist. Yet powerful enough to reach anyone. Anywhere in the world.

Is this technique effective? It probably works for the readers of *Wired,* a very trendy magazine. But appropriate occasions for such a style are limited, and any writer needs to think carefully about purpose and audience before risking such informality.

• 10b-1 Use intentional fragments sparingly. You might use them in narratives or in an article that's light and informal, but think carefully about whether you have a specific reason for writing a fragment. If you don't have one, it's better to get rid of it.

• 10b-2 As a rule, avoid intentional fragments in academic writing, formal articles, or business writing. Don't use them in research papers, technical reports, job applications, or any piece of serious writing for an audience about whom you know little.

10c Comma Splices

Comma splices occur when a writer incorrectly joins two independent clauses with a comma, as shown in the following example.

Local shopkeepers are concerned about a recent outbreak of graffiti, they fear it indicates renewed gang activity in the neighborhood.

Notice that the group of words on each side of the comma could stand alone as a sentence.

• 10c-1 Remember that the comma is a weak mark of punctuation. A comma marks such a brief pause that it doesn't provide the strong separation needed between two independent clauses. As a result, the reader tends to run right through the gap. A comma between two independent clauses can also hide the relationship between the two parts of a sentence.

Comma Splice: Shawna is a surprising musician, she has no formal training in music.

• 10c-2 Correct a comma splice by substituting a semicolon for the faulty comma. Unlike a comma, a semicolon indicates a strong separation. Choose a semicolon to correct a comma splice, especially if the two independent clauses are closely related.

As the diplomat approached the podium, he balanced his briefcase, top hat, earphones, and white gloves, he had everything that he needed to meet the demands of protocol.

• 10c-3 Correct a comma splice by substituting a period for the faulty comma. A period is especially appropriate if the two independent clauses are *not* closely related.

Like a chef laying out the ingredients for making bouillabaisse, the Honorable Thomas Calhoun spread his notes before him and set his pocket watch squarely on the podium. ⊙He ~~he~~ made sure that nothing could go wrong this time.

•10c-4 Correct a comma splice by keeping the comma but inserting a co-ordinating conjunction such as but, and, or, yet, for or after it. For example:

The reason the legislation got so bogged down in committee was that the new congresswoman was naive, for she had no inkling her colleagues could talk so long.

•10c-5 Correct the comma splice by rewriting the sentence and making one of the independent clauses a subordinate clause. For example:

When Congresswoman Harrison left the legislative session after midnight, she felt grateful that she still had her voice.

10d Run-on Sentences

A run-on sentence occurs when no punctuation separates two independent clauses. The reader is left to figure out where one sentence ends and the next one begins.

The police were suspicious of the package they called for an X-ray machine.

I left the room was too cold.

•10d-1 Correct a run-on by separating the two clauses with a period. For example:

In the affluent 1980s, advertisers counted on snob appeal and consumer insecurity to sell items such as Rolex watches and luxury cars. In ~~in~~ the thrift-minded 1990s, they are stressing high quality and long use.

•10d-2 Correct a run-on by putting a semicolon between two independent

clauses that have been run together. For example:

> Conversation ∧ in the office revolved around the boss's moods⁄ ∧ everyone else's moods were ignored.

> I left ∧ʹthe room was too cold. ∧

• 10d-3 Correct a run-on by joining the independent clauses with a comma and a coordinating conjunction. (See Section 10c-4.) For example:

Poisonous giant toads were introduced to Australia in the 1930s to control beetles ∧but they ∧ have since become an ecological menace.

The police were suspicious of the package ∧ʹso ∧ they called for an X-ray machine.

• 10d-4 Correct the run-on by making one of the independent clauses subordinate to the other. For example:

> McAndrews had to finish the report by himself because ∧ his assigned partner was inept.

chapter [11]

Modifiers

*U*sed well, adjectives and adverbs give writing color and make it more precise. But adjectives, and especially adverbs, can sometimes be tricky to use. If they're misplaced or used inaccurately, they can be confusing.

11a Placement of Adjectives

In English, adjectives usually come before the word or phrase they modify: **red** apple, **outstanding** athlete, and so on. You must, however, place adjectives carefully to avoid ambiguity and awkward pileups.

> The president had the (enthusiastic) stockholders' support.
> Does *enthusiastic* modify *stockholders* or *support?*

> The much-decorated, ~~popular, colorful~~ young sailor will make an attractive candidate.
> Too many adjectives pile up together.

• 11a-1 Relocate adjectives that are potentially confusing or ambiguous. Ask a second reader to look over your draft and point out any modifiers that might possibly be confusing.

> The (long-lost) spy's memoirs were revealing.
> Does *long-lost* go with *spy* or *memoirs?*

• 11a-2 Consider placing some adjectives after the words or phrases they modify. You can avoid piling up adjectives by occasionally varying their position.

> A new ~~powerful, quick, and easy-to-use~~ —powerful, quick, and easy to use— computer system was installed today.

11b Problems with Adjectives: Good, Well, and Other Confusions

Predicate adjectives are words that follow linking verbs (*is, are, was, seem, feel, looks,* and so on) and describe the subject. (See Section 14c-7 for more information.) In the following examples, the linking verb is in italics and the predicate adjective is boldface.

> I *feel* **bad.**
> He *seems* **uneasy.**
> Mike *looks* **strong.**

When you're confused about whether to follow a linking verb with an adjective or an adverb ending in -*ly,* locate the word you're going to modify. If it's a noun or a pronoun, finish it with an adjective. If it's a verb, modify it with an adverb. In the following examples, the linking verbs require an adverb.

> He *felt* **carefully** through the grass.
> She *looked* **suspiciously** at her brother.

• 11b-1 Remember that only adjectives, not adverbs, can modify a noun.

envious
Gordon feels ~~enviously~~ of Jerry's promotion.
           ^
(The word being modified here is *Gordon*.)

flawless
The tenant kept the woodwork ~~flawlessly~~.
                              ^

• 11b-2 Learn to use well and good properly.

Good is always an adjective; *well* is usually an adverb, but sometimes it too can be an adjective. Here are some guidelines.

Use *good* (or *bad*) after a linking verb if you are modifying the subject of the sentence.

>Jasper Hays looks **good.**

>His record is **good.**

>Janet looks **bad** since her divorce.

Use *well* when you're referring to someone's health.

>Madeline has felt **well** since she returned from New York.

But don't use *good* as an adverb. For example:

>   *well*
>The system doesn't run ~~good~~.
>   ^
>   *well*
>Jobs in social work don't usually pay ~~good~~.
>   ^

11c Absolute Adjectives

Adjectives such as *unique, perfect,* and *equal* are called absolute adjectives because logically they can't be modified. They are absolute in

Absolute Adjectives

Don't add modifiers to these words.

absolute	equal	pregnant
complete	full	singular
definite	perfect	unique
empty		

themselves. For example, it is illogical to say that something is "most unique," because something is either unique or it isn't. It is illogical to write "completely full" or "totally empty," since "full" and "empty" describe absolute conditions. Of course, such expressions do make sense; we know what they mean. But careful writers avoid such phrases, if only because they annoy some readers.

11d Forms of Adverbs

Adverbs modify verbs, adjectives, or other adverbs. They often end in *-ly,* and some have both long and short forms.

deep/deeply	fair/fairly	quick/quickly
rough/roughly	slow/slowly	tight/tightly

The short form of adverbs sounds more casual and colloquial than the long form. Thus, if you're writing for a professor or for an audience of businesspeople, you'll do better to use the *-ly* form of an adverb.

The Jets play **rough.** *or* Her teammates play **roughly.**

Drive **slow.** *or* It's best to drive **slowly.**

The judge played **fair.** *or* He played that hand **fairly.**

IIe Placement of Adverbs

Adverbs can take any of several positions in a sentence, as shown in the following examples.

> The legislator talked **endlessly** about his accomplishments.

> The legislator talked about his accomplishments **endlessly.**

But it's also easy to misplace adverbs.

• IIe-1 When editing, check to see that you haven't placed adverbs in positions that could cause confusion. For example:

> Seeing the security officer approach ^ **quickly**
> quickly
> James ^ concluded his speech.
> ^
> If *quickly* is intended to modify *concluded* instead of *approach,* it must be moved.

Negative Pronouns and Adverbs

barely	no	not any
hardly	nobody	nothing
never	none	scarcely

• IIe-2 Place the adverbs even and only directly before the words they modify in order to avoid confusion. For example:

> A true workaholic, Jan (**even**) thinks time spent driving to work should be used productively.

> The accountant (**only**) knew of one person who could do the job properly.

> Sonja (**only**) wrote on the day of her wedding three lines in her journal.

> Virginia had (**almost**) dated every man at the party.

IIf Double Negatives

Although double negatives are common in other languages (French, for example), in English they're nonstandard and will jolt your readers' sense of good usage.

• IIf-1 Check that you haven't used two no words in the same sentence or independent clause. If you have, drop one or alter the phrasing. For example:

> That newspaper **doesn't ~~never~~** take a stand.

> The manager **didn't want ~~no~~** young help.
> any

• 11F-2 Don't mix the negative adverbs hardly, scarcely, and barely with another negative word or phrase. For example:

The crowd's mood was so enthusiastic that the candidate ~~couldn't~~ **hardly** wait to speak.
_{could}

He ~~didn't scarcely~~ ~~get~~ started when the mood
_{got}
began to change.

11g Misplaced and Dangling Modifiers

Modifiers tend to attach themselves to the nearest noun or pronoun, so if you put the modifier in the wrong position, the sentence can go askew. Two forms of this problem are misplaced modifiers and dangling modifiers. A misplaced modifier is shown in the following example.

Short of money, the plans for the new stadium ~~had to be scrapped by the city.~~
_{city scrapped}
Does *short of money* modify *plans* or *city?*

A dangling modifier occurs when a writer uses a modifying phrase but doesn't supply anything in the sentence that it could modify. For example:

Before announcing the winners, a date must be set for the runoff.

• 11g-1 When editing, check that an introductory modifying phrase is followed by the word it modifies. Often you simply need to rearrange the sentence. For example:

~~Insulting and gross,~~ **fewer** and fewer televi-
_{Fewer}
sion viewers were attracted to the comedian's late-night diatribes.
_{insulting and gross}

• 11g-2 When editing, check for dangling modifiers and, if necessary, find a word for them to modify. This may mean rewriting a sentence. For example:

On returning to the room, the furniture had
_{she saw that}
been rearranged.

• 11g-3 Distinguish between absolute modifiers and misplaced modifiers. Some phrases are called absolute modifiers; that is, they are complete in themselves, serving only to give more information about the whole sentence. You have some flexibility about where to place such phrases in a sentence.

Given their lethal capabilities, it is not surprising that pit vipers frighten people.

or

It is not surprising that pit vipers frighten people, **given their lethal capabilities.**

His chances for reinstatement are very slim, **to be quite honest.**

or

To be quite honest, his chances for reinstatement are very slim.

11h Comparatives and Superlatives

The comparative and superlative forms of most adjectives and a few adverbs can be expressed in two ways.

ugly (an adjective)

comparative	uglier	more ugly
superlative	ugliest	most ugly

slowly (an adverb)

comparative	slower	more slowly
superlative	slowest	most slowly

Trust your ear when choosing a form. As a rule, use *-er* and *-est* endings with words of one syllable and *more* and *most* with words of more than one syllable.

Their group is **brighter** than ours.

This group is the **most conservative.**

The candidate talked **faster** than the moderator.

The incumbent speaks **more decisively** than the challenger.

• 11h-1 Use the comparative, not the superlative, form when you are comparing two items. For example:

That building is the **tallest** of the two.
^ taller

Of the two speakers, Casey drones **most loudly.**
^ more

• 11h-2 Use the superlative form when comparing more than two items. For example:

Of all the onlookers, the children yelled **most loudly.**

Given the choice of three applicants, Claude chose the **best dressed.**

• 11h-3 Avoid using two comparative or two superlative terms in the same phrase.

McDougal is a **more tougher** boss than Gonzalez is.

Paula Sung is the **most smartest** lawyer in her firm.

[12]

chapter

Subject-Verb Agreement

*P*roblems with subject-verb agreement are among the errors careful readers are most likely to notice. You can avoid difficulties with agreement by recalling just a few principles and guidelines.

12a Agreement with Singular and Plural Subjects

A verb changes form, depending on the person of its subject and whether its subject is singular or plural. The verb is then said to agree in person and number with its subject. In the present tense, agreement is fairly simple.

First person singular:	I wait.
Second person singular:	You wait.
First person plural:	We wait.
Second person plural:	You go.
Third person plural:	They go.

The notable exception in this pattern occurs with third person singular subjects (for example, *he, she, it, the carpenter, Mr. Jones*). For these sub-jects, a regular verb ends in *-s* or *-es.*

Third person singular:	Mr. Jones wait**s**.
	She wait**s**.
	It go**es**.

So, to choose a correct verb form in the third per-son, you need to know whether the subject of the sentence is singular or plural. Sometimes it's not easy to tell.

• 12a-1 Pay attention only to the subject itself when a subject is linked to other nouns by phrases such as along with, as well as, or together with. The verb agrees with the subject, not with the second noun.

sing. subj.
The *National Weather Service,* as well as
plural noun   sing. verb
local authorities, **wishes** amateurs wouldn't

chase tornadoes in their cars.

The same principle holds when a plural subject (*amateurs* in this example) is linked to a singular noun (*press* in this case).

plural subj.   sing. noun
Many *amateurs,* along with the *press,*
plural verb
chase tornadoes in the Midwest.

• 12a-2 In most cases, treat subjects joined by and as plural. Joining two sub-jects in this way creates a compound subject.

1st subj.   2nd subj.   plural verb
Storm chasers and reporters alike **want** great

pictures of storms.

However, a few subjects joined by *and* do describe a single thing or idea. Treat such expressions as singular.

sing. subj.   sing. verb
Peace and quiet **is** rare on the Texas plains in

the spring.

sing. subj.   sing. verb
Ham and eggs **is** his favorite breakfast.

Similarly, when a compound subject linked by *and* is preceded by *every* or *each,* the verb takes a singular form.

subj. + subj.   sing. verb
Each spring and each fall **brings** the danger of

more storms.

However, when *each* follows a compound subject, usage varies.

> *The meteorologist and the storm chaser each* **have** *their own reasons for studying the weather.*

> *The meteorologist and the storm chaser each* **has** *his or her story to tell.*

• *12a-3 When the subjects are joined by or, neither ... nor, or either ... or, be sure the verb (or its auxiliary) agrees with the subject closer to it.*

plural subj.   sing.
Neither the local authorities nor the National
subj.   sing. verb
Weather Service **is** able to prevent people

from tracking dangerous tornadoes.

sing. subj.   plural subj.
Either severe lightning or powerful bouts of hail
plural verb
are apt to accompany the development of a

supercell.

Summary: Indefinite Pronouns

Singular	Variable, Singular or Plural	Plural
anybody	all	few
anyone	any	many
anything	either	several
each	more	
everybody	most	
everyone	neither	
everything	none	
nobody	some	
no one		
nothing		
somebody		
someone		
something		

12b Agreement with Indefinite Pronouns

Indefinite pronouns are those that don't refer to a particular person, thing, or group. With such terms, agreement can get tricky because it's sometimes hard to tell whether these pronouns—words such as *everyone, none, each,* and *any*—are singular or plural.   The most troublesome indefinite pronouns are *each* and *none. Each* is singular; *none* varies but is usually singular. *Either* and *neither* are usually singular in formal writing but often plural in informal writing. The examples that follow demonstrate conservative usage.

Singular: *Each* **believes** the agency must take decisive action.

Singular: *Nobody* **knows** what the governor-elect will do.

Variable: *None* of the proposals **is** easy to understand.

Variable: *Most* of the voters **favor** the reform legislation.

Plural: *Many* in sports clubs **hope** for a new stadium.

Plural: *Few* **intend** to pay higher ticket prices.

12c Agreement with Collective Nouns

Collective nouns are singular in form but name a group: *team, choir, band, jury, committee, family,* and so on. Such nouns can be either singular or plural. A collective noun is singular if the group is thought of as acting as a unit. A collective noun is plural if the members of the group are thought of as acting separately.

      sing. subj.   sing. verb

The *Bucci family* **believes** that its pizzeria business is helped by the Korean deli around the corner.

      plural subj.   plural verb

The *Bucci family* **believe** that their pizzeria business is helped by the Korean deli around the corner.

Both versions are acceptable.

Decide whether a collective noun used as a subject acts as a single unit (the jury) or as separate individuals or parts (the members of the jury). Then be consistent, making the verb and any pronouns agree in number with the subject.

Singular: The *choir* **expects** to choose a variety of hymns.

Plural: The *choir* **raise** *their* voices in song.

Singular: The *public* **is** satisfied.

Plural: The *public* **are** here in great number.

Usually you'll do better to treat collective nouns as singular subjects.

12d Agreement When the Subject Is Hard to Identify

Subject-verb agreement errors often occur when subjects are separated from their verbs by modifying words or phrases. Thus when you're editing for subject-verb agreement, first identify the subject; then you can put the right verb with it.

• 12d-1 Be sure that a verb agrees in number with its real subject, not with other words that may stand between the subject and the verb. A string of modifiers doesn't affect the subject.

```
  sing. subj.                 modifying phrase
```
The *killer whale,* the most widely distributed of
```
     modifying phrase               sing. verb
```
all mammals except humans, **demonstrates**

complex social behavior.

Problems are most likely when the subject is an indefinite pronoun (see Section 12b) followed by a
prepositional phrase.

• 12d-2 Remember that a singular pro-noun remains singular even when it is modified by a phrase with a plural noun in it.

```
     sing. subj.              sing. verb
```
Each of the whales **makes** a unique sound.

```
     sing. subj.                         sing. verb
```
One of the witnesses at the scene **is** willing to

talk.

• 12d-3 When the subject is a pronoun that is indefinite—such as some, all, or none—choose the verb according to the content of the phrase that modi-fies it.

```
     sing. subj.              sing. verb
```
Some of the research **is** contradictory.

```
     plural subj.                      plural verb
```
Some of the younger whales **are** playful.

Occasionally you may lose track of the subject because the sentence is complicated. Just remember
to keep your eye on the subject.

• 12d-4 Keep track of your subject when a sentence or clause begins with here or there. In such cases, the verb still agrees with the subject, which often trails after it.

Singular Subjects:

Here **is** a surprising *turn* of events.

There **is** a *reason* for his disappearance.

Plural Subjects:

Here **are** the *reports*.

There **are** already *calls* for the warden's resig-
nation.

• 12d-5 Don't be misled by linking verbs.
The most common are *to be, to seem, to appear, to
feel, to look,* and *to become.* A linking verb agrees
with its subject even when it connects the subject
to a plural noun.

```
        sing. subj.                    l. v. plural noun
```
The *key* to a coach's success **is** victories.

• 12d-6 Don't be misled by inverted sen-tence order.
In inverted sentences, some por-
tion of the verb precedes the subject. A verb
agrees with its subject, no matter where the subject appears in the sentence.

```
    plural verb                     plural subj.    verb
```
Do the stock market *fluctuations* **make** you

nervous?

sing. verb   verb   sing. subj.
Also **ruined** in the crash **is** the *director* of the company.

• 12d-7 Watch out for subject-verb agreement in the clause one of those who. The verb is always plural because it always refers to *those,* which is plural.

> Hemingway is one of *those authors* who **are** [not **is**] not much read today.

To understand the situation more clearly, rearrange the sentence this way.

> Of the authors *who* **are** not much read today, Hemingway is one.

Now watch what happens if we add the word *only* to the mix.

> Hemingway is the *only* one of my favorite authors who **is** not much read today.

Why is the verb now singular? The subject of the verb *is* is still the pronoun *who*, but its antecedent is now the singular pronoun *one*, not the plural *authors*. Again, it helps to rearrange the sentence to appreciate who is doing what to whom.

> Of my favorite authors, Hemingway **is** the only one who is not much read today.

As you might guess, this subject-verb agreement issue confuses many writers

chapter [13]

A Verb Tenses
B Verb Forms
C Active and Passive Voice
D Subjunctive Mood

Verb Tense, Voice, and Mood

Writers need to know how to handle the forms and tenses of English verbs in order to express complex relationships between time and action.

13a Verb Tenses

Tense is that quality of a verb that expresses time and being. Tense is expressed through changes in verb forms and endings (for example, *see, saw, seeing; work, worked, working*) and through the use of auxiliaries (for example, *had seen, will have seen; had worked, had been working*).

• 13a-1 Know verb tenses and what they do. Here is a summary of English tenses—past, present, and future—in the active voice. (See Section 13c on voice.)

As you can see, many tenses require auxiliary verbs such as *will, be,* and *have*. Other auxiliary verbs, such as *can, could, may, might, should, ought,* and *must,* help to indicate possibility, necessity, permission, desire, capability, and so on. These verbs are called modal auxiliaries.

Summary: Verb Tenses in the Active Voice

What It Is Called	What It Looks Like
Simple present	I **answer** when I must.
Present progressive	I **am answering** the phone now.
Simple past	I **answered** quickly.
Past progressive	I **was answering** the phone when the alarm went off.
Present perfect	I **have answered** that question before.
Past perfect	I **had answered** that question twice before.
Simple future	I **will answer** it tomorrow too.
Future progressive	I **will be answering** the phones all day.
Future perfect	I **will have answered** all the questions by then.
Future perfect progressive	I **will have been answering** the phones for three hours by the time you arrive.

Juan **can** write well.

Audrey **might** write well.

Thuchpong **should** write well.

• *13a-2 Use the present tense appropriately.* It has several special roles. Use the present tense to introduce the words of authors you are quoting, whether living or dead.

> Lincoln **defines** conservatism as "adherence to the old and tried, against the new and untried."

Use the present tense to describe action in literary works or to introduce quotations.

> Hester Prynne **wears** a scarlet letter.

> The doctor in Macbeth **warns** a gentlewoman, "you know what you should not" (V.i.46–47).

Use present tense to express general scientific truths.

> Einstein **argues** that the principle of relativity **applies** to all physical phenomena.

• *13a-3 Use perfect tenses appropriately.* Perfect tenses enable writers to show exactly how events stand in relationship to each other in time. Avoiding the use of perfect tenses can produce imprecise sentences. (See also Section 15a.)

Lightning already ^(had) **struck** the house twice when Ivette decided that she **had** ^(had) enough and moved out.

13b Verb Forms

• *13b-1 Understand regular verbs.* All verb tenses are built from three basic forms, which are called the principal parts of a verb. The three principal parts are these.

- **Present** (or **Infinitive**). This is the base form of a verb, what it looks like when preceded by *to:* **to walk, to go, to choose.**
- **Past.** This is the form of a verb that shows action that has already occurred: **walked, dropped, warmed.**
- **Past participle.** This is the form a verb takes when accompanied by an **auxiliary verb** to show a more complicated past tense: *had* **walked,** *will have* **dropped,** *would have* **warmed,** *was* **hanged,** *might have* **argued.**

Regular verbs form their past and past participle forms simply by adding *-d* or *-ed* to the infinitive. Here are the three principle parts of two regular verbs.

Present	Past	Past Participle
talk	talk**ed**	talk**ed**
coincide	coincid**ed**	coincid**ed**

Checklist: *Irregular Verbs*

Present	Past	Past Participle	Present	Past	Past Participle
arise	arose	arisen	hang (an object)	hung	hung
bear (carry)	bore	borne	hang (a person)	hung, hanged	hung, hanged
bear (give birth)	bore	borne, born	know	knew	known
become	became	become	lay (to place)	laid	laid
begin	began	begun	lead	led	led
bite	bit	bitten, bit	leave	left	left
blow	blew	blown	lend	lent	lent
break	broke	broken	lie (to recline)	lay	lain
bring	brought	brought	light	lit, lighted	lit, lighted
burst	burst	burst	lose	lost	lost
buy	bought	bought	pay	paid	paid
catch	caught	caught	plead	pleaded, pled	pleaded, pled
choose	chose	chosen	prove	proved	proved, proven
cling	clung	clung			
come	came	come	ride	rode	ridden
creep	crept	crept	ring (to sound)	rang	rung
dig	dug	dug	rise	rose	risen
dive	dived, dove	dived	run	ran	run
do	did	done	say	said	said
draw	drew	drawn	see	saw	seen
dream	dreamed, dreamt	dreamed, dreamt	set	set	set
			shake	shook	shaken
drink	drank	drunk	shine	shone, shined	shone, shined
drive	drove	driven	show	showed	shown, showed
eat	ate	eaten			
fall	fell	fallen	shrink	shrank, shrunk	shrunk
find	found	found	sing	sang, sung	sung
fly	flew	flown	sink	sank, sunk	sunk
forget	forgot	forgotten	sit	sat	sat
forgive	forgave	forgiven	speak	spoke	spoken
freeze	froze	frozen	spring	sprang, sprung	sprung
get	got	got, gotten	stand	stood	stood
give	gave	given	steal	stole	stolen
go	went	gone	sting	stung	stung
grow	grew	grown	swear	swore	sworn

Present	Past	Past Participle	Present	Past	Past Participle
swim	swam	swum	wake	woke, waked	woke, woken, waked
swing	swung	swung			
take	took	taken	wear	wore	worn
tear	tore	torn	wring	wrung	wrung
throw	threw	thrown	write	wrote	written

• 13b-2 Understand irregular verbs. Irregular verbs do not form their past and past participle forms simply by adding -d or -ed to the infinitive. Instead, they change forms variously. Unfortunately, the English verbs used most often tend to be irregular. When in doubt about the form of an irregular verb, consult a dictionary or refer to the preceding checklist.

13c Active and Passive Voice

Voice indicates whether the subject acts or is acted upon, although it is a concept easier to illustrate than to define. Verbs that take objects (called transitive verbs) can be either in the active voice or the passive voice. They are in the active voice when the subject of the sentence actually does what the verb describes.

subj.   action
Mr. Yeh **managed** the advertising.

They are in the passive voice when the action described by the verb is done *to* the subject.

subj.   action
The *advertising campaign* **was managed** by Mr. Yeh.

• 13c-1 Use active voice for more lively writing. Because they are simpler and more direct, active sentences are often stronger than passive sentences. By avoiding passive constructions, you can tighten and clarify your sentences. To turn a passive construction into an active one, make the doer of the action the subject of the sentence or clause.

Passive: The designs **were approved** by management well before work **was completed** on them by the engineering staff.

Active: Management **approved** the designs well before the engineering staff **completed** them.

Passive: Though the Equal Rights Amendment **had been approved** by Congress during the Carter administration, it still **had not been**

95

ratified by the states by the time Carter left office in 1981.

Active: Though Congress **approved** the Equal Rights Amendment during the Carter administration, the states **had not ratified** it by the time Carter left office in 1981.

• 13c-2 Use passive voice when necessary.

Not every passive verb can or should be made active. Sometimes, as in the following example, you simply don't know who or what performs an action.

> The van **had been loaded** with valuable electronic equipment shortly before it **was stolen.**

Passive verbs are useful when *who* did an action may be less important than *to whom it was done,* as shown in these two examples.

> *Thomas Sowell* **was interviewed** on C-SPAN.
>
> *Dozens* **were arrested** at the concert.

The passive is also useful when responsibility for an action is deliberately unspecified.

> Flight 107 **has been canceled.**

13d Subjunctive Mood

Mood is a term used to describe the way a writer intends the action to be taken: either as a fact or question (the indicative mood), as a command or request (the imperative mood), or as a wish, desire, supposition, or improbability (the subjunctive mood). Mood is indicated by changes in verb form.

Indicative: The driver **was** careful.
   Was the driver careful?
Imperative: Be careful!
   Please **write** me.
Subjunctive: If the driver **were** more careful . . .

• 13d-1 Understand the subjunctive mood.

The subjunctive is used to express ideas that aren't factual or certain and to state wishes or desires.

> I wish it **were** [not *was*] warmer.
>
> If I **were** [not *was*] rich, I'd drive a Mercedes.
>
> God **bless** [instead of bless*es*] you.

The subjunctive is employed in *that* clauses following verbs that make demands, requests, recommendations, or motions.

> General Clark asked *that* his troops **be** silent.
>
> "I ask only *that* all soldiers **give** their best," he said.

Finally, some common expressions require the subjunctive.

> **Be that** as it may . . .   **Come** what may . . .
>
> As it **were** . . .   Peace **be** with you.

•13d-2 Select the correct subjunctive form of the verb. For all verbs, the present subjunctive is simply the base form of the verb—that is, the present infinitive form without *to*.

Verb	Present Subjunctive
to be	be
to give	give
to bless	bless

The base form is used even in the third person singular for which you might ordinarily expect a verb to take another form.

It is essential that *Salah* **have** [not *has*] his lines memorized by tomorrow.

For all verbs except *be*, the past subjunctive is the same as the simple past tense.

Verb	Past Subjunctive
to give	gave
to bless	blessed

For *be*, the past subjunctive is always *were*, even in the first and third person singular, for which you might expect the form to be *was*.

First Person: I wish *I* **were** [not *was*] the director.

Second Person: Suppose *you* **were** the director.

Third Person: I wish *she* **were** [not *was*] the director.

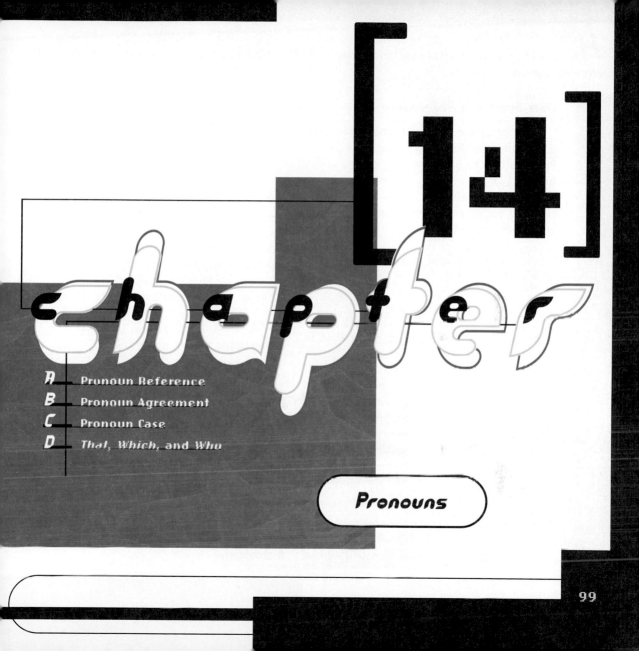

chapter [14]

Pronoun Reference
B **Pronoun Agreement**
C **Pronoun Case**
D **That, Which, and Who**

Pronouns

*H*andled well, pronouns help to make writing clear and economical. But you must pay attention to issues of *reference, agreement,* and *case.*

14a Pronoun Reference

Pronouns stand in for and act like nouns but don't name specific persons, places, or things. Pronouns include *I, you, he, she, it, they, whom, this, that, one,* and so on. The person, place, or thing a pronoun refers to is called its antecedent, the word you'd need to repeat in a sentence if you couldn't use a pronoun.

> ant.
> *Jill* demanded that the clerk speak to
> pron.
> **her.**

> ant.   pron.
> *Workers* denied that **they** intended to strike.

A pronoun must agree with its antecedent in number (singular or plural), in case (subjective, nominative, objective, or possessive), and sometimes in gender (masculine or feminine).

• 14a-1 Revise sentences to make antecedents clear. Replace any vague pronouns with words or phrases that explain them clearly.

> Passengers had been searched for weapons,
> this precaution
> but ~~it~~ did not prevent the hijacking.
>   ^

A pronoun that is not possessive can't have a possessive antecedent. In the following example, *experts'* is possessive. Since the pronoun *they* isn't possessive, it can't refer to *experts'* (or even to *experts' view*). The sentence must be recast.

> As for the *experts'* ~~view of the Miata,~~ **they** ei-
>   the Miata
> ther praise ~~it~~ or wish it had more power.
>   ^

• 14a-2 Avoid ambiguous pronouns. Replace any pronoun that could refer to more than one antecedent with a more specific term. Alternatively, revise the entire sentence for clarity. Sometimes you have to do both.

>   they
> When ~~Claire~~ talked ~~to Audrey~~ at noon,
> Audrey ^   Claire
> ~~she~~ did not realize that ~~she~~ might be resign-
> ^   ^
> ing before the end of the day.

• 14a-3 Revise sentences to be sure readers know what the pronouns this, that, which, and it refer to. Constructions such as the following can be confusing.

> The novel is filled with violence, brutality,
> and refined language. I especially like
>   combination of toughness and grace
> **this**.
>   ^

When the unclear pronoun is *it* or *which,* either revise the sentence or supply a clear and direct antecedent.

While atomic waste products are hard to dispose of safely, ~~it~~ ^nuclear power^ remains a reasonable alternative to burning fossil fuels to produce electricity.

The house has a tiny kitchen and a slate roof which the owners intend to remodel.

•14a-4 Avoid using they or it to describe people or things in general in sentences in which there are no antecedents.

In Houston, ~~they~~ ^people^ live more casually than in Dallas.

•14a-5 Avoid sentences in which pronouns merely repeat the obvious subject.

The *mayor*, an Independent, ~~he~~ lost the election.

14b Pronoun Agreement

Pronouns and nouns are either singular or plural. Singular pronouns (such as *she, it, this, that, her, him, my, his, her, its*) connect with singular antecedents, and plural pronouns (such as *they, these, them, their*) refer to plural antecedents. This connection is called agreement in number.

•14b-1 Be sure pronouns agree in number with their antecedents.
Agreement is usually simple when pronouns and antecedents are close together and when antecedents are clearly either singular or plural.

The soccer *players* gathered **their** equipment.

The *coach* searched for **her** car.

When words and phrases come between pronouns and their antecedents, it is more difficult to keep single antecedents with singular pronouns and plural antecedents with plural pronouns.

A *quarterback* always enjoys hearing hometown crowds cheering in the stands for ~~them~~ ^him^.

•14b-2 Be sure pronouns that refer to collective nouns are accurate in number.
Collective nouns describe groups or collections of things: *class, team, band, orchestra, government, jury, committee, audience, family.* Such nouns can be either singular or plural, depending on how they are used in a sentence.

The *chorus* sang **its** heart out.
the chorus as a group

The *chorus* arrived and took **their** seats.
the individual members of the group

If you treat a collective noun as singular, pronouns referring to it must be singular. If you treat it as plural, pronouns referring to it must be plural.

Checklist: Indefinite Pronouns

Singular	Variable, Singular or Plural	Plural
anybody	all	few
anyone	any	many
anything	either	several
each	more	
everybody	most	
everyone	neither	
everything	none	
nobody	some	
no one		
nothing		
somebody		
someone		
something		

Did *anybody* misplace **her** notes?

Everyone is entitled to **his or her** opinion.

Each of the legislators had **his or her** say.

In speech, you'll often hear plural pronouns linked to antecedents that are singular indefinite pronouns. Such mismatches, common as they may be, are still considered wrong in writing.

Everyone is entitled to ~~their~~ opinion. *(his or her)*

Each of the legislators had ~~their~~ say. *(his or her)*

When an indefinite pronoun is plural, any pronouns that refer to it should be plural.

Several of the jet fighters had to have **their** wings stiffened.

Few, however, had given **their** pilots trouble.

If the number of an indefinite pronoun that is used as an antecedent is variable, words or phrases modifying the pronoun may determine its number.

All of the portraits had yellowed in **their** *(var.)* *(plural)* frames. *Some* will be restored to **their** *(var.)* *(plural)* original condition.

The *jury* rendered **its** decision.

The *jury* had **their** opinions polled.

In most cases, your sentences will sound more natural if you treat collective nouns as singular.

The *band* ~~are~~ unhappy with ~~their~~ latest re- *(is)* *(its)* cordings.

• 14b-3 Be sure that pronouns referring to indefinite pronouns are accurate in number. Use the checklist of indefinite pronouns or a dictionary to determine whether various indefinite pronouns are singular or plural. The

---

var.   sing.   var.
All of the wine is still in **its** casks. *Some* of the
                         sing.
vintage is certain to have **its** quality evaluated.

None is considered variable because it is regularly accepted as a plural form in much writing and
speech. However, in most writing, treat *none* as
singular.

> *None* of the women is reluctant to speak **her**
> mind.

> *None* of the churches has **its** doors open.

**• 14b-4 Be cautious with pronouns re-
ferring to antecedents joined by or, nor,
either . . . or, or neither . . . nor.** When two
singular antecedents are joined by *or, either . . .
or,* or *neither . . . nor,* be sure any pronoun referring to them is singular.

> *Neither Brazil nor Mexico* will raise
> sing.
> **its** oil prices today.

When two plural antecedents are joined by *or, either . . . or, or neither . . . nor,* be sure any pronoun referring to them is plural.

> It is expected that *either the players or the*
>   plural
> *managers* will file **their** grievances with the
> commissioner before the next negotiating ses-
> sion.

When a singular noun is joined to a plural noun by
or, either . . . or, or *neither . . . nor,* any pronoun
should agree in number (and gender) with the
nearer noun.

>   sing.   plural
> *Either a poor diet or long, stress-filled hours* in
>   plural
> the office will take **their** toll on the business
> executive.

>   plural
> *Either the long, stress-filled hours* in the office
>   sing.   sing.
> or *poor diet* will take **its** toll on the business
> executive.

14c Pronoun Case

Some personal pronouns (and *who*) change
form to show their function in a sentence. These
different forms are called case.

**• 14c-1 Understand subjective, objec-
tive, and possessive case.** Pronouns need
to be in the subjective (or nominative) case when
they are subjects of sentences or clauses or when
they follow linking verbs as predicate nominatives: It is **I**; It was **they** who held the proxy.

Pronouns take the objective case when something is done to them: IBM hired **her**; Elena
shipped **them**. Pronouns also take the objective
case after prepositions: to **me**, for **her**, between
him and **us**. The subjective and objective forms of
the pronouns *you* and *it* are identical.

Summary: Pronoun Case

Subject	Object	Possessive
I	me	my, mine
we	us	our, ours
you	you	your, yours
he	him	his
she	her	her, hers
it	it	its, of it
they	them	their, theirs
who	whom	whose

Pronouns take the possessive case to show ownership.

• 14c-2 Check pronoun case when pronouns are paired. The second pronoun is often troublesome. To choose the right pronoun, figure out what the pronoun does in the sentence: Is it a subject or predicate nominative? Is it an object? Does it show possession? Then use the preceding chart to select the right case.

You and (~~I~~ **me**) don't have the latest designs yet.
Pronouns are subjects.

The winners are (**he** ~~him~~) and (~~I~~ **me**).
Pronouns are predicate nominatives.

The memo praised you and (~~she~~ **her**).
Pronouns are objects.

Forward the e-mail to him and (~~I~~ **me**).
Pronouns are objects of a preposition.

• 14c-3 Check pronoun case when first person plural pronouns are followed by nouns. The pronoun and the noun must share the same case.

We *lucky sailors* missed the storm.
subject

The storm missed **us** *lucky sailors.*
object

For **us** *engineers,* the job market looks promising.
object of preposition

• 14c-4 Check pronoun case with *who* **and** *whom.* Select the subjective form (*who*) when pronouns act as subjects and the objective form (*whom*) when pronouns act as objects. The correct choice is especially important in prepositional phrases.

Subjective Form: **Who** wrote this letter?
Objective Form: You addressed **whom?**
Objective Form: To **whom** did you write?

When *who* or *whom* (or *whoever/whomever*) is part of a dependent clause, *who* or *whom* takes the form it would have in the dependent clause, not in the sentence as a whole. Constructions of this kind are quite common. The words in italics shown in the following examples are clauses within full sentences.

The system rewards ***whoever*** works hard.

Whomever the party nominates is likely to be elected.

The deficit will increase no matter **whom** we elect president.

• 14c-5 Check pronoun case with infinitives. When pronouns are the subjects of infinitives, they are in the objective case, not in the subjective case as you might expect.

> The panel found Iliana and **me** to be liable.
>
> We urged Jones and **her** to write the report.

• 14c-6 Check pronoun case in comparisons. To determine pronoun case after *than* or *as,* it helps to complete the comparison.

> I am taller *than* **(him? he?).**
>
> I am taller *than* **he (is).**
>
> We don't invest as much *as* **(she? her?).**
>
> We don't invest as much *as* **she (does).**

Some comparisons, however, can be expanded two ways:

> Politics does not interest me as much *as* **(she? her?)**
>
> 1. Politics does not interest me as much *as* **she (does).**
> 2. Politics does not interest me as much *as* **(it interests) her.**

In such cases, the pronoun you select will determine what the sentence means. In these situa-

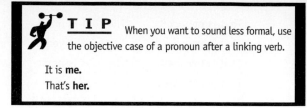

TIP When you want to sound less formal, use the objective case of a pronoun after a linking verb.

> It is **me.**
>
> That's **her.**

tions, it's probably better just to write out the full comparison.

• 14c-7 Check pronoun case after linking verbs. Linking verbs, such as *to be, to seem, to appear, to feel,* and *to become,* connect a subject to a word or phrase that extends or completes its meaning—the subject complement. In most cases, use the subjective case of a pronoun when it is the complement of a linking verb.

>   subj.   l. v.   subj. comp.
> The *culprits are* obviously **they.**

Such constructions are fairly common.

> It is **I.**
>
> The next CEO of the corporation will be **she.**
>
> You are **who?**

• 14c-8 Punctuate the possessive case of pronouns correctly. Do not use an apostrophe + *s* with personal pronouns to show ownership. This is true whether the possessive pronoun comes before or after a noun. In the following examples, the possessive pronoun comes before the noun in the first column and after the noun in the second column.

That is **my** *book*.	The *book* is **mine**.
That is **your** *book*.	The *book* is **yours**.
That is **her** *book*.	The *book* is **hers**.
That is **his** *book*.	The *book* is **his**.
That is **our** *book*.	The *book* is **ours**.
That is **their** *book*.	The *book* is **theirs**.
What is **its** *price?*	What is the *price* **of it?**
Whose *book* is this?	

Understand, too, that while some indefinite pronouns form the possessive by adding *'s,* others do not. Among the indefinite pronouns that cannot add *'s* to show possession are the following.

all	each	most	some
any	few	none	

Indefinite pronouns ending in *-body* or *-one* can form the possessive with *'s* or with *of*.

anybody's opinion	the opinion of **anybody**
someone's hope	the hope of **someone**

14d That, Which, and Who

These words require special attention when they serve as relative pronouns introducing modifying clauses.

• 14d-1 Understand that a modifying clause introduced by that is always restrictive (essential). Restrictive clauses are

essential to understanding the terms they modify or explain. Such clauses are not enclosed by commas.

The concept ***that*** *intrigued the shareholders most* involved profit sharing.

The report ***that*** *I wrote* recommended the concept.

• 14d-2 Understand that a modifying clause introduced by which is usually nonrestrictive (nonessential). The information in a nonrestrictive clause is important but not essential to the meaning of a sentence. When a nonrestrictive clause is deleted, the sentence still makes sense. Nonrestrictive clauses are bracketed by commas.

Nonrestrictive Clause: The concept, ***which*** *intrigued the shareholders a great deal,* was quite simple.

Nonrestrictive Clause: The report, ***which*** *the team dashed off at the last minute,* recommended profit sharing.

In rare cases, you may have to use *which* to introduce a restrictive clause.

Restrictive Clause: I can't say more about that ***which*** *we discussed earlier.*

• 14d-3 Use who rather than that or which when modifying a human subject.

The *woman* ~~that~~ waved was my boss.
who
^

chapter [15]

A — Verbs
B — Modals
C — Verbs Followed by a Noun or Pronoun
D — Articles and Number Agreement

Suggestions for ESL Writers

*T*his chapter is intended especially for the ESL (English as a second language) writer. It focuses on the areas in which ESL writers have the most problems. Native speakers of English may also find help here.

15a Verbs

Even after many years of studying English, you may be confused about verbs. This section will answer some of your questions.

• **15a-1 Choose the most appropriate verb tense.** The chart to the right shows the eight verb tenses that are used most often, along with a list of some common adverbs and expressions that accompany each tense. Use these as signposts to help you choose the best verb tense. A diagram illustrates the time line for each tense. In the diagram, an *X* indicates an action and a curved line indicates an action in progress.

past ——————+—————— future
now

• **15a-2 Learn which verbs are action verbs.** Some verbs in English can't be used in a progressive form because they express a state, not an activity. If you want to use one of these nonaction verbs, you must use a simple form of the verb, even though the time intended is now.

                   prefers
   Maria **is preferring** Carla's apartment to her own.
                   ^

The chart on page 110 indicates some of these nonaction verbs.

• **15a-3 Learn the difference between the simple past and present perfect tenses.** You can always use the simple

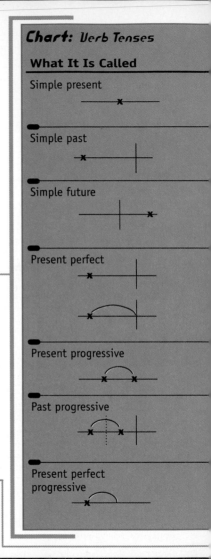

Chart: Verb Tenses

What It Is Called

Simple present

Simple past

Simple future

Present perfect

Present progressive

Past progressive

Present perfect progressive

What It Looks Like	What It Describes	Time Words Used with It
I **sleep** eight hours every day. Water **freezes** at 32°F.	habits, regular activities facts, general truths	every day often regularly always usually habitually
I **slept** only four hours yesterday.	a finished action in the past	yesterday last year ago
I **will try** to sleep more. *or* I **am going to sleep** early tonight.	a single action in the future a planned action in the future (with *be going to*)	tomorrow in *x* days next year
I **have** already **written** my paper. I **have lived** here for three months.	a past action that occurred sometime in the past an action that started in the past and continues to the present	already yet recently so far for *x* time period since *x* date
He **is sleeping** now.	a continuous activity in progress now	right now at this time
While he **was sleeping**, the telephone rang.	a continuous activity in progress in the past	while during that time between *x* and *y*
The woman **has been waiting** for many hours.	a continuous activity that began in the past and continues to the present, emphasizing the duration	for *x* time period since + exact date

Chart: Nonaction Verbs*

appear	forget	owe	seem
be	hate	own	smell
belong	have	possess	sound
consist	hear	prefer	surprise
contain	know	recognize	taste
deserve	like	remember	think
desire	love	require	understand
dislike	mean	resemble	want
feel	need	see	wish

*There are some exceptions to the nonaction rule (e.g., "I am thinking about getting a job"; "He is seeing a doctor about his back"). You will need to keep a list of these exceptions as you come across them.

past tense to describe an action that happened in the past and is finished. Use the present perfect tense to indicate that something happened in the past and may continue.

Simple Past: My grandmother never **used** a computer.

This implies that the grandmother may no longer be alive.

Present Perfect: My mother **has** never **used** a computer.

This sentence indicates that the mother is still alive and may use a computer in the future.

You must use the present perfect for an action that begins in the past and continues up to the present moment.

Present Perfect: This theater **has shown** the same film for three months.

Present Perfect: Cal **has studied** Greek for more than a decade.

• 15a-4 Learn the difference between intransitive and transitive verbs. An intransitive verb is complete without an object; in fact, you cannot put an object after it. For example:

Incorrect: She **grew up** her children.

Correct: Her children **grew up** without her.

There are two kinds of intransitive verbs—linking verbs and action verbs. (See the chart on the facing page for a list of these verbs.)

Linking Verb: This book **seems** very old.
<small>l. v.　subj. comp.</small>

Action Verb: Jorge **complained** bitterly.
<small>a. v.</small>

A transitive verb is a verb that has a direct object; that is, it has an effect on, or does something to, a person or thing.

Incorrect: She **raised.**

The thought is incomplete; you need to know what she raised.

Correct: She **raised** *her children* on a farm.

There are two types of transitive verbs. (See the chart on the facing page for a list.) One type—verb + direct object—*must* be followed directly by a noun or pronoun.

trans. v.   dir. obj.

The shopping center **needs** more parking spaces.

The other type—verb + (indirect object) + direct object—can be followed by an indirect object (a person or thing receiving the action) before the direct object. If you use to or for in front of the indirect object, the position changes, as the following examples show.

trans. v. dir. obj.

Akim **bought** a rose.

trans. v. indir. obj. dir. obj.

Akim **bought** his wife a rose.

trans. v.   dir. obj. + (for/to + indir. obj.)

Akim **bought** a rose for his wife.

15b Modals

A modal, which is an auxiliary, or helping, verb, expresses an attitude about a situation. Modals are used for many purposes; some of these are to express necessity, obligation, regret, and degrees of formality. Modals can be used to express ideas about the past, the present, and the future.

Past: She **could** speak Japanese as a child.

Present: My colleague **can** speak Japanese.

Future: More businesspeople **might** learn Japanese next year.

The chart on the following page summarizes the functions of modals and shows their present

tenses only. For information about other tenses, consult an ESL text.

Here are some specific tips to help you with modal formation.

1. Don't use to after the modal.

   Must I ~~to~~ hand this report in tomorrow?

2. There is no -s on the third person singular of a modal.

   Kwang **might~~s~~** go to graduate school.

3. You cannot use two modals together.

   The plane ~~**might**~~ **could** be delayed.

Chart: *Intransitive and Transitive Verbs*[*]

INTRANSITIVE VERBS

Linking Verbs: appear, be, become, look, seem
Action Verbs: arrive, come, get dressed, go, grow up, laugh, lie, listen, live, rise, run, sit, sleep, walk, work

TRANSITIVE VERBS

Verb + Direct Object: attend, bring up, choose, do, have, hit, hold, keep, lay, need, raise, say, spend, use, want, wear
Verb + (Indirect Object) + Direct Object: bring, buy, get, give, make, pay, send, take, tell

---

[*]These lists are not complete. You can always consult your dictionary to find out whether a verb is transitive or intransitive.

Chart: Modals

	What It Means	Present Form
Permission Informal → Formal	can could may would you mind*	**Can** I be excused? **Could** I be excused? **May** I be excused? **Would you mind if** I brought my dog?
Ability	can be able to	Joe **can** drive a car. Carl **is able to** study and sing at the same time.
Advice	should ought to had better	You **should** quit. You **ought to** quit. You **had** better quit.
Necessity	have to must	He **has to** pay a fine. She **must** pay her taxes.
Possibility More sure → Less sure	can may could might	It **can** get cold in May. It **may** get cold in June. It **could** get cold in July. It **might** get cold next week.
Expectation	should/ought to	Your keys **should** be on the desk where I left them.
Conclusion	must	José **must** have lost his job.
Polite Requests Informal → Formal	can will could would you mind + present participle	**Can** you give me a hand? **Will** you give me a hand? **Could** you give me a hand? **Would you mind** giving me a hand?

Would you mind is followed by *if* + the past tense of the verb.

15c Verbs Followed by a Noun or Pronoun

Some transitive verbs in English need to have a noun or pronoun after them. For example, when you use *tell* in a sentence, you need a direct object (what you told) or an indirect object (whom you told) to complete the sentence.

Incorrect: I told to write me a letter.

The object is missing; the sentence is incomplete.

Correct: I told **my son** to write me a letter.

My son is the indirect object; the sentence is complete.

Remember that an infinitive verb comes after a transitive verb + noun or pronoun construction. (The infinitive is the base of the verb: *to go, to see, to learn,* and so on.) The following chart lists the verbs that follow this pattern.

15d Articles and Number Agreement

Nonnative speakers of English are sometimes confused about the articles *a, an,* and *the* and may also be uncertain about whether to use *a few* or *a little* before some nouns. This section addresses those problems.

• 15d-1 Decide whether the noun is a count noun or a noncount noun.

A count noun refers to something that can be divided easily—*books, chairs,* or *minutes,* for example. A noncount noun refers to something that can't be counted or divided—*milk, traffic, or advice,* for example. If you have trouble deciding whether a noun is a count or a noncount noun, consult an ESL dictionary.

• 15d-2 Decide whether the count noun requires a definite article (the) or an

Chart: Verbs Followed by Nouns or Pronouns and Infinitives

These verbs must be followed by a noun or pronoun + infinitive.

advise	encourage	order	tell
allow	force	persuade	urge
cause	hire	remind	warn
challenge	instruct	require	
convince	invite		

indefinite article (a/an). When you refer to a noun for the first time, without having referred to it before, you will use the indefinite article, *a* or *an.* (*A* is used when the word following it begins with a consonant sound—a **b**oat, a **c**hurch, a **n**ew house. *An* is used when the word following it begins with a vowel sound—an **h**our, an **e**arly appointment, an **e**xperience.)

> Johann is buying **a** new car.
> Indefinite meaning
>
> He is tired of **the** car he's driving.
> Definite meaning

Some other situations require the definite article, **the.**

1. When there is only one of a noun

   The *earth* is round.

2. When the noun is a superlative

   This is **the** *best* brand you can buy.

3. When the noun is limited to show that it is a specific example

   The *book on Picasso* is out.

• 15d-3 Choose carefully the articles to be used before general nouns.

As a rule, you can use *a/an* or *the* with most singular count nouns to make generalizations.

> **A** *dog* can be good company for **a** *lonely person.*

Chart: Quantifiers

Used with Count and Noncount Nouns	Used with Count Nouns Only	Used with Noncount Nouns Only
some books/money **a lot of** books/money **plenty of** books/money **a lack of** books/money **most of the** books/money	**several** books **many** books **a couple of** books **a few** books	**a good deal of** money **a great deal of** money **not much** money **a little** money **little** money

The *computer* has changed the way people do their banking.

You can use a plural count noun to make general statements, but without *the*.

Capitalists believe in free enterprise.

Computers have changed the banking industry dramatically.

Noncount nouns in a general statement do not have an article before them.

Sugar is a major cause of tooth decay.

Many educators question whether **intelligence** can be measured.

• 15d-4 Be aware of possible problems with noncount nouns. Make sure that you don't use *a/an* with noncount nouns.

I need ~~a~~ work.

Also keep in mind that a noncount noun can never be plural.

The committee needs more **informations** about the stock.

• 15d-5 Pay careful attention to quantifiers. The words that come before nouns and tell you how much or how many are called quantifiers.

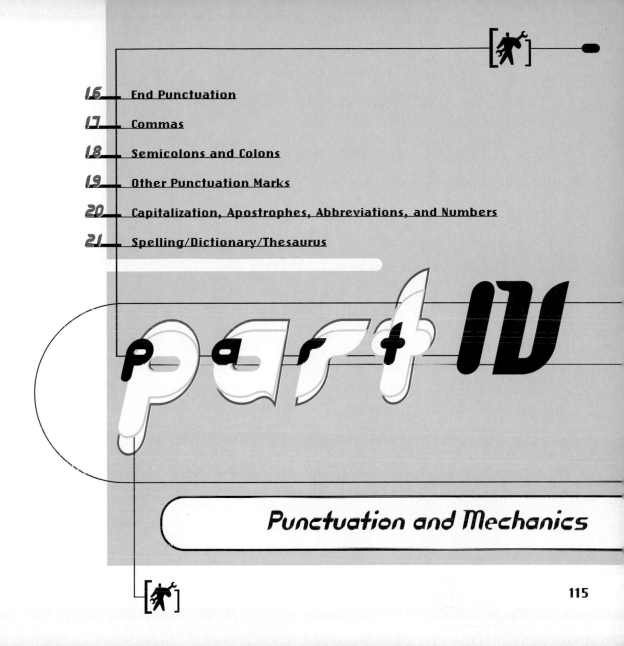

part IV

Punctuation and Mechanics

chapter

A — Periods
B — Question Marks
C — Exclamation Marks

End Punctuation

Periods terminate sentences and abbreviations.

• 16a-1 Use periods to end statements, indirect questions, and commands.

Hannibal, general of Carthage, has been hailed as a genius of military strategy.

Military theorists wonder whether any battle plan has been more tactically perfect than Hannibal's at Cannae (216 B.C.).

Just look at this mess.

Strong commands may be punctuated with exclamation marks. (See Section 16c-1.)

• 16a-2 Use periods to punctuate abbreviations.
Note that many abbreviations written with all-capital letters do not require periods. When in doubt, check a dictionary. (For appropriate uses of abbreviations, see Section 20c.)

abbr.   anon.   Cong.
HEW   GPO   U.S.

When a sentence ends with an abbreviation, don't add an end punctuation mark unless the sentence is a question or an exclamation.

We visited the Folger Library in Washington, D.C.

Have you ever been to Washington, D.C.?

How I love Washington, D.C.!

• 16a-3 Use periods to indicate decimals.

    0.01
 $189.00
   75.47

• 16a-4 Use periods (dots) in e-mail addresses.

ruszkiewicz@mail.utexas.edu

16b Question Marks

Question marks terminate questions or suggest doubt.

• 16b-1 Use question marks after direct questions.

Have you ever heard of the Battle of Cannae?

Who fought in the battle?

• 16b-2 Use question marks to indicate uncertainty about dates, numbers, or statements.

Hannibal (247?–183 B.C.) was a general and military tactician.

• 16b-3 Do not use question marks to terminate indirect questions.
Indirect

 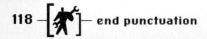

questions are statements that seem to have questions within them. Compare these examples to appreciate the difference.

Indirect Question: Varro wondered whether Hannibal's strategy would succeed.

Direct Question: Will Hannibal's strategy succeed?

Direct Question: Varro wondered, "Will Hannibal's strategy succeed?"

Indirect Question: Our guide asked if we knew who Hannibal was.

Direct Question: "Do you know who Hannibal is?"

Direct Question: The guide asked, "Who was Hannibal?"

• *16b-4 Punctuate as questions any sentences that begin with statements but end with questions.*

The strategy looked fine on paper, but would it work on the battlefield?

Don't confuse these sorts of constructions, however, with indirect questions as discussed in Section 16b-3.

• *16b-5 Place question marks outside quotation marks except when they are part of the quoted material itself.* Compare the examples.

Was it Terence who wrote "Fortune helps the brave"?

"Have you read any Cicero?" the teacher asked.

For more about quotation marks, see Section 19a.

• *16b-6 Place question marks after direct questions that appear in the middle of sentences.* Such questions are typically enclosed by parentheses, quotation marks, or dashes.

Skeptical of the guide—Would Hannibal really camp on such marshy ground?—the tourists consulted a map.

16c Exclamation Marks

Exclamation marks give emphasis to statements. They are rare in academic and business writing.

• *16c-1 Use exclamation marks to express strong feelings or commands.*

We are winning!   Come here now!

• *16c-2 Use only one exclamation point in a sentence.*

Don't overdo it!!

• *16c-3 Don't use commas after exclamations that fall in the middle of sentences.*

"Please check your records again!" the caller demanded.

• 16c-4 Use exclamations rarely in academic or business writing. Too many exclamatory sentences can make a paragraph or passage seem juvenile.

chapter

Commas

17a Commas That Separate

A comma is a signal to pause in a sentence, but it is a weaker signal than a semicolon and a much weaker one than a period. Thus you should insert a comma when you want only a slight pause to set off a word or phrase.

• 17a-1 Use a comma after an introductory phrase of more than three or four words.

At the end of the week, we'll be in California.

A comma isn't needed when an introductory phrase is only a few words long and the sentence is clear without it.

On Tuesday we'll be in New Mexico.

• 17a-2 Use a comma after an introductory dependent clause.
Dependent clauses are signaled by words such as *after, although, as, because, before, if, since, unless, when, while,* and so on. (See Section 10a-1.)

Although traffic problems are worsening in all American cities, almost no one suggests that Americans should buy fewer cars.

If the president of the university can avert this crisis, she'll be a star.

Without a comma after such an introductory clause, the reader may slide past the beginning of the main part of the sentence.

While the crevice had started months before the inspector who found it seemed surprised.

Without a comma after *before* in this example, the reader may slide over the separation between *before* and *the inspector.* A comma ends the confusion.

While the crevice had started months before, the inspector who found it seemed surprised.

• 17a-3 Use a comma to set off a contrasting clause that comes after a main clause.

The partners expect to work together, despite personal differences.

Marietta makes stunning pottery, though her prices are steep.

Do not use commas, however, when the additional clause is closely related to the main idea of the sentence. For example:

The stock market plunged *while the investors were looking the other way.*

• 17a-4 Use commas after conjunctive adverbs at the beginning of sentences or clauses.
Conjunctive adverbs—words such as *however, nevertheless, moreover,* and *therefore*—act as interrupters that mark a shift or contrast in a sentence. For example:

The questionnaire was poorly designed. *Nevertheless*, readers seemed to have faith in the answers.

The budget cuts are final; *therefore*, you'll have to reduce staff.

• 17a-5 Use commas to set off absolute modifiers. (See Section 11g-3 for more information on absolute modifiers.)

The question settled, the mediators returned to their homes.

The pioneers pressed on across the desert, their water almost gone.

Commas That Separate: Other Uses

- To separate words where repetitive phrases have been left out

  Brad Pitt once worked as a giant chicken; Rod Stewart, as a grave digger; Whoopie Goldberg, as a make-up artist for corpses.

- To keep ideas clear and distinct

  The motto of some critics seems to be, whatever is, is wrong.

- To separate conversational expressions from the main body of the sentence

  No, I'm sure the inspector wasn't there.

T I P It's not always easy to decide when to insert a comma before a clause. When you're editing, read carefully to decide whether you need a comma for clarity. Then make the best judgment you can. When it seems like a toss-up, omit the comma.

• 17a-6 Use commas to mark contrasts.
For example:

In most cities, owning a car is a necessity, *not a luxury*.

• 17a-7 Use commas to introduce quotations or to follow them.

The lawyer kept repeating, "He can't be held responsible."

"Don't tell *me* he can't be held responsible," bellowed the judge.

No commas are needed when the quotation fits right into the sentence without an introductory frame.

Oscar Wilde defined experience as "the name everyone gives to their mistakes."

17b Commas That Enclose

Commas often serve to set off certain parts of a sentence that add to content but are not essential to the primary meaning.

123

17 ,

• 17b-1 Use commas to set off non-restrictive (nonessential) modifiers.

Nonrestrictive Modifier: The police officers, *who had been carefully screened,* marched in front.

Modifier Removed: The police officers marched in front.

When you can't remove an enclosed modifier from a sentence without affecting the primary meaning, the modifier is restrictive (essential).

Restrictive Modifier: The car *that we received* was not the car *that we had custom-ordered.*

• 17b-2 Use commas to enclose appositives that are nonrestrictive (nonessential). An appositive is a noun or noun phrase that describes another noun or pronoun more fully. Usually it is nonrestrictive in nature.

Franklin Delano Roosevelt, *the only president to serve more than two terms,* died in office.

There are, however, essential appositives that follow a noun and give information necessary to the sentence.

The factory workers **who had been hired last** were the first to be let go.

17c Commas That Link

Though commas often mark separations, they can also tell readers that certain ideas belong together.

• 17c-1 Use commas before the coordinating conjunctions and, but, yet, for, so, or, and nor when those words link independent clauses together to form compound sentences.

Municipal bonds give a more reliable yield than stocks, and the income is also tax free.

Stocks have more growth potential than bonds, but the risk is higher.

A comma is especially important when the independent clauses it connects are long.

Amateur investors use financial newsletters, computer programs, and their own hunches to guide their ventures into the market, but not even the experts have figured out a reliable way to get rich in the stock market.

• 17c-2 Use commas to link more than two items in a series.

The group is planning to travel by plane, by bus, and by canoe.

• 17c-3 Use commas to link coordinate adjectives in a series.
Coordinate adjectives are those that modify the noun they precede, not each other.

The job calls for a *creative, imaginative, intelligent* manager.

When adjectives are coordinate, they can be switched around without affecting the sense of the phrase. Thus the sentence above could just as easily read as follows.

The job calls for *an imaginative, intelligent, creative* manager.

• 17c-4 Do not use commas to mark off noncoordinate adjectives in a series.
Noncoordinate adjectives

work together to modify a term, and they cannot be switched around.

She sent *her six completed* chapters by Federal Express.

He drives a *shiny blue Mustang* convertible.

17d Unnecessary Commas

Putting commas where they don't belong creates problems by breaking sentences in the wrong places. When you edit, delete commas that do not serve a specific purpose.

• 17d-1 Eliminate commas that interrupt the flow of a sentence.

Five years after joining the firm, Jolene found herself wondering when she was going to become a partner.

The writer doesn't mean "Jolene found herself," but rather that "Jolene found herself wondering."

The following is another example of a comma gone wrong.

CAUTION Be careful **not** to place a comma **after** a conjunction that joins independent clauses. Don't write "I lost too so, I know how it feels." Put the comma before the conjunction.

TIP In newspaper and magazine articles, writers and editors often omit commas after the next-to-last item in a series. Nevertheless, academic writers should include commas after all words in a series but the last.

CAUTION Remember not to join two independent clauses with only a comma. When you do, you create a comma splice, considered by many to be very bad form. (See Section 10c.)

125

17 ,

Although, Jolene is fifty-one years old, she's ready to start studying for a new degree.

• 17d-2 Don't use a comma to separate a subject from its verb. This error usually occurs when the sentence subject is long or complex.

> What happened to the team since yesterday, isn't clear.
>
> *What happened to the team* is the subject, and *isn't* is the verb.

Of course, when modifiers separate subjects from their verbs, they are set off by commas. Compare these sentences.

No Modifier/No Commas: Jolene is determined to improve her credentials.

Modifier/Commas: Jolene, who just turned fifty-one, is determined to improve her credentials.

• 17d-3 Don't use commas before coordinating conjunctions—and, but, yet, or, nor, for, so—unless the clause that comes after the conjunction is an independent clause.

> The visiting business executives toured the factory, and then visited the corporate offices.
>
> The author broke his promise to his agent, and his contract with his publisher.

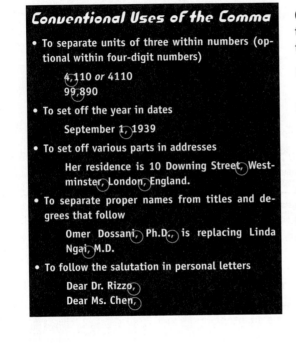

Conventional Uses of the Comma

- To separate units of three within numbers (optional within four-digit numbers)

  4,110 *or* 4110
  99,890

- To set off the year in dates

  September 1, 1939

- To set off various parts in addresses

  Her residence is 10 Downing Street, Westminster, London, England.

- To separate proper names from titles and degrees that follow

  Omer Dossani, Ph.D., is replacing Linda Ngai, M.D.

- To follow the salutation in personal letters

  Dear Dr. Rizzo,
  Dear Ms. Chen,

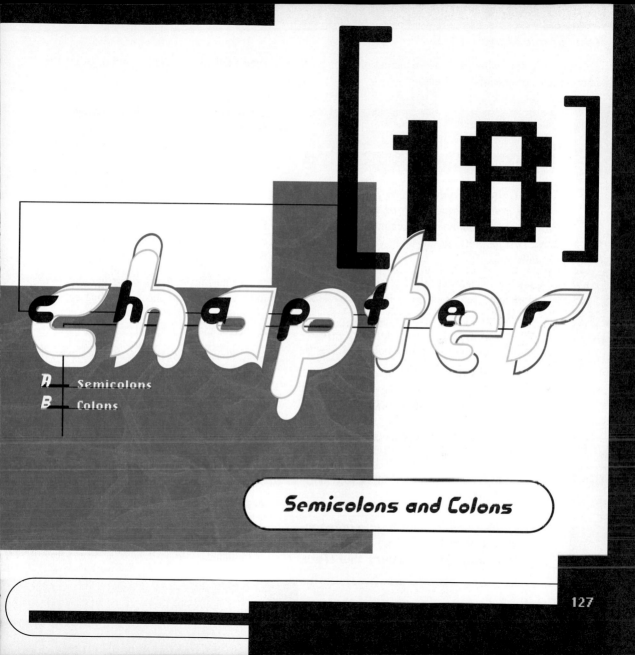

chapter [18]

A — Semicolons
B — Colons

Semicolons and Colons

18a Semicolons

Use semicolons when you need punctuation stronger than a comma but weaker than a period. Insert them between similar grammatical items.

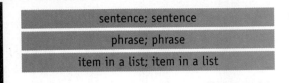

sentence; sentence
phrase; phrase
item in a list; item in a list

• 18a-1 Use semicolons to join two (or more) related independent clauses. You don't need a coordinating conjunction (such as *and, but, for, yet, nor, so*) when you use a semicolon.

> Italian cinema flourished after World War II; directors such as de Sica, Fellini, and Antonioni won worldwide acclaim.

> Ethel Waters was a distinguished African-American actress; her autobiography is entitled *His Eye Is on the Sparrow*.

If you use a comma to join independent clauses, you must use a coordinating conjunction. (See Section 10c on comma splices.) The only exception occurs when the clauses are very short.

> As best film director ever, Xavier nominated Kurosawa, Adele picked Hitchcock, Toshiya chose Agnes Varda.

• 18a-2 Use semicolons to join independent clauses connected by conjunctive adverbs such as however, therefore, nevertheless, nonetheless, moreover, and consequently. These words, on their own, cannot link sentences; they require a semicolon.

> Bob Hope started his entertainment career in vaudeville; however, he made his major mark as a film star and television comic.

> Films about British spy 007 have been in decline for years; nevertheless, new James Bond films continue to appear.

Using a comma instead of a semicolon before the conjunctive adverb produces a comma splice—a serious punctuation error. To correct the error, replace the comma with a semicolon.

> Good films often spawn sequels; however, the sequels rarely match the originals in quality.

When words such as *however* and *therefore* occur in the middle of independent clauses, they are preceded and followed by commas. Compare these examples.

> Some teens in the audience had never seen *Gone with the Wind; moreover,* many had not even heard of Clark Gable.

> Some teens in the audience had, moreover, never seen *Gone with the Wind* or heard of Clark Gable.

• 18a-3 Use semicolons between independent clauses connected by expressions such as indeed, in fact, at any rate, for example, and on the other hand. Be sure that you have an independent clause on both sides of the semicolon.

The film's prerelease publicity had been enormous; as a result, opening day crowds broke all box office records.

• 18a-4 Use semicolons to separate items in a series that contain commas or other punctuation. Using semicolons in such situations makes complicated sentences easier to read.

Bob Hope's films include *Road to Morocco,* which also features Bing Crosby and Dorothy Lamour; *The Paleface,* a comic western with Jane Russell as Calamity Jane; and *The Seven Little Foys,* a biography about vaudeville performer Eddie Foy, Sr.

Chart: Frequently Used Conjunctive Adverbs

consequently	meanwhile	rather
furthermore	moreover	then
hence	nonetheless	therefore
however	otherwise	thus

The sound track for the film included the Supremes' "Stop in the Name of Love!"; Bob Dylan's "Rainy Day Women #12 & 35"; and Rodgers and Hart's "Glad to Be Unhappy."

• 18a-5 Do not use semicolons between dependent clauses and independent clauses. Use commas instead. (See Section 17a-2.)

Although director Alfred Hitchcock once said that actors should be treated like cattle, he won fine performances from many of them.

• 18a-6 Do not use semicolons between independent clauses and prepositional phrases. When punctuation is needed, use a comma.

In the tradition of the finest Hollywood directors, many young filmmakers regularly exceed their budgets.

• 18a-7 Do not use semicolons to introduce quotations or lists. Use commas or colons instead.

Wasn't it Mae West who said, "When I'm good I'm very good, but when I'm bad I'm better"?

Paul Robeson, performed in several distinguished films, *Showboat, Song of Freedom, King Solomon's Mines.*

•18a-8 Place semicolons outside of quotation marks.

The first Poe work filmed was "The Raven"; movies based on the poem appeared in 1912, 1915, and 1935.

18b Colons

Colons point to ideas, lists, quotations, or clauses you wish to highlight.

•18b-1 Use colons to direct readers to examples, explanations, or significant words and phrases.
Such a colon should follow an independent clause.

Orson Welles's greatest problem may also have been his greatest achievement: the brilliance of his first film, *Citizen Kane.*

Citizen Kane turns on the meaning of one word uttered by a dying man: "rosebud."

Do not use colons immediately after linking verbs or in the middle of prepositional phrases.

America's most bankable film star is: Tom Hanks.

Katharine Hepburn starred in: *Little Women, The Philadelphia Story,* and *The African Queen.*

•18b-2 Use colons to direct readers to lists.
Colons that introduce lists ordinarily follow independent clauses.

Besides *Citizen Kane,* Welles directed, produced, or acted in many movies: *The Magnificent Ambersons, Journey into Fear, The Lady from Shanghai,* and *Macbeth,* to name a few.

Use colons after phrases that specifically announce lists, indicated by expressions such as *including these, as follows,* and *such as the following.*

The director intended to trim her production budget by cutting out some frills *such as these*: special lighting equipment, rental costumes for the cast, and lunches for the crew.

But don't use colons after expressions such as *for example, such as,* and *that is.*

Shoestring budgets have produced many financially successful films such as: *Flashdance, Breaking Away,* and *Halloween.*

•18b-3 Use colons to direct readers to quotations or to dialogue.

Orson Welles commented poignantly on his own career: "I started at the top and worked down."

We recalled Dirty Harry's memorable challenge: "Make my day!"

But don't introduce colons after very short tag lines. Use commas or no punctuation at all.

Dirty Harry said "Make my day!"

As Dirty Harry said, "Make my day!"

•18b-4 Use colons to join two independent clauses when the second clause explains the first.

Making a film is like writing a paper: it absorbs all the time you give it.

•18b-5 Use colons in special situations.

Colons separate titles from subtitles and separate numbers when marking time or citing biblical passages. They also follow the salutation in business letters.

"Darkest Night: Hollywood and *Film Noir*"

12:35 p.m.

Matthew 3:1

Dear Mr. Ebert:

T I P S

• **Colons and semicolons are not interchangeable.** However, you can use both pieces of punctuation in the same sentence. For example, a colon might introduce a list of items separated by semicolons.

Errol Flynn played many different roles: an Indian in *Kim*; a pirate in *Against All Flags*; a famous outlaw in *The Adventures of Robin Hood*.

• **Don't use more than one colon in a sentence.** A dash can usually replace one of the colons. (See Section 19d.)

Almost every film critic agrees on this point: Orson Welles is responsible for one of the greatest films of all time—/ *Citizen Kane*.

131

[19]

chapter

Other Punctuation Marks

19a Quotation Marks

Quotation marks, which always occur in pairs, highlight what appears between them. Use double quotations (" ") around most quoted material; use single quotations (' ') to mark quotations within quotations.

• 19a-1 Use quotation marks around material you are borrowing word for word from sources.

Notice the punctuation before and after the quotations in the following examples.

A quotation introduced or followed by *said, remarked, observed,* or a similar expression takes a comma.

> Benjamin Disraeli *observed,* "It is much easier to be critical than to be correct."

> "Next to the originator of a good sentence is the first quoter of it," *said* Ralph Waldo Emerson.

Commas are used, too, when a single sentence quotation is broken up by an interrupting expression such as *he asked* or *she noted.*

> "If the world were a logical place," *Rita Mae Brown notes,* "men would ride sidesaddle."

When such an interrupting expression comes between two successive sentences quoted from a single source, a comma and period are required.

> "There is no such thing as a moral book or an immoral book," *says Oscar Wilde.* "Books are well written or badly written. That is all."

No extra punctuation is required when a quotation runs smoothly into a sentence you have written.

> Abraham Lincoln observed that "in giving freedom to the slave we assure freedom to the free."

See 23b-5 for guidelines on introducing and framing quotations.

• 19a-2 Use quotation marks to mark dialogue.

When writing a passage with several speakers, start a new paragraph each time the speaker changes.

> Mrs. Bennet deigned not to make any reply; but unable to contain herself, began scolding one of her daughters.
>
> "Don't keep coughing so, Kitty, for heaven's sake! Have a little compassion on my nerves. You tear them to pieces."
>
> "Kitty has no discretion in her coughs," said her father; "she times them ill."
>
> "I do not cough for my own amusement," replied Kitty fretfully.
>
> —Jane Austen, *Pride and Prejudice*

• 19a-3 Use quotation marks to highlight the titles of short works.

These include titles of songs, essays, magazine and newspaper articles, TV episodes, unpublished speeches, chapters of books, and short poems. (Titles of longer works appear in *italics*; see Section 19b-1).

"Love Is Just a Four-Letter Word"

song

"Love Is a Fallacy"

title of an essay

•19a-4 Use quotation marks to draw attention to specific words. Italics can be used in these situations too. (See Section 19b-3.)

People clearly mean different things when they write about "democracy."

•19a-5 Use quotation marks to show when you are using words or expressions ironically, sarcastically, or derisively.

The clerk at the desk directed the tourists to their "suites"—bare rooms crowded with cots. A bathroom down the hall would serve as the "spa."

But don't overdo the use of quotation marks for this purpose. This technique for adding emphasis loses punch quickly. Highlighting clichés, for example, just makes them more tedious.

Working around electrical fixtures makes me more nervous than "a long-tailed cat in a room full of rocking chairs."

•19a-6 Place quotation marks correctly with other pieces of punctuation.

Commas and periods go *inside* closing quotation marks except when a parenthetical note is given.

"This must be what the sixties were like," I thought.

Down a corridor lined with antiwar posters, I heard someone humming "Blowin' in the Wind."

Rose argues that we hurt education if we think of it "in limited and limiting ways" *(3)*.

Colons and semicolons go *outside* closing quotation marks.

Riley claimed to be "a human calculator": he did quadratic equations in his head.

The young Cassius Clay bragged about being "the greatest"; his opponents in the ring soon learned he wasn't just boasting.

Question marks and exclamation points can fall either inside or outside the closing quotation mark. They fall *inside* when they apply only to the quotation.

When Mrs. Rattle saw her hotel room, she muttered, "Good grief!"

She turned to her husband and said, "Do you really expect me to stay here?"

They fall *outside* the closing quotation mark when they apply to the complete sentence.

Who was it that said, "Truth is always the strongest argument"?

19b Italics

Italics, as with quotation marks, draw attention to a title, a word, or a phrase. In a printed text, italics appear as *slanted letters*. In typed or handwritten papers, italics are often signaled by underlining the appropriate words.

• 19b-1 Use italics to set off some titles. Some titles and names are italicized; others appear between quotation marks. But neither italics nor quotation marks are used for the names of *types* of trains, ships, aircraft, or spacecraft.

Trident submarine	Boeing 767
space shuttle	Atlas Agena

Neither italics nor quotation marks are used with titles of major religious texts, books of the Bible, or classic legal documents.

the Bible	Genesis
the Qur'an	The Declaration of Independence

• 19b-2 Use italics to set off foreign words and phrases. Foreign terms that haven't become an accepted item of English vocabulary and scientific names are given special emphasis.

Chart: Titles *Italicized* or "*In Quotations*"

Titles *Italicized*

books	*Microserfs*
magazines	*Men's Journal*
journals	*Written Communication*
newspapers	*The New York Times* or the New York *Times*
films	*Casablanca*
TV shows	*Seinfeld*
radio shows	*All Things Considered*
plays	*Othello*
long poems	*Paradise Lost*
long musical pieces	*The Mikado*
albums	*Revolver*
paintings	the *Mona Lisa*
sculptures	Michelangelo's *Pietà*
ships	*Titanic*
	U.S.S. *Saratoga*
trains	the *Orient Express*
aircraft	*Enola Gay*
spacecraft	*Apollo 13*
software programs	*Microsoft Word*

Titles "In Quotation Marks"

chapters of books	"Lessons from the Pros"
articles in magazines	"Afoot in Godzone"
articles in journals	"Vai Script and Literacy"
articles in newspapers	"Inflation Heats Up"
sections in newspapers	"Living in Style"
TV episodes	"The Understudy"
radio episodes	"McGee Goes Crackers"
short stories	"Araby"
short poems	"The Red Wheelbarrow"
songs	"God Bless America"

Pierre often described his fellow-workers as *les bêtes humaines.*

However, the many foreign words and phrases absorbed by the English language over the centuries should not be italicized. Check a recent dictionary to make this determination.

crèche	gumbo
gestalt	arroyo

Common abbreviations from Latin also appear without italics or underscoring.

etc.	et al.
i.e.	viz.

• 19b-3 Use italics (or quotation marks) to emphasize or clarify a letter, a word, or a phrase.

Does that word begin with an *f* or a *ph?*

"That may be how *you* define fascist," she replied.

When some people talk about *school spirit,* they really mean *let's have a party!*

19c Ellipses

Three spaced periods or dots mark an ellipsis (. . .), a gap in a sentence or passage.

• 19c-1 Place ellipses where material has been omitted from direct quota-

tions. This material may be a word, a phrase, a complete sentence, or more.

Complete Passage: Abraham Lincoln closed his First Inaugural Address (March 4, 1861) with these words: "We are not enemies, but friends. We must not be enemies. Though passion may have strained it must not break our bonds of affection. The mystic chords of memory, stretching from every battlefield and patriot grave to every living heart and hearthstone all over this broad land, will yet swell the chorus of the Union, when again touched, as surely they will be, by the better angels of our nature."

Passage with Ellipses: Abraham Lincoln closed his First Inaugural Address (March 4, 1861) with these words: "We are not enemies, but friends. . . . The mystic chords of memory . . . will yet swell the chorus of the Union, when again touched, as surely they will be, by the better angels of our nature."

• 19c-2 Use ellipses to indicate pauses of any kind or to suggest that an action is incomplete or continuing.

We were certain we would finish the report on time . . . until the computer crashed and wouldn't reboot.

The rocket rumbled on its launch pad as the countdown proceeded, "four, three, two, . . ."

• 19c-3 Use correct spacing and punctuation before and after ellipsis marks.
When an ellipsis mark appears in the middle of a sentence, leave a space before the first and after the last period.

> chords of memory (. . .) will yet swell

If a punctuation mark occurs immediately before the ellipsis, include the mark when it makes your sentence easier to read. The punctuation mark is followed by a space and then the ellipsis mark.

> We are not enemies, (. . .) must not be enemies

When an ellipsis occurs at the end of a complete sentence or when you delete a full sentence or more, place a period at the end of the sentence, followed by a space and then the ellipsis.

> We must not be enemies (. . .) The mystic chords

• 19c-4 Use a full line of spaced dots when you delete more than a line of verse.

> For Mercy has a human heart,
> Pity a human face,
> (. . . . .)
> And Peace, the human dress.
>
> —William Blake, "The Divine Image"

19d Dashes

Dashes can link or separate ideas in sentences. They are bold punctuation marks to be used with care and a little flair.

• 19d-1 Use dashes to add illustrations, examples, or summaries to the ends of sentences. A dash gives emphasis to any addition.

> Beethoven's Ninth Symphony was a great accomplishment for an artist in bad health— and completely deaf.

• 19d-2 Use pairs of dashes to insert information into a sentence. Information between dashes gets noticed.

> Many regard Verdi's *Otello*—based upon Shakespeare's story of a marriage ruined by jealousy—as the greatest of Italian tragic operas.

• 19d-3 Use dashes to highlight interruptions, especially in dialogue. The interruption can even be punctuated.

> "When—perhaps I should say *if?*—I ever sit through Wagner's *Ring* again, I expect to be paid for it," Joshua remarked.

• 19d-4 Don't use a hyphen when a dash is required. Keyboarded dashes are made up of two unspaced hyphens [--]. No space is left before or after a dash.

```
Much of Beethoven's music--unlike
that of Mozart--is autobiographical.
```

•19d-5 Don't use too many dashes in a sentence or passage. Certainly use no more than one pair of dashes per sentence.

Mozart⟨—⟩recognized as a genius while still a child⟨—⟩produced more than 600 compositions during his life⟨—⟩including symphonies, operas, and concertos.

19e Hyphens

Hyphens either put words together or divide them between syllables.

•19e-1 Use hyphens to link some compound nouns and verbs. The conventions for hyphenating words are complicated and inconsistent. Here are expressions that take hyphens.

bes⟨-⟩seller	mother⟨-of-⟩pearl	strong⟨-⟩arm
mother⟨-in-⟩law	right⟨-⟩hander	way⟨-⟩out

Here are some compounds that aren't hyphenated.

best man	cabdriver	seabird
blockhouse	cab owner	sea dog

When in doubt, check a dictionary or style manual.

•19e-2 Use hyphens to link unit modifiers before a noun. When putting a comma between modifying words produces nonsense, you probably have a unit modifier that requires a hyphen.

bare⟨,⟩chested warrior

an English⟨,⟩speaking city

But don't use hyphens to link compound modifiers following a noun.

The warrior was *bare chested*.

The candidate is hardly awe inspiring.

Nor should you use hyphens with *very* or with adverbs that end in *-ly*.

a very hot day   a sharply honed knife

•19e-3 Use hyphens when you write out numbers from twenty-one to ninety-nine. Fractions also take hyphens, but use only one hyphen per fraction.

twent⟨y-⟩nine	one fort⟨y-⟩seventh of a mile
one⟨-⟩quarter inch	two hundred fort⟨y-⟩six

•19e-4 Use hyphens to link prefixes to proper nouns.

*pre⟨-⟩*Columbian

*anti⟨-⟩*American

• 19e-5 Use hyphens in technical expressions or to prevent words from being misread.

uranium-235	A-bomb
co-op	re-create

• 19e-6 Don't hyphenate words or numbers at the ends of lines.
Most style manuals advise against such divisions when you are typing. If you are using a computer, word wrap automatically eliminates end-of-line divisions. When you must divide a word, break it only at a syllable and then check a dictionary for the syllable break. Don't guess. Divide any compound expressions between words, not syllables.

Wrong: self-confi- dent

Right: self- confident

19f Parentheses

Parentheses add an extra bit of information, a comment, or an aside to sentences. They are much more common than brackets, which are used in only a few situations. (See Section 19g.)

• 19f-1 Use parentheses to separate material from the main body of a sentence or paragraph.
This added material may be a word, a phrase, a list, or even a complete sentence.

The flight to Colorado was quick (*only about ninety minutes*) and uneventful.

The emergency kit contained all the expected items (*jumper cables, tire inflator, and roadside flares*).

• 19f-2 Use parentheses to highlight numbers or letters used to list items in running text.

The labor negotiators realized they could **(1)** concede on all issues immediately, **(2)** stonewall until the public demanded a settlement, or **(3)** hammer out a compromise.

• 19f-3 Place parentheses properly either inside or outside of end punctuation.
When a complete sentence standing alone is surrounded by parentheses, its end punctuation belongs *inside* the end parenthesis.

The neighborhood was run-down and littered. (Some houses looked as if they hadn't been painted in decades.)

However, when a sentence concludes with parentheses, the end punctuation for the complete sentence falls *outside* the final parenthesis mark.

> On the corner was a small church (actually, a converted stores).

• 19f-4 Don't use punctuation before parentheses in the middle of sentences.

A comma before a parenthesis is incorrect; however, if necessary, a parenthesis may be followed by a comma.

> Although the Crusades failed in their announced objective (Jerusalem remained in Muslim hands when they ended) the expeditions changed the West dramatically.

19g Brackets

Like parentheses, brackets are enclosures. But they have fewer and more specialized uses. Brackets and parentheses are usually *not* interchangeable.

• 19g-1 Use brackets to insert comments or explanations into direct quotations.

> "He [George Lucas] reminded me a little of Walt Disney's version of a mad scientist."
> —Steven Spielberg

• 19g-2 Use brackets to avoid one set of parentheses falling within another.

Turn the inner pair of parentheses into brackets.

> The paper included a full text of the resolution (expressing the sense of the House of Representatives on the calculation of the Consumer Price Index [H.RES.99]).

• 19g-3 Use brackets to acknowledge or highlight errors that originate in quoted materials.

In such cases the Latin word *sic* ("thus") is enclosed in brackets immediately after the error. See Section 23b-9 for an example.

19h Slashes

Slashes are used to indicate divisions. They are rare pieces of punctuation with just a few specific functions.

• 19h-1 Use slashes to divide lines of poetry quoted within sentences.

When used in this way, a space is left on either side of the slash.

> Only then does Lear understand that he has been a failure as a king: "O, I have taken / Too little care of this!"

If you quote more than three lines of verse, set the passage as a block quote and break the lines as they appear in the poem itself.

• 19h-2 Use slashes to separate expressions that indicate a choice. In these cases, no space is left before or after the slash.

either/or   he/she   yes/no   pass/fail

Some readers object to these expressions, especially *he/she* (sometimes written as *s/he*).

• 19h-3 Use slashes in typing World Wide Web addresses.

http://nps.gov/glac/press.htm

19i Other Marks

You may encounter various marks in electronic discourse.

• 19i-1 Recognize the symbol for "at": @. It appears in e-mail addresses:

feedback@www.whitehouse.gov

• 19i-2 Recognize "smileys." These characters, created from various typographical elements, may appear in electronic writing environments. They are also called "emoticons."

smiley face :-)
frowney face :-(
wink ;-)
bored :-|
yawn :-o
hug [ ]

chapter [20]

Capitalization, Apostrophes, Abbreviations, and Numbers

143

20a Capitalization

Capital letters can cause problems simply because you have to remember the conventions guiding their use. Fortunately, you can observe the guidelines for capital letters in almost every sentence you read.

• 20a-1 Capitalize the first word of a sentence.

It was a dark and stormy night.

The rule varies with sentences falling within parentheses. Such sentences are capitalized when they stand alone but not capitalized when they fall within other sentences.

Click on the icon. (**T**he icon will be highlighted.)

Insert the disk into the disk drive (**s**ee Appendix 3).

• 20a-2 Capitalize the first word of a direct quotation when it is a full sentence.

Ira asked, "**W**here's the Air and Space Museum?"

Summary: *Capitalizing Titles*

To capitalize a title follow these three steps.

- **Capitalize the first word.**
- **Capitalize the last word.**
- **Capitalize all other words** *except*
  - **Articles (***a, an, the***)**
  - **Prepositions with fewer than five letters**
  - **Coordinating conjunctions**
  - **The** *to* **in infinitives**

Use lowercase for quotations that continue after an interruption.

"It's on the Mall," the guide explained, "**n**ot far from the Hirschhorn Gallery."

• 20a-3 Don't capitalize the first word after a colon unless you want to emphasize the word or it is part of a title.

No Caps After Colon: They ignored one detail while parking the car: **a** no-parking sign.

Caps for Emphasis: The phrase haunted her: **Y**our license has expired!

Caps for Title: *Marilyn: The Untold Story*

• 20a-4 Capitalize the major words in the titles of papers, books, articles, poems, and so on.

All the Trouble in the World

"**S**topping by **W**oods on a **S**nowy **E**vening"

• 20a-5 Capitalize the first word in lines of quoted poetry unless the poet has used lowercase letters.

Sumer is ycomen in,
Loude sing cuckoo!
—"The Cuckoo Song"

• 20a-6 Capitalize the names and initials of people as well as titles identified with specific people.

Virginia Woolf

Justice Clarence Thomas

I. M. Pei

J. Hector St. Jean Crèvecoeur

Anzia Yezierska

Aunt Josephine

Rosa Eberly, Ph.D.

Robert King, the Dean of Liberal Arts

But don't capitalize titles used less specifically or minor titles that stand alone—that is, unattached to a particular person.

Josephine, my favorite aunt

Robert King, a dean at the university

a commissioner in Cuyahoga County

the first president of our club

More prestigious titles may be capitalized even when they stand alone, though style manuals disagree on this point.

the President *or* the president

the Secretary of State *or* the secretary of state

the Chair of the Classics Department

• 20a-7 Capitalize the names of national, political, or ethnic groups.

Kenyans

Australians

African Americans

Do not capitalize the titles of racial groups, economic groups, and social classes.

blacks	the proletariat
whites	the knowledge class

• 20a-8 Capitalize the names of institutions and specific objects. These include the following.

businesses	Chrysler Corporation
organizations	National Rifle Association
unions	Teamsters
schools	Memphis State University
religious figures	the Blessed Virgin
religions	Buddhism
sacred books	the Bible, the Torah
place names	Asia, France
geographic features	the Gulf of Mexico
buildings	the Empire State Building
structures	Jacob's Field
monuments	the Alamo
ships and planes	S.S. *Titanic,* Boeing 767
automobiles	Cadillac Catera
brand-name products	Xerox, Frigidaire
documents	the Constitution
	the Magna Carta
cultural movements	Romanticism, Vorticism
historical periods	Pax Romana, Victorian Age

days and months	Monday, July
holidays	Halloween, Fourth of July
course titles	History 101

Do not capitalize seasons of the year (*winter, spring*); compass directions unless they are part of a place name (*north, North America*); or school subjects unless they are themselves proper nouns (*mathematics, Russian history, English*).

• 20a-9 Capitalize abstractions when you want to give them special emphasis. Compare the following examples.

What is this thing called Love?

Adil had fallen in love again.

• 20a-10 Capitalize all the letters in most acronyms. (See Section 20c-2 for more details.)

NATO   OPEC   SALT Treaty

Do not capitalize acronyms that have become so familiar they seem like ordinary words (*radar, sonar*). When in doubt, check a dictionary.

20b Apostrophes: Contractions and Possessives

• 20b-1 Use apostrophes in contractions to show where letters have been omitted. Such apostrophes are not optional.

can't—cannot

it's—it *is*

you're—you *are*

who's—who *is*

• 20b-2 Use apostrophes to form the possessives of nouns. Add an apostrophe + s to most singular nouns and to plural nouns that do not end in *s*.

a dog's life

geese's behavior

the NCAA's ruling

children's imaginations

Form the possessive of singular nouns ending in *s* or *z* with either an apostrophe + s or just the apostrophe. Use one form or the other consistently.

the countess's jewels *or* the countess' jewels

Katz's menu *or* Katz' menu

Add an apostrophe (but not an *s*) to plural nouns that end in *s*.

the hostesses' jobs

the senators' parking spaces

• 20b-3 Use apostrophes to show possession in compound or hyphenated words.

the president-elect's decision

both fathers-in-law's Cadillacs

• 20b-4 Use apostrophes to show joint ownership. When two nouns share ownership, only the second noun needs an apostrophe.

> Peg and John's research grant
>
> Vorhees and Goetz' project

But when ownership is separate, each noun shows possession.

> Peg's and John's educations
>
> Vorhees' and Goetz' offices

• 20b-5 Do not use apostrophes to make personal pronouns possessive. Personal pronouns—*my, your, her, his, our, their, its*—form possessives without them. Don't confuse the possessive pronouns *its* and *whose* with the contractions *it's* and *who's.*

> **It's** an idea that has **its** opponents in arms.
>
> **Who's** to say **whose** opinion is right?

Indefinite pronouns form their possessives regularly: *anybody's, each one's, everybody's.* For more about possessive pronouns, see Section 14c-8.

• 20b-6 Use apostrophes to mark certain types of plurals. These might include the plurals of numbers, symbols, individual letters, abbreviations, and dates and words used as words.

> 8's and 9's
>
> two +'s

two .45's and a .22

three *the's* and four *an's*

Many writers omit the apostrophe for such plurals, especially when the 's might be mistaken as a possessive.

> the three CEO**s**
>
> the ACT**s**

20c Abbreviations

Some abbreviations (*a.m., p.m., Mrs., Mr., Dr., B.C., B.C.E., A.D.*) may appear in all kinds of writing. Others (*Jan., ft, no.*) should be limited to forms and technical reports.

• 20c-1 Be consistent in punctuating abbreviations and acronyms.

Summary: *Punctuating Abbreviations*

- Abbreviations of single words usually take periods: *vols., Jan., Mr.*
- Some abbreviations that are spoken letter by letter may have periods after each letter but are usually written without them: *HBO, IRS, WWW, AFL-CIO.*
- Acronyms (spoken as complete words) do not require periods: *CARE, NATO, NOW.*
- Periods are usually omitted after abbreviations in technical writing unless an item might be misread without the period: *ft* for foot, *km* for kilometer, but *in.* for inch.

147

20c-2 Be consistent in capitalizing abbreviations and acronyms.

Summary: Capitalizing Abbreviations

- Capitalize abbreviations of words that are capitalized when written out in full: *General Motors—GM, 98° Fahrenheit—98°F.*
- Do not capitalize abbreviations of words not capitalized when written out: *pound—lb, minutes—min.*
- Capitalize most acronyms: *IRS, CRT, UCLA, NBC.*
- Always capitalize *B.C.* and *A.D.*
- You may capitalize *A.M.* and *P.M.*, but they now ordinarily appear in small letters: *a.m.* and *p.m.*

20c-3 Use the appropriate abbreviations for titles, degrees, and names.

Some titles are almost always abbreviated (*Mr., Ms., Mrs., Jr.*). Other titles are normally written out in full, though these may be abbreviated when they precede a first name or initial.

President	President Bush	**Pres.** George Bush
Professor	Professor Campbell	**Prof.** K. Campbell
Reverend	Reverend Eagle	**Rev.** Ann Eagle
	the Reverend Dr. Eagle	**Rev. Dr.** Eagle
Secretary	Secretary Perry	**Sec.** William Perry

Never use abbreviated titles of this kind alone in a sentence.

        governor   senator
The g̶o̶v̶. urged the s̶e̶n̶. to support the resolutions in Congress.

Give credit for academic degrees either before a name or after—not both. Don't, for example, use both *Dr.* and *Ph.D.* in the same name. Abbreviations for academic titles can stand by themselves, without names attached.

Professor Kim received her **Ph.D.** from Illinois and her **B.S.** from St. Vincent College.

> **T I P** An abbreviation in the middle of a sentence retains its period. Such a period may even be followed by another punctuation mark.
>
> Though he had not yet earned his **Ph.D.**, Enrique knew his job prospects were bright.

20c-4 Use appropriate common abbreviations.

The following are appropriate in all types of writing.

businesses	**IBM, A&P, MTV**
organizations	**NCAA, GOP**
time	43 **B.C.E., A.D.** 1996, 4:13 **a.m.**, 10:00 **p.m.**
temperature	13°**C.**, 98°**F.**
places	**USSR;** Washington, **D.C.**

The following abbreviations are appropriate in special situations, such as technical reports, footnotes, recipes, forms, and addresses. In most writing, however, the terms should be written out in full.

months	**Jan., Aug.**
days	**Mon., Fri.**
time	60 **mins.**, 3 **hrs.**
weights	30 **lb**
measures	3 **tsp**, 26 **km**
book terms	**p., vols., ch.**
states (postal)	**CA, NY, TX, WY**

• 20c-5 Use appropriate technical abbreviations. Specialized abbreviations (*DNA, GNP, kW*) are often used in professional and technical writing. When writing for nontechnical audiences, spell out technical terms in full the first time you use them. Then in parentheses give the specialized abbreviation you will use in the rest of the paper.

The two candidates debated the effects that the tax increase would have on the *gross national product* **(GNP).**

20d Numbers

• 20d-1 Write out numbers from one to nine; use numerals for numbers larger than nine. This guideline, however, has variations and exceptions. The MLA style manual, for example, recommends spelling out any number that can be expressed in one or two words.

thirteen	twenty-one	three hundred

When you need to express large round numbers, combine words and figures.

100 billion	432 million	103 trillion

• 20d-2 Use numbers appropriately. Numerals are needed or preferred in the following situations.

dates	July **4, 1776**
addresses	**1900** East Blvd.
measurements	**2.5** miles, **33°**F.
percentages	**75** percent
time	**10:00** a.m., **2:15** p.m.
	(*but **ten** in the morning, **six** o'clock*)

TIPS

- In large figures, use commas to separate thousands, millions, billions, and so on. Commas are omitted, however, in dates (unless there is a day and year combination), after street numbers, and sometimes in four-digit numbers.
- In most cases, spell out ordinal numbers (that is, numbers that express a sequence): *first, second, third, fourth,* and so on. Don't make these words adverbs by adding *-ly.*

· 20d-3 Don't begin sentences with numerals. Either spell out the number or rephrase the sentence so that the numeral is not the first word.

~~32~~ Thirty-two people were standing in line.

Sentences may, however, begin with dates.

1989 marked the end of world communism.

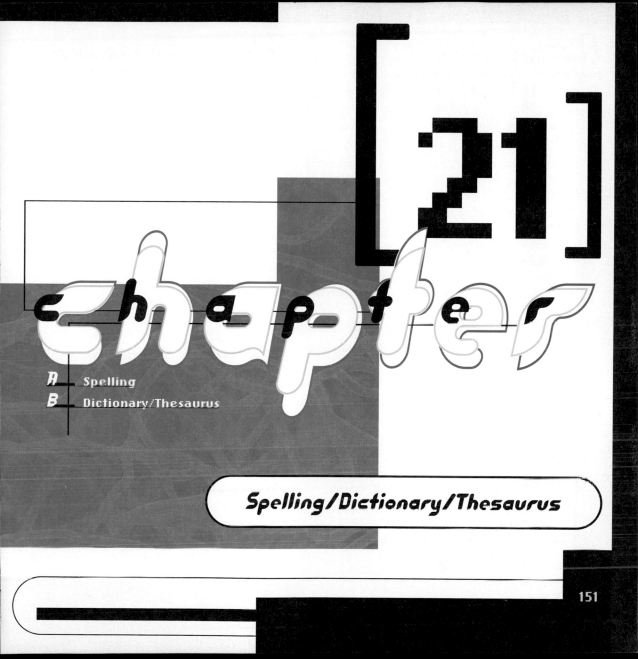

chapter [21]

A — Spelling
B — Dictionary/Thesaurus

Spelling/Dictionary/Thesaurus

*R*eaders react very strongly to errors in spelling. That is why you should carefully edit the final draft of any paper you write, looking especially for the types of misspellings you make habitually. And don't depend on a spelling checker to edit a final draft. Review the paper yourself.

21a Spelling

Most spelling errors involve simple words rather than difficult ones, and the toughest errors to catch are habitual ones, such as mistaking *its* for *it's* or *too* for *to*. You have to develop techniques for locating and correcting such mistakes.

• 21a-1 Proofread carefully to eliminate obvious errors.

There's no easy way around the need to proofread all your academic and professional writing carefully. Here are three effective proofreading techniques.

- Read a draft aloud, slowly.
- Read a draft with a pencil in hand, touching each word as you read.
- Read a draft backward to isolate individual words.

When you find a misspelling, check the next few words very carefully too. Finding a mistake sometimes makes writers miss other errors in the immediate vicinity.

Be especially careful at those points where English spelling is most apt to go wrong.

- Words that contain *ei* or *ie*: rec**ei**ve, bel**ie**ve, for**ei**gn, counterf**ei**t
- Words with silent letters: **p**neumonia, de**b**t, ans**w**er

- Words that end in

  -able or *-ible:* laugh**able**, vis**ible**
  -ance or *-ence:* guid**ance**, obedi**ence**
  -ant or *-ent:* attend**ant**, differ**ent**
  -cede, -ceed, or *-sede:* pre**cede**, pro**ceed**, super**sede**

- Words that contain double consonants: o**cc**u**rr**ence, emba**rr**ass, exa**gg**erate, a**cc**umulate, a**cc**o**mm**odate, reco**mm**end
- Contractions: *who's, it's, you're, don't, won't, can't*
- Possessive forms: *Jones's, Boz's* (see Section 20b)
- Irregular plurals: *geese, media, women*
- Hyphenated words: *double-edged, mothers-in-law*

• 21a-2 Eliminate errors that result from problems with pronunciation or misreading.

No one spells English words correctly just because he or she pronounces them correctly; the language refuses to be consistent. You may not recognize some spelling errors until an editor or reader points them out.

• 21a-3 When in doubt about the spelling of words, look them up.

Looking words up takes less time than you may imagine. But don't go to a dictionary until after you've drafted a section, or you'll lose momentum. While writing, circle or underline doubtful spellings and then return to them. Verify the correctness of words that look right when you know they're the sort you often misspell—words that end in *-ible,* for example.

Keep in mind that not all words in English have a single correct spelling. Some dictionaries offer variant spellings, but in general, you should avoid variants labeled *chiefly British (colour, judgement, theatre), archaic,* or *obsolete* unless you have a special reason for using them. You would use British spellings, for example, in quoting a London newspaper or a speech by the Prime Minister.

•21a-4 Apply spelling rules—if helpful.

Spelling rules for English tend to be complicated, hard to remember, and unreliable. You can find most of them in a reputable dictionary. Unfortunately, the only rule most people find helpful—or even remember—is that *i* comes before *e* except after *c*—except when *ei* has a long *a* sound.

bel**ie**ve	**ei**ght
rec**ei**ve	w**ei**gh

Significant exceptions weaken even this familiar guideline.

counterfeit	either	seize
weird	foreign	

Checklist: Common Spelling Errors

Wrong	Right
alot	a lot
alright	all right
arguement	argument
athelete	athlete
beleive	believe
definately	definitely
enviroment	environment
Febuary	February
goverment	government
hankerchief	handkerchief
knowlege	knowledge
mispell	misspell
neccesary	necessary
noticable	noticeable
occured	occurred
perscription	prescription
privlege	privilege
recieve	receive
roomate	roommate
seperate	separate
suprise	surprise
surppress	suppress
temperture	temperature
truely	truly
villian	villain

•21a-5 Pay close attention to the spelling of words that sound alike.
Words that sound exactly alike—called homonyms—

all ready [set to go]	already [by now]
altar [table]	alter [change]
bare [empty, clear]	bear [carry]
bored [uninterested]	board [group/plank/climb on]
brake [stop]	break [fracture]
capital [seat of government]	capitol [government building]
cite [point out]	sight [see]; site [location]
compliment [praise]	complement [make complete]
council [group]	counsel [advice/lawyer]
dessert [treat]	desert [abandon/arid place]
gorilla [large ape]	guerrilla [soldier]
hear [perceive sound]	here [this place]
its [possessive form]	it's [contraction for *it is*]
lead [to direct/metal]	led [past tense of *to lead*]
lessen [decrease]	lesson [instruction]
past [what's occurred]	passed [went/met standards]
patience [tolerance]	patients [people under medical care]
peace [harmony]	piece [part or portion]
principal [head of school/ most important]	principle [standard/moral guide]
road [highway]	rode [past tense of *ride*]
stationary [not moving]	stationery [writing material]
their [possessive]	there [in that place]; they're [*they are*]
threw [past tense of *throw*]	through [across]
throne [royal seat]	thrown [past participle of *throw*]
weak [not strong]	week [seven days]
wear [to have on]	where [place]
weather [climate]	whether [if/choice]
whose [possessive]	who's [contraction for *who is*]
your [possessive]	you're [contraction for *you are*]

cause many errors. Keep track of your most common homonym problems and check them in every paper you write.

• 21a-6 Pay close attention to the spelling of words that look alike. Words similar in spelling or appearance often differ widely in meaning. Unfortunately, no simple tricks prevent the misspelling (or misuse) of such common terms. The best you can do is gradually accumulate a list of habitual troublemakers. Here is just a sampling of the many problem clusters in English.

• 21a-7 Spell plurals correctly. Forming the plurals of nouns is usually easy, but some plurals are irregular or tricky (*ox → oxen; fungus → fungi*). When in doubt, check a dictionary. The basic rules are simple.

Add -s to most nouns to form the plural.

   toy → toy**s**

demonstration → demonstration**s**

picture → picture**s**

Add *-es* when the plural adds a syllable to the pronunciation of a noun. If the noun already ends in *-e,* add only *-s.*

dish → dish**es**

summons → summons**es**

• 21a-8 Use a spelling checker carefully. A spelling checker on a word processor will find all typos and errors in a draft—as long as the mistakes aren't legitimate words on their own. A spelling checker, for example, will signal if you spell *supposed* as "suposed"; but it won't tell you that you've omitted the *d* at the end of the word, because *suppose* is a correctly spelled term by itself.

Even after a spelling checker has examined a draft, proofread it again to find the kind of errors computers can't detect. A typical spelling checker, for example, would find no mistakes in the following sentence:

Their our to many excuses for the prejudice attitudes we sea every wear in the whirled around us.

21b Dictionary/Thesaurus

Everyone needs a dictionary and a thesaurus. But which of the many volumes available is right

---

Checklist: Troublesome Pairs

accept [allow]	except [not including]
adverse [difficult]	averse [opposed to]
advice [n.—counsel]	advise [v.—to give counsel]
affect [to influence]	effect [consequence]
allusion [a reference]	illusion [a false impression]
are [form of *to be*]	our [possessive]
breath [n.—an inhalation]	breathe [v.—to inhale]
conscience [moral guide]	conscious [aware of]
elicit [to evoke]	illicit [illegal]
eminent [famous]	imminent [about to occur]
loose [not fastened]	lose [to misplace]
personal [private]	personnel [work force]
quiet [not noisy]	quite [very]
than [compared with]	then [at that time]
wear [to have on]	were [past tense of *to be*]

---

for you? The answer depends on the type of work you do.

• 21b-1 Own a desk-sized college dictionary. So-called desk, or collegiate, dictionaries are an ideal compromise between large, unabridged dictionaries and paperback "pocket" dictionaries. They typically contain between 140,000 and 200,000 entries—enough for most routine writing jobs. College dictionaries may differ in their willingness to give guidelines for correct usage. A few, called *prescriptive,* offer advice about how English is properly employed. Most current dictionaries, however, give usage rules

Checklist: *Selecting a Dictionary*

✔ Does the dictionary have at least 100,000 words in its lexicon? Are the definitions full and clear?
✔ Does an entry explain a word's history (etymology)?
✔ Does an entry include information about capitalization, division, variations in spelling, synonyms, antonyms, and homonyms?
✔ Is the pronunciation guide helpful and in type large enough to read?
✔ Does the dictionary provide stylistic labels (for example, *archaic, slang, chiefly British*)?
✔ Does the dictionary offer guidance about mechanics and usage?
✔ Does the dictionary list the names of important persons, places, countries, cities?
✔ Are the introductions and appendixes useful and readable?
✔ Are pages laid out well? Does the dictionary include drawings, maps, charts, tables, and illustrations?
✔ Is the book bound well?

The Random House Dictionary of the English Language.

• 21b-3 Use a pocket dictionary as a convenience. You can rely on a pocket dictionary for correct spellings and basic meanings, but it contains fewer entries, shorter definitions, and sketchier etymologies (word origins) than college dictionaries.

• 21b-4 Use a thesaurus judiciously. A thesaurus is a collection of synonyms to help you find the best word for a particular situation. Whether you use a printed or electronic version, be certain that any synonyms you select match both denotatively and connotatively the words you intend to replace. The differences in connotation between words of the same denotation can be enormous, as these synonyms for *thin* demonstrate: *sheer, bony, lanky, watery, diluted, fragile, feeble.*

sparingly (and are therefore considered *descriptive*). They explain how words *are* used, but not how they *should* be used.

• 21b-2 Consult an unabridged dictionary when necessary. When you are looking for a rare, obscure, or old word, or when you need comprehensive or historical information about a term, you may wish to consult an unabridged dictionary. These works, routinely available in library reference rooms, attempt to record standard vocabulary items as fully as practicable. The *Oxford English Dictionary* is the most famous unabridged dictionary. Also useful are *Webster's Third International Dictionary of English* and

 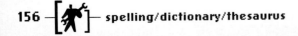

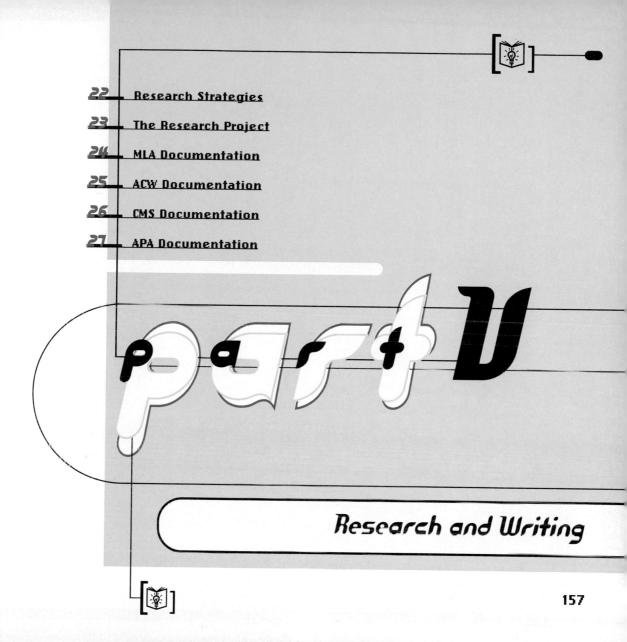

part **V**

Research and Writing

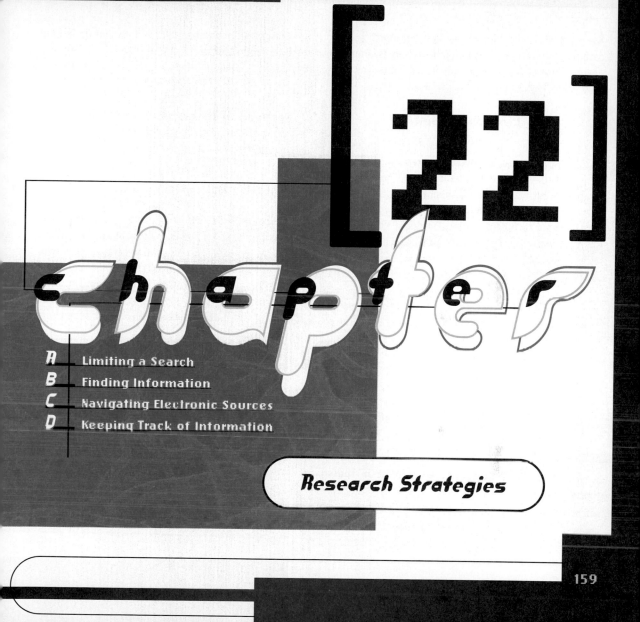

chapter [22]

A — Limiting a Search
B — Finding Information
C — Navigating Electronic Sources
D — Keeping Track of Information

Research Strategies

*O*nly a few years ago, writers doing research spent much of their time locating sources of information in card catalogs, printed indexes, and bibliographies. Today, with computerized library catalogs, electronic indexes, and on-line information services widely available, you can identify dozens—even hundreds—of potential leads with only a few keystrokes.

22a Limiting a Search

The importance of a "good" subject to research can be overestimated. In and of themselves, subjects aren't either "good" or "bad." What makes the difference is treatment—that is, how well you shape any topic to your readers and your own capabilities. Finding a fertile subject to explore is not a matter of chance or luck. It involves, instead, deciding what you want to achieve and carving a path to that goal.

• 22a-1 Choose a manageable subject.
Be sure to understand how many words or pages you are expected to produce. In general, the shorter the project, the more specific the subject should be. To narrow a subject, look for an angle, or a hook—an idea that will grab and hold your audience. The point seems elementary: your article should convey information that surprises readers. Compare the topic proposed in the first example with those in the next two.

General Subject: An interest in the space program

Focused Subject: What the *Voyager* mission to Neptune discovered about the moon Triton

Focused Subject: What America might gain from spending billions of tax dollars on a Mars landing

Follow your inclinations in choosing a subject. You'll write better papers when you have a stake in them.

• 22a-2 Size up projects carefully.
Pay attention to key words in any assignment from an instructor or editor. Be sure you understand what you are asked to do. Are you expected to *analyze, examine, classify, define, discuss, evaluate, explain, compare, contrast, argue, prove, disprove,* or *persuade?* Each of those words means something different.

• 22a-3 Choose topics sensibly.
Select a topic you can live with for days or weeks. Avoid stale topics. For example, don't prepare yet another piece on gun control, abortion, capital punishment, or the legalization of marijuana. Consider exploring what is unique to your community, taking advantage of information not available to writers living elsewhere.

• 22a-4 Read in the subject area.
Do selective background reading in your most promising areas.

Summary: *Key Research Terms*

- **Analyze. Examine.** Break your subject into its parts or components. Discuss their relationship or function.
- **Classify. Define.** Place your subject into a more general category. Distinguish it from other objects in that category. What are its significant features? What makes it unique? recognizable?
- **Discuss.** Talk about the problems or issues your subject raises. Which issues are the most significant? What actions might be taken? Look at the subject from several points of view.
- **Evaluate.** Think about the subject critically. What criteria would you use to judge it? How well does it meet those standards? How does it compare to similar subjects?
- **Explain.** Show what your subject does or how it operates. Provide background information about it. Put your subject in its historical or political context so readers understand it better.
- **Compare.** Show how your subject resembles other things or ideas.
- **Contrast.** Show how your subject differs from other things or ideas.
- **Prove.** Provide evidence to support an idea or assertion.
- **Disprove.** Provide evidence to contradict or undermine an idea or assertion.
- **Persuade.** Come to a conclusion about your subject, and explain why you believe what you do. Use evidence to persuade others to agree, or provide good reasons for someone to think or act in a particular way.

The most efficient sources for *preliminary* reading are encyclopedias, beginning with any that deal specifically with your subject. The more specialized the encyclopedia, the better its coverage of a subject area is going to be. Library reference rooms have dozens of specialized encyclopedias covering many fields. Ask reference librarians for help.

If no specialized encyclopedia is available or if the volume you select proves too technical, use one of the general encyclopedias, available in print or electronically.

Checklist

Background reading should

✔ Confirm whether you are, in fact, interested in a topic.
✔ Survey the main points of a subject so you can begin narrowing it.
✔ Determine whether the local resources will support your subject in the time available.

Bound	Electronic
The Encyclopaedia Britannica	*Britannica Online*
Encyclopedia Americana	*Encarta*
Colliers Encyclopedia	*Groliers Electronic*
Columbia Encyclopedia	*Columbia Electronic*

Checklist: *Specialized Encyclopedias*

Writing about . . . ?	Begin by checking . . .
American history	*Encyclopedia of American History*
Art	*Encyclopedia of World Art*
Astronomy	*Encyclopedia of Astronomy*
Computers	*Encyclopedia of Computer Science*
Ethical issues in life sciences	*Encyclopedia of Bioethics*
Film	*International Encyclopedia of Film*
Health/medicine	*Health and Medical Horizons*
Law	*The Guide to American Law*
Literature	*Cassell's Encyclopedia of World Literature*
Music	*The New Grove Dictionary of American Music*
Philosophy	*Encyclopedia of Philosophy*
Political science	*Encyclopedia of American Political History*
Psychology	*Encyclopedia of Psychology*
Religion	*The Encyclopedia of Religion*
Science	*McGraw-Hill Encyclopedia of Science and Technology*
Social sciences	*Encyclopedia of the Social Sciences*

· 22a-5 Narrow the topic.

Narrowing a subject makes it easier to search library catalogs, indexes, and databases. Formulate a hypothesis or a question to answer. For example, you might narrow a general article on bicycling to the history of mountain biking in the United States. Or you might ask a question: Should mountain bikes be permitted on hiking trails in state and national parks?

22b Finding Information

Once you've narrowed your topic, you can proceed to the next step, finding information about it. However, locating information is only half the job. You also have to keep track of it, which is discussed in Section 22d. Fortunately, in libraries with electronic catalogs and indexes, you can now print out lists of sources and sometimes whole articles. You can also use index cards to record information and keep track of sources (3-by-5-inch cards are ideal).

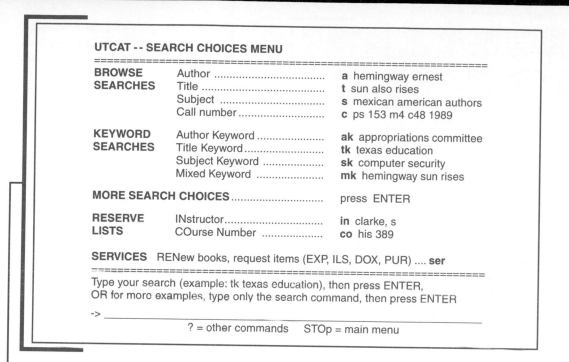

```
UTCAT -- SEARCH CHOICES MENU
==================================================================
BROWSE          Author .................................    a hemingway ernest
SEARCHES        Title ...................................    t sun also rises
                Subject ...............................    s mexican american authors
                Call number ..........................    c ps 153 m4 c48 1989

KEYWORD         Author Keyword ....................    ak appropriations committee
SEARCHES        Title Keyword ........................    tk texas education
                Subject Keyword ...................    sk computer security
                Mixed Keyword .....................    mk hemingway sun rises

MORE SEARCH CHOICES ...........................    press ENTER

RESERVE         INstructor ..............................    in clarke, s
LISTS           COurse Number ...................    co his 389

SERVICES   RENew books, request items (EXP, ILS, DOX, PUR) .... ser
==================================================================
Type your search (example: tk texas education), then press ENTER,
OR for more examples, type only the search command, then press ENTER

->  _____
           ? = other commands      STOp = main menu
```

Cards work efficiently because you can add, delete, alphabetize, and annotate entries quickly.

· 22b-1 Use library catalogs efficiently.
Most larger libraries now provide access to their resources via computer terminals. Electronic catalogs can be searched in various ways (by author, title, subject, and keywords) and may indicate when books have been checked out, lost, or recalled. Spend a few minutes learning to use all your library catalog's search techniques and commands.

Some catalogs, for example, can search periodical indexes and on-line encyclopedias. Here, for example, is the search menu screen for the library catalog at the University of Texas at Austin. Notice that the screen allows you to begin many different searches simply by typing an appropriate command. Note, too, the combinations of keyword searches that this system offers.

Librarians find that most people search on-line catalogs by keyword searches. A keyword search identifies all the titles in a catalog containing the keyword(s) you have selected. The keywords you choose determine the scope of your search. For example, if you were exploring whether mountain bikes should be permitted on park trails, you might begin with these keywords: *bicycle, bike, mountain bike,* and *trail bike.* Each search will generate a different number of library items. In a sample search, for example, one library catalog listed 211 items for *bicycle,* 51 items for *bike,* 7 items for *mountain bike,* but 0 items for the less familiar term *trail bike.* If your search used only *trail bike,* you might mistakenly assume the library has no materials on your subject.

• 22b-2 Locate suitable bibliographies.
Bibliographies list books, articles, and other materials that deal with specific subjects or subject areas.

An up-to-date bibliography on your subject is invaluable. To find such a bibliography, ask the reference librarian or an expert in your subject area. Only a few of the many bibliographies in specific academic fields are shown in the following list.

• 22b-3 Locate periodical indexes. You shouldn't undertake any college-level research paper without searching the periodical literature on your topic. Fortunately, you can track articles on almost any subject by using periodical indexes. Some are general and wide ranging, while others are more specialized and sophisticated. These tools—usually housed in the library's reference room—indicate which journals, magazines, and periodicals contain articles about given subjects during given periods of time. To take advantage of

Checklist: Bibliographies

Doing research on . . . ?	Check this bibliography . . .
American history	*Bibliographies in American History*
Anthropology	*Anthropological Bibliographies: A Selected Guide*
Art	*Guide to the Literature of Art History*
Astronomy	*A Guide to the Literature of Astronomy*
Classics	*Greek and Roman Authors: A Checklist of Criticism*
Communications	*Communication: A Guide to Information Sources*
Engineering	*Science and Engineering Literature*
Literature	*MLA International Bibliography*
Mathematics	*Using the Mathematical Literature*
Music	*Music Reference and Research Materials*
Philosophy	*A Bibliography of Philosophical Bibliographies*
Physics	*Use of Physics Literature*
Psychology	*Harvard List of Books in Psychology*
Social work	*Social Work Education: A Bibliography*

these powerful tools, read the front matter of printed indexes and the on-line help screens or the handouts of computerized indexes.

All major academic fields have indexes and guides to their essential periodical literature, and most such indexes are now computerized. Because new indexes may be added to a library's collection at any time, check with your reference librarian about the latest and best resources for your subject area. Be aware, though, that you are more likely to find specialized indexes at university libraries or in large municipal collections. Smaller libraries may not have comprehensive resources or access to electronic sources.

Electronic indexes, such as on-line catalogs, allow you to do many kinds of valuable searches, again by author, title, subject, and keywords. Sometimes the indexes will provide you not only with the titles of useful sources, but also with the articles themselves. Here, for example, is an item

```
18 Pedal power. (popularity of bicycling; includes related
article on mountain biking). / Chisholm, Patricia /
Maclean's : July 26 1993,
v106, n30, p48 / 4 page(s)

*** TEXT AVAILABLE ONLINE - TYPE 18 AND PRESS ENTER ***
```

Checklist: Periodical Indexes

A project in this area?	Check this index . . .
Art	Art Index
Astronomy	INSPEC
Biography	Biography Index
Business	Business Periodicals Index
Computer science	Computer Literature Index
Contemporary events	NewsBank
Education	Education Index; ERIC
Film	Film Literature Index; Art Index
Humanities	Social Science & Humanities Index; Humanities Index; InfoTrac
Literature	Essay and General Literature Index; MLA Bibliography
Mathematics	MATHFILE
Philosophy	The Philosopher's Index
Psychology	Psychological Abstracts; Psyc Lit
Public affairs	PAIS (Public Affairs Information Service)
Science	General Science Index
Social science	Social Science & Humanities Index; Social Sciences Index
Technology	Applied Science and Technology Index

listed in an on-line periodical index that can be called up on screen should the user want to see it.

To search an electronic index by keyword, identify several key terms that define and position your topic. Focus your topic and your search by combining keywords with *and;* look for related material by allowing the search to include synonyms with *or;* disallow subjects or specific types of sources by prefacing words with *not* or *no.*

AND   video games AND gender
OR   juvenile OR youth
NOT   united states AND civil war
       NOT book review

The more specific your keyword search, the more focused and useful the list of sources you will generate. Don't be frustrated by searches that turn up either more information than you can use or no items at all. Keep plugging away, refining your keyword combinations until you find exactly what you need.

• 22b-4 Consult dictionaries of biography. When you need information about people, good sources are the *Biography Index: A Cumulative Index to Biographic Material in Books and Magazines, Bio-Base, Current Biography,* and *The McGraw-Hill Encyclopedia of World Biography.* There are also various *Who's Who* volumes, which cover living British, American, and world notables, and volumes on African Americans, women, politics, and fashion. Deceased notables are listed in *Who Was Who.* The two most famous dictionaries of biography are the *Dictionary of National Biography* (British) and the *Dictionary of American Biography.* Specialized dictionaries cover scientists, authors, architects, lawyers, scholars, and so on.

• 22b-5 Locate statistics. Libraries have many volumes of statistics. Be sure to locate figures that are up-to-date and authoritative.

Checklist: Biographical Information

Your subject is in . . . ?	Check this biographical info . . .
Art	*Index to Artistic Biography*
Education	*Biographical Dictionary of American Educators*
Music	*The New Grove Dictionary of Music and Musicians*
Politics	*Politics in America*
Psychology	*Biographical Dictionary of Psychology*
Religion	*Dictionary of American Religious Biography*
Science	*Dictionary of Scientific Biography*

Your subject is . . . ?	Check this biographical info . . .
African	*Dictionary of African Biography*
African American	*Dictionary of American Negro Biography*
Asian	*Encyclopedia of Asian History*
Canadian	*Dictionary of Canadian Biography*
Female	*Index to Women; Notable American Women*
Hispanic	*Chicano Scholars and Writers: A Bibliographic Directory*

Checklist: Statistics

To find . . .	Check these sources . . .
General statistics	*World Almanac*
Statistics about U.S.	*Historical Statistics of the United States; Statistical Abstract of the United States*
World information	*The Statesman's Yearbook; National Intelligence Factbook; UN Demographic Yearbook*
Business facts	*Handbook of Basic Economic Statistics; Dow Jones Irwin Business Almanac*
Public-opinion polls	*Gallup Poll*

• 22b-6 Check news sources. If you know the date of an event, you can usually locate the information you want from newspapers. If your subject isn't an event, you may have to trace it through newspaper indexes such as those for *The New York Times* or *The Wall Street Journal.* Another reference tool for current events (available since 1982 in computer format) is *Newsbank,* an index of more than 400 newspapers from across the country keyed to a microfiche collection. Also helpful are *Facts on File,* which summarizes national and international news weekly, and *Editorial Research Reports,* which gives background information on major problems and controversies. To discover what editors are thinking, examine *Editorials on File,* a sampling of world and national opinion.

• 22b-7 Check book reviews. To locate reviews of books, consult *Book Review Digest* (1905), *Book Review Index* (1965), or *Current Book Review Citations* (1976). *Book Review Digest* does not list as many reviews as the other two collections, but it summarizes those it does include, a helpful feature.

• 22b-8 Consult experts. People are often the best sources of up-to-date and authoritative information. If you can discuss your subject with an expert (without being a nuisance), you'll add authority and immediacy to any research report. For instance, talk to medical professionals if you are writing about high health-care costs. Interview local producers or theater managers if you are exploring community theaters. If you are examining problems in the construction industry, find a builder or banker with twenty minutes to spare. Get the story directly and accurately from people immediately involved.

• 22b-9 Write to professional organizations. Ask for pamphlets, brochures, propaganda, tracts, leaflets, reports, and so on. The *Encyclopedia of Associations,* published by Gale Research, provides addresses. Also remember that the U.S. government publishes information on many subjects of public interest. Check the *Index to U.S. Government Periodicals* or the *Monthly Catalog of United States Government Publications* for listings.

•22b-10 Select reputable sources.

Thanks to electronic searches, it's easy now to locate more books and articles than you can possibly use for a writing project. So study carefully the items you have turned up to find those that will be most useful to you. •

22c Navigating Electronic Sources

Electronic research tools can serve everyone. But it's easy to be intimidated by the complexity of some computer tools and frustrated by the various irritations that plague electronic searches—difficulty logging on, systems going down, or machines that lack adequate memory to download large files. The fact remains, however, that a researcher on a computer can accomplish in a few minutes what may take a print-bound colleague days or weeks.

•22c-1 Decide whether an electronic source will serve you better than a printed one.

Much research information available on the computer (especially periodical indexes) has been adapted from more traditional printed formats. These databases in electronic form can be searched much more quickly and accurately than printed resources.

For example, electronic keyword searches allow you to choose the exact terms for studying your subject; you are not limited just to descriptors assigned by the person who created the research

tool. You can also direct the computer to explore various combinations of keywords until you find the material you want. You may even discover a subject you did not anticipate. (See Section 22b-1.) When you get a disappointing response from a search, ask Why? Look for clues in the items the search produced, and then test new search terms. Try synonyms and check your spellings too.

•22c-2 Evaluate your electronic search.

In an electronic format such as ProQuest, Lexis/Nexis, or Homework Helper, you can retrieve results quickly and then decide whether (or how) new material illuminates your chosen subject: Did you get the information you expected or something quite different? Don't be satisfied with your initial search, even if it seems to have been successful. Because computer searches generate material so quickly, novices often terminate their explorations too soon when another combination of keywords or a different search path might provide still better material.

Be sure to evaluate the materials you do find, especially when searching on-line catalogs and periodical indexes. What keyword searches worked best? Are there other combinations to try? What kinds of sources are you finding?

• 22c-3 Explore various electronic indexes.

Don't search just your library's on-line catalog or a single CD-ROM index. Different sources provide different kinds of electronic information. Consider alternative ways of searching too, such as tracing ideas or controversies by following the names of people involved.

Don't assume that quantity of information outweighs quality. *More* information does not automatically produce *better* arguments or *better* articles.

• 22c-4 Use the Internet and World Wide Web.

A totally different kind of exploration is possible with the on-line resources available on the Internet (the Net) or the World Wide Web (WWW), many of which have no print equivalents. The Internet is an expanding worldwide network of millions of computers and supercomputers. Some information on the Net is fairly traditional, including news stories, press releases, books, articles, research reports, and software. In addition, the Internet also supports electronic conversations on a global bulletin board called Usenet, more restricted conversations called Listservs, and virtual reality environments of all sorts with acronyms such as *MUD, MUSH,* and *MOO,* and, of course, *e-mail.*

The World Wide Web is a hypertextual pathway into the Internet that presents information via "pages" that can contain text, graphics, and sound. Web users can move through different "sites" just by clicking on words or graphics that link to other related resources.

You can gain access to information on the Internet or WWW by learning to manipulate a few basic tools. (Look for classes on computer literacy at libraries and colleges.)

Depending on the Net browser you are using (for example, Mosaic, Netscape, Microsoft Web Explorer), you can search by keyword, individual word, or categories. Web search engines are frequently refined and improved, and new search engines are constantly being developed. Popular web search tools include Yahoo, EINet Galaxy, and AltaVista.

Yahoo (http://www.yahoo.com/), for example, enables you to explore the Web in several ways. Its opening screen presents a series of general categories that should lead you toward your topic: Arts, Business and Economy, Computers and Internet, Education, Entertainment, Government, Health, News, Recreation and Sports, Reference, Regional, Science, Social Science, Society and Culture. Click on any of these topics and subtopics to make them appear. "Education," for example, divides into more than two dozen subtopics, each of which divides further until you find precisely the sites that interest you. At any point in this hierarchy, you can do a keyword search, either of the entire Yahoo database or of a narrower subtopic you have identified. Yahoo searches can even include mentions of your keyword topic in newsgroups.

Another powerful Web search tool is AltaVista (http://www.altavista.digital.com). It can quickly find all occurrences of a word or phrase in tens of millions of Web pages. Needless to say, AltaVista offers various options for organizing and limiting these explorations; as with all search engines, you should study the instructions to learn how best to focus your work. But even a novice can perform quick and powerful searches using AltaVista.

The Web is also searchable in more specialized ways. Individual colleges or universities may have

> **CAUTION** Information on the Internet and World Wide Web often hasn't been refereed, edited, or checked for accuracy (or grammar or spelling, for that matter). Anyone can join the conversation School children publish their essays on some of these electronic sources, and college students sometimes post their term papers—even the ones that got *Ds*.

tools for locating information on local Web sites so that you can quickly find out about faculty, courses, or library holdings. Many periodical indexes, too, are searchable via the Web, though access may be restricted to users from specific sites. For example, libraries may acquire access to indexes such as the *MLA Bibliography*, Lexis/Nexis, or *Readers' Guide Abstracts* for students working on their campuses. In some cases, library catalogs themselves can be examined via Web searches.

It is easy to be overwhelmed by the amount of information available on the steadily growing Web and by the need to sort through frivolous or irrelevant material to find what is truly valuable. You also have to train yourself to keep track of information on the Internet.

Fortunately, the software tools you'll use for browsing the Web also allow you to record Web sites you've visited by specifying them with "bookmarks." Use this feature when you do research because you may have to document Web pages as sources later.

• 22c-5 Join electronic conversations.
You can find information and participate in online discussions by using the Internet's Usenet newsgroups and Listserv discussion groups. Web browsers such as Netscape now give easy access to such forums. Usenet groups are publicly accessible conferences on every manner of subject from "alt.activism.death-penalty" to "talk.religion.buddhism." Almost every political group, social interest, religion, hobby, and fantasy has a Usenet group. Listservs are more restrictive mail programs that serve subscribers sharing a common interest. Lists may even be moderated to screen irrelevant or inappropriate material. Information about how to use both Usenets and Listservs is typically available in FAQ (frequently asked questions) files attached to these groups.

The better Usenet and Listserv groups can provide up-to-the-minute insight into important topics and issues, with participants drawn from across the world. Here you can sometimes watch or participate in conversations between scholars and researchers before they publish their findings in traditional journals. But many of the groups are far from scholarly or even polite.

You must exercise judgment in deciding when and how to use information from Usenet groups or Listservs. Remember that on-line information usually hasn't been selected for publication, checked for accuracy, or edited for style. Anyone with a computer and a server can join a conversation on the Web.

22d Keeping Track of Information

After you've located all your sources, you need to keep tabs on *what* you've read and *where* to use that information later. Although it may seem easier initially to rely on luck and memory than on system and strategy to manage research material, that's a false impression.

• 22d-1 Check your computer printouts.
When you need to document an article formally, most on-line catalogs provide the necessary data for a Works Cited or References list: title of work, author, edition, publication information, date, and page numbers for periodicals. But check your printouts while you're still at a terminal. You don't want to discover at the last minute that your entries omit necessary details.

• 22d-2 Prepare accurate bibliography cards. It still makes sense (especially for longer projects) to prepare 3-by-5-inch bibliography cards for the sources you examine, one source per index card. Each bibliography card should contain all the information you may need to find a source again later or record it in the Works Cited or References list if the paper must be formally documented. Be sure to include a library call number or location (current periodicals may not have call

Checklist: Necessary Bibliographic Information

✔ Call number/location in the library
✔ Full name of author(s)
✔ Title of work—underlined for a book and between quotation marks for an article
✔ For a book: place of publication, publisher, and publication date
✔ For a scholarly article: name of the journal (underlined); volume number; date (usually just the year); and page numbers of the article
✔ For an article in a popular magazine or newspaper: name of the periodical or paper (underlined); date, month, and year of publication; and relevant page numbers or location

```
TL
410
V36
1989
PCL Stacks

van der Plas, Rob. The Mountain Bike
    Book: Choosing, Riding and
    Maintaining the Off-Road
    Bicycle. 3rd ed. San Francisco:
    Bicycle, 1993.
```

numbers). A typical bibliography card might look like the one shown here.

For the exact Works Cited or References form of any bibliography card entry, check the MLA, CMS or APA Form Directories (pp. 195, 234, and 244).

• 22d-3 Photocopy or download passages you know you will quote from directly and extensively. Most researchers now routinely photocopy their major sources, work with sources such as ProQuest that furnish complete articles, or download materials from the Internet. In any of these situations, be sure that your copies are complete and legible (especially the page numbers for photocopied materials). Record any and all bibliographical information directly onto any printed sheets so you don't forget where a photocopied or downloaded article came from. Highlight passages you expect to quote or refer to later, and keep your copies in a folder. When you cut and paste directly from a computer source to your own draft, be sure to mark the material as a direct quote.

• 22d-4 Keep a set of note cards. When doing any type of research, you'll probably want to record some information on index cards. While 3 by 5-inch cards are fine for bibliography entries, larger ones work better for notes. Be sure each note card for a source includes the author's last name and (if necessary) a short title so that you can later connect the notes with the right bibliography card or printout. For example, a note card using information from Rob van der Plas's *The Mountain Bike Book* might be headed simply: van der Plas, *Mountain*.

Don't crowd too much information onto a single card; it's better to record only one major point, quotation, or statistic on each one. That way you'll later find it easy to arrange cards into an outline of your article, with the facts exactly where you want them. For the same reason, write on only one side of a note card. Information on the flip side of a card is easily ignored.

• 22d-5 Record page numbers for all material. Whether you use note cards or photocopies for your sources, you may later have to cite page numbers for ideas and quotations you borrow. So, to save backtracking to the library, be sure you have page numbers either on the cards or on the photocopies. With some electronic sources, you may not have traditional pages. In such cases, you will need to record electronic addresses. A World Wide Web site may have an electronic address like the following: http://www.stsci.edu/pubinfo/PR/96/09.htm/.

Chapter 23

A Sharpening Your Focus
B Using Sources and Quotations
C Handling Sources Responsibly
D Preparing the Paper

The Research Project

*T*hanks to new research tools available online or in most libraries, finding information for a research project is easier than ever before. But good information must still be shaped into a coherent report or persuasive argument, one that presents significant ideas supported by reliable information. To achieve that goal, you need a powerful thesis backed up by sources handled skillfully and appropriately. Shaping the thesis means doing much more than just breaking a big subject into smaller parts. There's an art, too, in selecting material for citation, introducing quotations, and presenting tables and figures attractively. Your goal is to produce a project that readers will find convincing, authoritative, and readable.

23a Sharpening Your Focus

Writers using sources need to focus their work, often with the help of a statement—called a thesis—that clearly explains the purpose of their project. Thesis statements that merely break large subjects into smaller parts may indicate lack of focus. An effective thesis makes a coherent and engaging claim that can be supported by research materials.

• 23a-1 Make sure you have a point to make. Here are questions to use in testing potential theses or subjects.

• Is it a substantial issue?
• Is it a debatable issue?
• Will the issue affect or interest readers?
• Will readers understand how the issue affects them?
• Can I interest readers in the subject?

• 23a-2 Focus on problems and conflicts. Look for unconventional subjects or new perspectives on familiar ideas.

Tentative Thesis: People who don't pump iron or run marathons might live longer than those who do.

You may find, however, that a claim you hope to make isn't supported by hard evidence. If that's the case, share your discovery with readers.

Final Thesis: If you think exercise won't extend the quality of your life, you're flat wrong.

• 23a-3 Ask basic questions about your subject, particularly how and why. Examine issues that matter. Here are two dull thesis statements revised to interest and challenge more people.

Dull: Child abuse is a serious problem with three major aspects: cause, detection, and prevention.

Challenging: The charge of child abuse sometimes serves the interest of political groups eager to have the government define the relationship between parents and children.

Dull: The most common types of white-collar criminals are people who work in business, in the military, and in the government.

Challenging: White-collar crime is rarely punished severely because—down deep—many people admire the perpetrators.

Be prepared to refine and reshape a thesis until it says something surprising or important. Make a commitment.

• 23a-4 Use a thesis to help organize an entire piece.
Begin by making a scratch outline for the whole essay—nothing elaborate, just a thesis followed by the four or five supporting ideas suggested by your research and directly connected to your claim. Then ponder the order of those ideas. Would a reader understand why your first point comes before your second one, the second before the third, and so on? If not, recast the outline. Consider, too, how much background information you must give so readers understand your claim. The less readers know about your subject, the more background you'll have to provide.

23b Using Sources and Quotations

Documentation is the trail you leave in a paper or article to help readers identify and (if necessary) track down the sources of information you have used. You identify sources so readers can judge the quality, credibility, and originality of your work.

Documentation can be either informal or formal. It is informal when writers simply identify sources and quotations as they appear in the body of their work. You'll find informal documentation in newspapers and most popular magazines and books. Documentation is formal when writers support every major claim by endnotes or footnotes backed up by bibliography entries. Usually codified by a professional society such as the Modern Language Association (MLA) or the American Psychological Association (APA), formal documentation is required in most scholarly journals, formal research reports, and academic papers.

Specific guidelines for formal documentation appear in Chapters 24–27. This section examines more general principles for acknowledging and using sources.

• 23b-1 Provide a source for every direct quotation.
A direct quotation is any material repeated word for word from a source. Direct quotations in a college paper require some form of parenthetical documentation—that is, a citation of author and page number (MLA) or author, date, and page number (APA).

MLA: It is possible to define literature as simply "that text which the community insists on having repeated from time to time intact" **(Joos 51–52).**

accept	allege	insist	say
add	argue	mention	state
admit	believe	propose	think
affirm	confirm	reveal	verify

APA: Hashimoto (1986) questions the value of attention-getting essay openings that "presuppose passive, uninterested (probably uninteresting) readers" **(p. 126).**

You are similarly expected to identify the source for any diagrams, statistics, charts, or pictures in your paper. You need not document famous sayings, proverbs, or biblical citations.

For nonacademic writing, you should identify the author, speaker, or the work from which you borrow any passage and indicate why the words you are quoting are significant. Many phrases of introduction or attribution are available. Here are just a few.

One expert **reported** that ". . ."

The members of the board **declared** that ". . ."

Marva Collins **asserts** that ". . ."

"The figures," **according to** the GAO, "are . . ."

• **23b-2 Document all ideas, opinions, facts, and information that you acquire from sources and that cannot be considered common knowledge.** Common knowledge includes the facts, dates, events, information, and concepts that an educated person can be assumed to know. You may need to check an encyclopedia to recall that the Battle of Waterloo was fought on June 18, 1815, but the fact itself belongs to common knowledge and for this reason you don't have to document it. You may also make assumptions about common knowledge within a field. What experts know collectively constitutes the common knowledge within a field; what they claim individually—their opinions, studies, theories, research projects, and hypotheses—is the material you *must* document in a paper.

• **23b-3 Document all ideas, opinions, facts, and information that readers might question or wish to explore further.** If your subject is controversial, you may want to document even facts or ideas considered common knowledge. When in doubt, document. Also, date important events, and identify people, places, or things most readers might not recognize.

Henry Highland Garnet **(1815–1882),** American abolitionist and radical, once wrote . . .

• **23b-4 Select direct quotations strategically.** Every quotation in an article should contribute something your own words cannot. Use quotations for various reasons.

• To focus on a particularly well-stated key idea in a source
• To show what others think about a subject—either

experts, people involved with the issue, or the general public

- To give credence to important facts or concepts
- To add color, power, or character to your argument or report
- To show a range of opinion
- To clarify a difficult or contested point
- To demonstrate the complexity of an issue
- To emphasize a point

Never use quotations to avoid putting ideas in your own words or to pad your work.

• 23b-5 Introduce all direct and indirect borrowings in some way. To be sure readers pay attention to important ideas, give borrowed passages a context or frame. Such frames can precede, follow, or interrupt the borrowed words or ideas. You may choose to integrate the borrowed material with one of your own sentences. Alternatively, you may frame the borrowed material with sentences in the surrounding paragraph but present it as its own separate sentence. Here are ways borrowed material can be introduced.

- Frame precedes borrowed material

> **In 1896, Woodrow Wilson, who would become Princeton's President in 1902, declared,** "It is not learning but the spirit of service that will give a college a place in the public annals of the nation."
>
> —Ernest L. Boyer,
> "Creating the New American College"

- Frame follows borrowed material

> "One reason you may have more colds if you hold back tears is that, when you're under stress, your body puts out steroids which affect your immune system and reduce your resistance to disease," **Dr. Broomfield comments.**
>
> —Barbara Lang Stern, "Tears Can Be Crucial to Your Physical and Emotional Health"

- Frame interrupts borrowed material

> "Whatever happens," **he wrote grimly to Engels,** "I hope the bourgeoisie as long as they exist will have cause to remember my carbuncles."
>
> —Paul Johnson, *Intellectuals*

- Borrowed material integrated with passage

> **The study concludes that a faulty work ethic is not responsible for the decline in our productivity; quite the contrary, the study identifies** "a widespread commitment among U.S. workers to improve productivity" and suggests that "there are large reservoirs of potential upon which management can draw to improve performance and increase productivity."
>
> —Daniel Yankelovitch,
> "The Work Ethic Is Underemployed"

- Surrounding sentences frame borrowed material

> **In the meantime, [Luis] Jimenez was experimenting with three-dimensional form.** "Perhaps because of the experience of working in the sign shop, I realized early on that I

wanted to do it all—paint, draw, work with wood, metal, clay." **His images were those of 1960s pop culture, chosen for their familiarity and shock value.**

—Chiori Santiago, "Luis Jimenez's Outdoor Sculptures Slow Traffic Down"

• 23b-6 Tailor direct quotations to fit the grammar of your sentences.
You may have to tinker with the frame around the quotation or modify the quotation itself by careful selections.

> ˄the chemical
> ~~The chemical~~ capsaicin that makes chili
> ˄is so strong ≡ ⌄
> hot: ~~"it is so hot~~ it is used to make antidog
>   ˄
> and antimugger sprays" (Bork 184).

• 23b-7 Use ellipses, three spaced periods (...), to show where you have cut material from direct quotations.
Only part of a long quotation may suit your essay; ellipses enable you to present only the appropriate portion. Ellipses in the following passage indicate that the source being cited is not used in its entirety.

> Although working with any part of an original scripture text is difficult, Barry Hoberman, author of "Translating the Bible," describes the text of the Old Testament as "the stuff of scholarly nightmares." He explains that while "the entire New Testament was written within fifty to a hundred years, the books of the Old Testament were composed and edited over a period

of about a thousand....The oldest portions of the Old Testament...are probably a group of poems that appear...to date from roughly the twelfth and eleventh centuries B.C."

Whenever you use ellipses, be sure the shortened quotation doesn't change the meaning of the original passage. For more details about ellipses for this purpose, see Section 19c-1.

• 23b-8 Use square brackets [ ] to add necessary information to a quotation.
Including bracketed additions (see Section 19g-1) enables you to identify to whom or what a pronoun refers, to provide a helpful date, or to explain a puzzling word.

> Some critics clearly prefer Wagner's *Lohengrin* to *Tannhäuser*. Says Grout, "the well-written choruses [*of Tannhäuser*] are combined with solo singing and orchestral background into long, unified musical scenes" (629).

Don't overdo using brackets for this purpose. Readers will resent the explanation of obvious details.

• 23b-9 Use [sic] to indicate an obvious error copied faithfully from a quotation.
Quotations must be copied accurately, word for word from your source—errors and all. To show that you have copied a passage faithfully, place the expression *sic* (the Latin word for "thus" or "so") in square brackets one space after any mistake.

Mr. Vincent's letter went on: "I would have preferred a younger bride, but I decided to marry the old window **[sic]** anyway."

If *sic* can be placed outside of the quotation itself, it appears between parentheses, not brackets.

Molly's paper was entitled "Understanding *King Leer*" **(sic).**

• 23b-10 Place short prose quotations between quotation marks.
MLA style defines *short* as no more than four typed lines; APA defines *short* as fewer than forty words.

In *On Liberty* (1859), John Stuart Mill declares that **"**if all mankind minus one were of one opinion, mankind would be no more justified in silencing that one person than he, if he had the power, would be justified in silencing mankind.**"**

Longer quotations should be indented. MLA form recommends an indention of one inch or ten spaces; APA form requires five spaces. Quotation marks are *not* used around the indented material. In typed papers, an indented passage—like the rest of the article—is double-spaced.

23c Handling Sources Responsibly

Some writers do not realize that taking notes carelessly or documenting sources inadequately can destroy the credibility of their research. Indeed, representing the words or ideas you found in a source as your own constitutes plagiarism, a serious charge against any writer. Quite simply, you should respect and acknowledge the work you borrow from other writers or colleagues.

• 23c-1 Understand the special nature of collaborative projects.
In many situations today, writers work in groups on collaborative projects for their companies, schools, or institutions. In such collaborative projects, it can be tough to remember who wrote what. Problems are less likely to arise, however, when everyone understands the ground rules of a project. Nevertheless, legitimate questions do arise.

- Must we write the whole project together?
- Can we break the project into separately authored sections?
- Can one person research a section, another write it, a third edit and proofread it?
- What do we do when someone is not pulling his or her weight?
- Who gets credit for what?

The time to answer such questions is at the beginning of a collaborative effort. First, determine what the project guidelines are. Then sit down with the members of your team and hammer out the rules.

If your research project involves creating a World Wide Web site, be sure you understand your instructor's ground rules for borrowing text and downloading images from the Internet. Most sites will necessarily contain some borrowed information, as well as helpful links to other locations on the Web.

Example 1   106

You will probably use forest service or fire roads and trails intended for hikers most of the time. Don't stray off these trails, since this may cause damage, both to the environment and to our reputation. As long as you stay on the trails and do it with a modicum of consideration for others, you have nothing to fear and should not risk being banned from them by public agencies.

In many areas a distinction is made between single-track trails and wider ones. Single tracks are often considered off-limits to mountain bikers, although in most cases they are perfectly suitable and there are not enough hikers and other trail users to worry about potential conflicts. In fact, single trails naturally limit the biker's speed to an acceptable level.

Example 2

As Rob van der Plas reminds bikers, they need only use common sense in riding public trails: "As long as you stay on the trails and do it with a modicum of consideration for others, you have nothing to fear and should not risk being banned from them by public agencies" (106).

Works Cited

van der Plas, Rob. The Mountain Bike Book: Choosing, Riding and Maintaining the Off-Road Bicycle. 3rd ed. San Francisco: Bicycle, 1993.

182 — the research project

•23c-2 For conventional projects, acknowledge all direct or indirect uses of anyone else's work. Suppose, for example, that in preparing an article on mountain biking, you come across this sample passage from *The Mountain Bike Book* by Rob van der Plas.

If you decide to quote all or part of example 1 in your article, you must use quotation marks (or indention, as appropriate) to indicate that you are borrowing the writer's exact words. If writing an academic paper, you must also identify the author, work, publisher, date, and location of the passage through formal documentation—MLA, APA, CMS, or any other system used by professionals. If you are using MLA documentation, for example (see Chapter 24), the parenthetical note and corresponding Works Cited entry would look like example 2.

You must use *both* quotation marks and the parenthetical note when you quote directly. Quotation marks alone do not tell your

readers what your source is. A note alone acknowledges that you are using a source, but it does not explain that the words in a given portion of your paper are not entirely your own. (By the way, the author in this case spells his last name exactly as shown, so *van der* is not capitalized in the Works Cited entry, though most last names, of course, are capitalized.)

On some occasions, you might need to use the material

in example 1 indirectly, borrowing the information in van der Plas's paragraphs but not his words or arrangement of ideas. Here are two acceptable summaries of the passage on mountain biking that report its facts appropriately and originally. Notice that both versions, following MLA documentation style, include a parenthetical note acknowledging van der Plas's *The Mountain Bike Book* as the source of information.

Example 3

Rob van der Plas asserts that mountain bikers need not fear limitations on their rights-of-way if they ride trails responsibly (106).

Example 4

Though using so-called single-track trails might put mountain bikers in conflict with the hikers, such tracks are often empty and under-utilized (van der Plas 106).

Example 5—Plagiarized

. . . In trail cycling today, access and right-of-way are the two intangibles. The sport of mountain biking is getting too popular too quickly, and defensive authorities have banned cyclists from many potentially suitable areas out of fear.

Mountain bikers typically use forest service or fire roads and trails intended for hikers most of the time. Bikers shouldn't stray off these trails, since this may cause damage, both to the environment and to the reputation of cyclists. As long as mountain bikers remain on the trails and do it with a modicum of consideration for others, they need not fear and should not risk being banned from them by public agencies.

In many areas, mountain bikers make a distinction between single-track trails and wider ones. Single tracks are often considered off-limits to mountain bikers, although in most cases they are quite suitable and there are not enough hikers and other trail users to worry about possible conflicts. In fact, single trails naturally lower the mountain biker's speed to a more acceptable level.

Without documentation, both examples 3 and 4 would be considered plagiarized even though only van der Plas's ideas—and not his actual words—are borrowed. You must acknowledge ideas and information you take from your sources in some way (even in nonacademic papers) unless you are dealing with common knowledge (see Section 23b-2).

• 23c-3 Summarize and paraphrase carefully. A proper summary or paraphrase of a source should be entirely in your own words (as in examples 3 and 4 presented earlier). Some writers mistakenly believe that they can avoid a charge of plagiarism by rearranging or changing a few words in a selection; **they are wrong.** The passage in Example 5 would be considered plagiarism—with or without formal documentation—because it takes the source's basic words and ideas and varies them only slightly.

23d Preparing the Paper

Since academic research papers represent a first level of serious professional work, they must usually meet more exacting standards in composition and form than less formal writing. These requirements vary from discipline to discipline, but the principles examined in this section apply to most such papers.

• 23d-1 Check the organization. Organizing a long paper is rarely an easy job. Here are some suggestions for evaluating the organization of a long paper.

- **Underline the topic idea, or thesis, in your draft.** It should be clearly stated somewhere in the first few paragraphs.
- **Underline just the first sentence in each subsequent paragraph.** If the first sentence is very short or closely tied to the second, underline the first two sentences.
- **Read the underlined sentences straight through as if they formed an essay in themselves.** Ask whether each sentence advances or explains the main point, or thesis statement. If the sentences—taken together—read coherently, chances are good the paper is well organized.
- **If the underlined sentences don't make sense, re-examine those paragraphs not clearly related to the topic idea.** If the ideas really are not related, delete the whole paragraph. If the ideas are related, consider how to revise the paragraph to make the connection clearer. A new lead sentence for the paragraph will often solve the problem of incoherence. Pay attention to transitions.

• 23d-2 Test your conclusion against your introduction. Sometimes the conclusions of essays contradict their openings because of changes that occurred as the paper developed. When you've completed a draft, set it aside for a time and then reread the entire piece. Does it hang together? If not, revise it.

• 23d-3 Use headings to organize a lengthy piece. A short essay (five to six pages) ordinarily needs only a first level heading —that is, a title. With longer papers, you may need subheads to explain the content of major sections. Such headings should be brief and parallel in phrasing. For most academic papers, you probably won't use more than two levels of headings: a title and one set of parallel subheads.

Titles of MLA papers (described in more detail in Chapter 24) are ordinarily centered on the first page of an essay, while headings and subheadings appear flush with the left-hand margin. If you descend to a third-level head, you'll have to distinguish between second- and third-level heads by numbering or lettering them or by varying them with capitalization or underlining. MLA does not specify how these headings should be handled in undergraduate papers.

APA style (described in more detail in Chapter 27) defines five levels of headings for professional articles, which is more than you'll likely ever use in an academic paper. Here's how to handle three or fewer levels of headings.

- Titles (first-level heads) use both uppercase and lowercase letters and are centered
- Second-level heads use uppercase and lowercase letters like titles but also are underlined. They are placed flush with the left-hand margin.
- Third-level heads use only an initial capital letter. They are underlined and indented as paragraph headings. Third-level heads conclude with a period.

These APA guidelines produce headings such as the following.

Mountain Biking and the Environment	**1st level**
The Mountain Bike	**2nd level**
History of Mountain Biking	**2nd level**
Mountain Bikes and the Environment	**2nd level**
Trail damage.	**3rd level**
Conflicts with hikers.	**3rd level**
Mountain Bikes and Responsible Riding	**2nd level**

• 23d-4 Pay attention to the design of the document. At a minimum, be sure the paper is typed cleanly without distracting strikeovers, whiteouts, and wandering margins. Use good-quality paper, type only on one side, and double-space the body of your essay and the notes.

If you use a word processor, take advantage of its features. Keep fonts simple, and use boldface consistently to highlight important headings.

The features of an MLA and APA paper are explained in Sections 24d and 27d, respectively. These formats, which define where page numbers go, the size of margins, and the use of headings, can be applied even to papers that don't follow a specific professional style.

• 23d-5 Insert tables and figures as needed. Computer technology now makes it easy to download illustrations and complex graphics into papers. You should do so whenever graphics might help readers understand your ideas better than words alone. For example, bar graphs and pie charts make numbers easier to interpret and trends more evident.

Learn to use the graphics tools available in your word-processing or data management programs. In the latter, you can usually choose how you want your information presented (tables, bar graphs, pie charts); the program itself produces the actual image, which you can modify to suit your needs. If you have access to the World Wide Web, you can download pictures and other visual items for your papers, properly acknowledging the borrowing. However, be careful not to clutter your work with what one design expert calls "chartjunk." Just because you have easy access to graphics doesn't mean you must illustrate every page. Develop an eye for clean and attractive presentations on paper or screen.

MLA form requires that you label tables (columns of data) and figures (pictures or illustrations), number them, and briefly identify what they illustrate. Spell out *table,* and position the heading above the table, flush left. For example: *Figure* is usually abbreviated in the caption, which appears below the illustration, flush left.

For an APA paper, check the detailed coverage of tables and figures in the *Publication Manual of the American Psychological Association,* fourth edition.

• 23d-6 Include all the parts your project requires. Before submitting an academic or professional paper, reread the specifications either of the instructor or the professional society to which you are submitting the paper. Must you, for instance, include an abstract or an outline? Check to see what leeway (if any) you have in arranging the title page, notes, bibliography, or other features. Then put the parts of your research essay in the proper order.

- **Title page** (not recommended in MLA; required in APA)
- **Outline** (optional; begins on its own page; requires separate title page)
- **Abstract** (optional, but common in APA; usually on its own page)
- **Body of the essay** (Arabic pagination begins with body of the essay in MLA; in APA, Arabic pagination begins with title page)

Table 1 First-Year Student Applications by Region

	Fall '95	Fall '94	Difference	Percent Change
Texas	12,022	11,590	432	+ 4
Out of state	2,121	2,058	63	+ 3
Foreign	756	673	83	+ 11

Fig. 7. Mountain bike.

- **Content or bibliographic notes**
- **Works Cited/References** (begins on its own page separate from the body of the essay or any content or bibliographic notes)

187

The sample research essay on pages 211–24 presents a model paper in MLA style, and the essay on pages 251–59 presents a paper in APA style.

For a more complex paper such as a master's thesis or doctoral dissertation, follow the order recommended either by an instructor or a volume such as *The MLA Style Manual* (MLA) or *Publication Manual of the American Psychological Association* (APA).

• 23d-7 Submit your paper sensibly.
Bind it modestly with a paper clip. Nothing more elaborate is needed, unless an instructor or professional society specifies otherwise. Some instructors, for example, may ask you to place the essay (still clipped) in a folder along with all materials you used in developing it.

If you submit an article for publication, be sure to follow all instructions for submission provided by the editors. Note in particular how many clean copies they require of your work, to whom those copies should be sent, and whether they expect you to furnish a self-addressed, stamped envelope for return of your work.

chapter

MLA Documentation

In many professional fields in the humanities, writers are expected to follow the conventions of documentation and format recommended by the Modern Language Association (MLA). The basic procedures for MLA documentation are spelled out in this chapter. If you encounter documentation problems not discussed here, you may want to refer to the *MLA Handbook for Writers of Research Papers,* fourth edition, by Joseph Gibaldi. To handle any system of documentation, you need to know the basic procedure and to check the details. The two basic steps of MLA documentation are outlined in Sections 24a and 24b.

24a MLA In-Text Notes

· [Step 1] In the text of your paper, place a note in parentheses to identify the source of every passage or idea you must document. For example, here is a sentence that includes a direct quote from *Ralph Bunche: An American Life* by Brian Urquhart:

> Ralph Bunche never wavered in his belief that the races in America had to learn to live together: "In all of his experience of racial discrimination Bunche never allowed himself to become bitter or to feel racial hatred" (Urquhart 435).

The basic MLA note consists of the author's last name and a page number, both placed between parentheses. An author's name and the page number(s) are separated by a single typed space. Page numbers are *not* preceded by *p.* or *pp.* or by a comma.

> (Urquhart 435)
> (Bly 253–54)

You can shorten a note by naming the author of the source in the body of the essay; then the note consists only of a page number. This is a common and readable form, one you should use regularly.

> Brian Urquhart, a biographer of Ralph Bunche, asserts that "in all of his experience of racial discrimination Bunche never allowed himself to become bitter or to feel racial hatred" (435).

As a general rule, make all parenthetical notes as brief and inconspicuous as possible. Remember that the point of a note is to identify a source of information, not to distract or impress readers.

The parenthetical note is usually placed right after a passage needing documentation, typically at the end of a sentence and *inside the final punctuation mark.* However, with a quotation long enough (more than four typed lines) to require indention, the parenthetical note falls *outside the final punctuation mark.* Compare the following examples.

Short Quotation

The quote is not indented.

Ralph Bunche never wavered in his
belief that the races in America had
to learn to live together: "In all
of his experience of racial discrim-
ination Bunche never allowed himself
to become bitter or to feel racial
hatred" (Urquhart 435). He continued
to work . . .

The note is placed inside the final punctuation mark.

Long Quotation

The quote is indented ten spaces.

Winner of the Nobel Peace Prize in
1950, Ralph Bunche, who died in
1971, left an enduring legacy:

>   His memory lives on,
>   especially in the long
>   struggle for human dignity
>   and against racial dis-
>   crimination and bigotry,
>   and in the growing effec-
>   tiveness of the United
>   Nations in resolving con-
>   flicts and keeping the
>   peace. (Urquhart 458)

The note is placed outside the final punctuation mark.

Following are some guidelines to use when
preparing in-text notes.

**1. When two or more sources are cited within
a single sentence,** the parenthetical notes appear right after the statements they support.

> While the budget cuts might go
> deeper than originally reported
> (Kinsley 42), there is no reason to
> believe that "throwing more taxpay-
> ers' dollars into a bottomless pit"
> (Doggett 62) will do much to reform
> "one of the least productive job
> training programs ever devised by
> the federal government" (Will 28).

Notice that a parenthetical note is always placed
outside of any quotation marks but before the period that ends the sentence.

**2. When you cite more than one work by a sin-
gle author** in a paper, a parenthetical note in the
paper that gave only the author's last name could
refer to more than one book or article on the
Works Cited page. To avoid confusion, place a
comma after the author's name and identify the
particular work being cited, using a shortened
title. For example, a Works Cited page (see Section
24b) might list the following four works by
Richard D. Altick:

> Works Cited
>
> Altick, Richard D. The Art of
>   Literary Research. New York:
>   Norton, 1963.

---. _The Shows of London_. Cambridge: Belknap-Harvard, 1978.

---. _Victorian People and Ideas_. New York: Norton, 1973.

---. _Victorian Studies in Scarlet_. New York: Norton, 1977.

The first time—and every subsequent time—you refer to anything by Richard Altick, you need to identify the work by a shortened title in the parenthetical note.

(Altick, _Shows_ 345)

(Altick, _Victorian People_ 190-202)

(Altick, _Victorian Studies_ 59)

3. When you need to document a work without an author—an article in a magazine, for example, or a newspaper story—simply list the title, shortened if necessary, and the page number.

("In the Thicket" 18)

("Students Rally" A6)

Works Cited

"In the Thicket of Things." _Texas Monthly_ Apr. 1994: 18.

"Students Rally for Academic Freedom." _The Chronicle of Higher Education_ 28 Sept. 1994: A6.

4. When you need to cite more than a single work in one note, separate the citations with a semicolon.

(Polukord 13-16; Ryan and Weber 126)

5. When a parenthetical note would be awkward, refer to the source in the body of the essay itself.

In "Hamlet's Encounter with the Pirates," Wentersdorf argues . . .

Under "Northwest Passage" in _Collier's Encyclopedia_ . . .

The _Arkansas State Highway Map_ indicates . . .

Software, such as Microsoft's _FoxPro_ . . .

Occasions when parenthetical notes might be awkward include the following.

- When you wish to refer to an entire article, not just to a passage or several pages
- When the author is a group or institution—for example, the editors of _Time_ or the Smithsonian Institution
- When the citation is to a personal interview or an unpublished speech or letter
- When the item doesn't have page numbers—for example, a map, a cartoon, a work of art, a videotape, or a play in performance
- When the item is a reference work arranged alphabetically
- When the item is a government document with a name too long for a convenient in-text note
- When the item is computer software or an electronic source without conventional page numbers

Individual entries in the MLA Form Directory (24c) indicate when to avoid an in-text parenthetical note.

24b MLA Works Cited Page

· [Step 2] On a separate page at the end of your paper, list every source cited in a parenthetical note. This alphabetical list of sources is labeled "Works Cited." The Works Cited entry for Brian Urquhart's biography of Bunche discussed in Section 24a would look like this.

```
Urquhart, Brian. Ralph Bunche: An
     American Life. New York:
     Norton, 1993.
```

A typical **MLA Works Cited entry for a book** includes the following basic information.

- Author, last name first, followed by a period and one space.
- Title of work, underlined, followed by a period and one space.
- Place of publication, followed by a colon.
- Publisher, followed by a comma and one space.
- Date of publication, followed by a period.

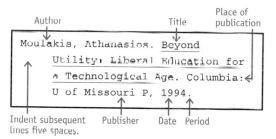

Author   Title   Place of publication

```
Moulakis, Athanasios. Beyond
     Utility: Liberal Education for
     a Technological Age. Columbia:
     U of Missouri P, 1994.
```

Indent subsequent lines five spaces.   Publisher   Date Period

A typical **MLA Works Cited entry for an article in a scholarly journal** (where the pagination is continuous throughout a year) includes the following basic information.

- Author, last name first, followed by a period and one space.
- Title of article, followed by a period (or other final punctuation mark) and enclosed between quotation marks.
- Name of the periodical, underlined, followed by one space.
- Volume number, followed by one space.
- Date of publication in parentheses, followed by a colon.
- Page or location, followed by a period. Page numbers should be inclusive, from the first page of the article to the last, including notes and bibliography.

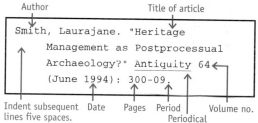

Author   Title of article

```
Smith, Laurajane. "Heritage
     Management as Postprocessual
     Archaeology?" Antiquity 64
     (June 1994): 300-09.
```

Indent subsequent lines five spaces. Date   Pages Period   Volume no.
Periodical

A typical **MLA Works Cited entry for an article in a popular magazine or newspaper** includes the following basic information.

- Author, last name first, followed by a period and one space.
- Title of article, followed by a period and enclosed between quotations marks.
- Name of the periodical or newspaper, underlined, followed by one space.

- Date of publication, followed by a colon and one space. Abbreviate all months except May, June, and July.
- Page and/or location (section number for newspapers), followed by a period. Pages should be inclusive.

Author   Title of article

```
Wolkomir, Richard. "Squalls Ahead,
     East or West, These Storm
     Chasers Never Rest."
     Smithsonian Oct. 1994: 52-61.
```

Indent subsequent Periodical Date   Pages Period
lines five spaces.

A typical **MLA Works Cited entry for an electronic source** includes the following information.

- Author, last name first, followed by a period and one space.
- Title of work, followed by a period and one space. Book titles are underlined; article titles appear between quotation marks.
- Publication information, followed by a period and one space.
- Publication medium, followed by a period and one space.
- Name of the computer service or network, followed by a period and one space.
- The date you accessed the information, followed by a period and one space.
- The electronic address, preceded by the word *Available* and followed by a period. The period is not part of the electronic address. Electronic addresses are optional, but many instructors expect them.

Author   Title   Publication information

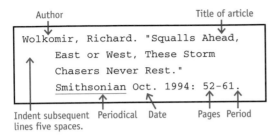

```
Lawrence, D. H. Sons and Lovers. New
     York: Viking, 1913. Online. U of
     Virginia Electronic Text Center.
     Internet. 22 Apr. 1995. Available
     WWW: http://etext.lib.virginia.
     edu/english.html.
```

Computer   Electronic   Date of Publication
service   address (optional)   access medium

There are so many variations to these general entries, however, that you will want to check the MLA Form Directory that follows in Section 24c for the correct format of any unusual entry.

The Works Cited page itself follows the body of the essay (and a footnote page, if there is one). It lists bibliographical information on all the materials you used in composing an essay. You do not, however, include sources you examined but did not cite in the body of the paper itself. For a sample Works Cited list, see pages 223–24.

When an author has more than one work on the list, those works are listed alphabetically under the author's name using this form.

```
Altick, Richard D. The Shows of
     London. Cambridge: Belknap-
     Harvard, 1978.
---. Victorian People and Ideas. New
     York: Norton, 1973.
---. Victorian Studies in Scarlet.
     New York: Norton, 1977.
```

Works published since 1900 include a publisher's name. Publishers' names should be shortened whenever possible. Drop words such as *Company, Inc., LTD, Bro., Books,* and so on. Abbreviate *University* to *U* and *University Press* to *UP*. When possible, shorten a publisher's name to one word. Here are some suggested abbreviations.

Barnes and Noble Books	Barnes
Doubleday and Co., Inc.	Doubleday
Harvard University Press	Harvard UP
University of Chicago Press	U of Chicago P

24c MLA Form Directory

In this section are MLA Works Cited forms for nearly sixty kinds of sources. They are listed in the following order.

Books
Articles and magazines
Newspapers
Reference works and electronic sources
Miscellaneous

You will find a detailed index of these entries on pages ii and iii at the front of this book.

1. Book, One Author—MLA

Works Cited
Weinberg, Steven. Dreams of a Final
    Theory. New York: Pantheon, 1992.

Parenthetical note: (Weinberg 38)

2. Book, Two or Three Authors or Editors—MLA
The names of second and third authors are given in normal order, first names first.

Works Cited
Collier, Peter, and David Horowitz.
    Destructive Generation: Second
    Thoughts about the '60s. New
    York: Summit, 1989.

Parenthetical note: (Collier and Horowitz 24)

3. Book, Four or More Authors or Editors—MLA
You have two options. You can name all the authors in both the Works Cited entry and any parenthetical notes.

Works Cited
Curtin, Philip, Steve Feierman,
    Leonard Thompson, and Jan
    Vansina, eds. African History.
    Boston: Little, 1978.

Parenthetical note: (Curtin, Feierman, Thompson, and Vansina 77)

Alternatively, you can name just the first author on the title page and use the Latin abbreviation *et al.,* which means "and others."

Works Cited
Curtin, Philip, et al., eds. African
    History. Boston: Little, 1978.

Parenthetical note: (Curtin et al. 77)

4. Book Revised by a Second Author—MLA
Sometimes you may need to cite a book by its original author, even when it has been revised. In such a case, place the editor's name after the title of the book.

> Works Cited
> Guerber, Hélène Adeline. The Myths
> of Greece and Rome. Ed. Dorothy
> Margaret Stuart. 3rd ed.
> London: Harrap, 1965.

Parenthetical note: (Guerber 20)

5. Book, Edited—Focus on the Editor—MLA If you cite an edited work by the editor's name, identify the original author after the title of the work.

> Works Cited
> Noyes, George R., ed. The Poetical
> Works of John Dryden. By John
> Dryden. Boston: Houghton, 1950.

Parenthetical note: (Noyes v-vi)

6. Book, Edited—Focus on the Editor, More Than One Editor—MLA Treat multiple editors just as you do multiple authors, but place the abbreviation for editors (*eds.*) after their names.

> Works Cited
> Detweiler, Robert, John N.
> Sutherland, and Michael S.
> Werthman, eds. Environmental

Decay in Its Historical
Context. Glenview: Scott, 1973.

Parenthetical note: (Detweiler et al. 3)

7. Book, Edited—Focus on the Original Author—MLA Notice that because the sample Works Cited entry shown here is an edition of Shakespeare, the parenthetical note furnishes the act, scene, and line numbers for a particular play—not the author and page numbers one might expect with another kind of book.

> Works Cited
> Shakespeare, William. The Complete
> Works of Shakespeare. Ed. David
> Bevington. 4th ed. New York:
> HarperCollins, 1992.

Parenthetical note: (Ham. 4.5.179-85)

8. Book Written by a Group—MLA In the Works Cited entry, treat the group as the author. But to avoid a confusing parenthetical note, identify the group author in the body of your paper and place only relevant page numbers in parentheses. For example, you might use a sentence such as this: "Reader's Digest's *Fix-It-Yourself Manual* explains the importance of a UL label (123)."

> Works Cited
> Reader's Digest. Fix-It-Yourself
> Manual. Pleasantville, NY:
> Reader's Digest, 1977.

9. Book with No Author—MLA List it by its title, alphabetized by the first major word (excluding *The, A,* or *An*).

Works Cited
Illustrated Atlas of the World.
     Chicago: Rand, 1985.

Parenthetical note: (Illustrated Atlas 88)

10. Book, Focus on a Foreword, Introduction, Preface, or Afterword—MLA The note below, for instance, refers to information in Tanner's introduction, not to the text of Jane Austen's novel.

Works Cited
Tanner, Tony. Introduction.
     Mansfield Park. By Jane Austen.
     Harmondsworth, Eng.: Penguin,
     1966. 7-36.

Parenthetical note: (Tanner 9 10)

11. Work of More Than One Volume—MLA When you use only one volume of a multivolume set, identify both the volume you have used and the total number of volumes in the set.

Works Cited
Spindler, Karlheinz. Abstract
     Algebra with Applications.
     Vol. 1. New York: Dekker, 1994.
     2 vols.

Parenthetical note: (Spindler 17-18)

If you use more than one volume of a set, list only the total number of volumes in that set. Then, in your parenthetical notes, identify the specific volumes as you used them.

Works Cited
Spindler, Karlheinz. Abstract
     Algebra with Applications. 2
     vols. New York: Dekker, 1994.

Parenthetical notes: (Spindler 1: 17-18);
(Spindler 2: 369)

12. Book, Translation—Focus on the Original Author—MLA

Works Cited
Freire, Paulo. Learning to Question:
     A Pedagogy of Liberation.
     Trans. Tony Coates. New York:
     Continuum, 1989.

Parenthetical note: (Freire 137-38)

13. Book, Translation—Focus on the Translator—MLA

Works Cited
Swanton, Michael, trans. Beowulf.
     New York: Barnes, 1978.

Parenthetical note: (Swanton 17-18)

14. Book in a Foreign Language—MLA Copy the title of the foreign work exactly as it appears on the title page, paying special attention both to accent marks and capitalization.

Works Cited

Bablet, Denis, and Jean Jacquot. <u>Les Voies de la création théâtrale</u>. Paris: Editions du Centre National de la Recherche Scientifique, 1977.

Parenthetical note: (Bablet and Jacquot 59)

15. Book, Republished—MLA Give original publication dates for works of fiction that have been through many editions and reprints.

Works Cited

Herbert, Frank. <u>Dune</u>. 1965. New York: Berkeley, 1977.

Parenthetical note: (Herbert 146)

16. Book, Part of a Series—MLA Give the series name just before the publishing information. Do not underline or italicize a series name.

Works Cited

Kirk, Grayson, and Nils H. Wessell, eds. <u>The Soviet Threat: Myths and Realities</u>. Proceedings of the Academy of Political Science 33. New York: Academy of Political Science, 1978.

Parenthetical note: (Kirk and Wessell 62)

17. Book, a Reader or Anthology—MLA When you quote from the frontmatter of the collection, the page numbers for a parenthetical note may sometimes be Roman numerals. (To cite a selection within an anthology, see model 29.)

Works Cited

Lunsford, Andrea, and John Ruszkiewicz, eds. <u>The Presence of Others</u>. New York: St. Martin's, 1994.

Parenthetical note: (Lunsford and Ruszkiewicz xiii-xv)

18. Book, a Second, Third, or Later Edition—MLA

Works Cited

Rombauer, Marjorie Dick. <u>Legal Problem Solving: Analysis, Research, and Writing</u>. 5th ed. St. Paul: West, 1991.

Parenthetical note: (Rombauer 480-81)

19. Chapter in a Book—MLA

Works Cited

Owens, Delia, and Mark Owens. "Home to the Dunes." <u>The Eye of the Elephant: An Epic Adventure in the African Wilderness</u>. Boston: Houghton, 1992: 11-27.

Parenthetical note: (Owens and Owens 24-27)

20. Book Published Before 1900—MLA Omit the name of the publisher in citations to works published prior to 1900.

Works Cited

Bowdler, Thomas, ed. <u>The Family</u>
    <u>Shakespeare</u>. 10 vols. London,
    1818.

Parenthetical note: (Bowdler 2: 47)

21. Book Issued by a Division of a Publisher—A Special Imprint—MLA Attach the special imprint (Vintage in this case) to the publisher's name with a hyphen.

Works Cited

Hofstader, Douglas. <u>Gödel, Escher,</u>
    <u>Bach: An Eternal Golden</u> Braid.
    New York: Vintage-Random, 1980.

Parenthetical note: (Hofstader 192-93)

22. Dissertation or Thesis—Published (Including Publication by UMI)—MLA If the dissertation you are citing is published by University Microfilms International (UMI), be sure to provide the order number as the last item in the Works Cited entry.

Works Cited

Rifkin, Myra Lee. <u>Burial, Funeral</u>
    and <u>Mourning Customs in</u>
    <u>England, 1558-1662</u>. Diss. Bryn
    Mawr, 1977. Ann Arbor: UMI,
    1977. DDJ78-01385.

Parenthetical note: (Rifkin 234)

23. Dissertation or Thesis—Unpublished—MLA Note that the titles of unpublished dissertations appear between quotation marks. *Diss.* indicates that the source is a dissertation.

Works Cited

Altman, Jack, Jr. "The Politics
    of Health Planning and
    Regulation." Diss.
    Massachusetts Institute of
    Technology, 1983.

Parenthetical note: (Altman 150)

24. Book Review—Titled or Untitled—MLA Not all book reviews have titles, so the Works Cited form for a book review can vary slightly.

Works Cited

Keen, Maurice. "The Knight of
    Knights." Rev. of <u>William</u>
    <u>Marshall: The Flower of</u>
    <u>Chivalry</u>, by Georges Duby. <u>The</u>
    <u>New York Review of Books</u> 16
    Jan. 1986: 39-40.

Parenthetical note: (Keen 39)

Works Cited

Baym, Nina. Rev. of <u>Uncle Tom's Cabin</u>
    and <u>American Culture</u>, by Thomas
    F. Gossett. <u>The Journal of</u>
    <u>American History</u> 72 (1985):
    691-92.

Parenthetical note: (Baym 691-92)

25. Article in a Scholarly Journal—MLA Scholarly journals are usually identified by volume number or season (rather than day, week, or month of publication). Such journals are usually paginated year by year, with a year's work treated as a volume.

```
          Works Cited
Wentersdorf, Karl P. "Hamlet's
     Encounter with the Pirates."
     Shakespeare Quarterly 34
     (1983): 434-40.
```

Parenthetical note: (Wentersdorf 434)

If a scholarly journal *is* paginated issue by issue, place a period and an issue number after the volume number.

26. Article in a Popular Magazine—MLA Magazines are paginated issue by issue and identified by the monthly or weekly date of publication (instead of by volume number). If an article does not appear on consecutive pages in the magazine, give the first page on which it appears followed by a plus sign—for example, 64+.

```
          Works Cited
Sabbag, Robert. "Fear & Reloading
     in Gun Valley." Men's Journal
     Oct. 1994: 64+.
```

Parenthetical note: (Sabbag 64)

27. Article in a Weekly or Biweekly Magazine—MLA Give the date of publication as listed on the issue.

```
          Works Cited
Gray, Paul. "Hurrah for Dead White
     Males." Time 10 Oct. 1994: 62-63.
```

Parenthetical note: (Gray 62)

28. Article in a Monthly Magazine—MLA

```
          Works Cited
Hudson, Elizabeth. "Hanging Out
     with the Bats." Texas Highways
     Aug. 1994: 14-19.
```

Parenthetical note: (Hudson 15)

29. An Article or Selection from a Reader or Anthology—MLA List the item on the Works Cited page by the author of the piece you are actually citing, not the editor(s) of the collection. Then provide the title of the particular selection, the title of the overall collection, the editor(s) of the collection, and publication information. Conclude with the page numbers of the selection.

```
          Works Cited
Paglia, Camille. "Madonna--Finally,
     a Real Feminist." The Presence
     of Others. Ed. Andrea Lunsford
     and John Ruszkiewicz. New York:
     St. Martin's, 1994. 486-89.
```

Parenthetical note: (Paglia 486)

When you will cite two or more selections from a reader or an anthology, list that collection fully on the Works Cited page.

Lunsford, Andrea, and John
    Ruszkiewicz, eds. The Presence
    of Others. New York: St.
    Martin's, 1994.

Then, elsewhere in the Works Cited list, identify the authors and titles of all articles you cite from that reader or anthology, followed by the name of the editors and page numbers of those selections.

Dyson, Freeman. "Engineer's Dreams."
    Lunsford and Ruszkiewicz 222-
    31.
Paglia, Camille. "Madonna--Finally,
    a Real Feminist." Lunsford and
    Ruszkiewicz 486-89.

When necessary, provide the original publication information first and then give the facts about the collection.

Works Cited
Hartman, Geoffrey. "Milton's
    Counterplot." ELH 25 (1958):
    1-12. Rpt. in Milton: A
    Collection of Critical Essays.
    Ed. Louis L. Martz. Twentieth
    Century Views. Englewood
    Cliffs, NJ: Spectrum-Prentice,
    1966: 100-08.

Parenthetical note: (Hartman 101)

30. Article in a Newspaper—MLA For page numbers, use the form in the newspaper you are citing; many papers are paginated according to

sections. A plus sign following the page number (for example, 7+) indicates that an article continues beyond the designated page, but not necessarily on consecutive pages.

Works Cited
Peterson, Karen S. "Turns Out We Are
    'Sexually Conventional'." USA
    Today 7 Oct. 1994, 1A+.

Parenthetical note: (Peterson 2A)

31. Editorial in a Newspaper—Author Not Named—MLA

Works Cited
"Negro College Fund: Mission Is Still
    Important on 50th Anniversary."
    Editorial. Dallas Morning News
    8 Oct. 1994, sec. A: 28.

Parenthetical note: ("Negro College" 28)

32. Letter to the Editor—MLA

Works Cited
Cantu, Tony. Letter. San Antonio
    Light 14 Jan. 1986, southwest
    ed., sec. C: 4.

Parenthetical note: (Cantu 4)

33. Cartoon—MLA To avoid a confusing parenthetical note, describe any cartoon in the text of your essay. For example, you might use a reference such as this: "In 'Squib' by Miles Mathis . . . ."

```
            Works Cited
Mathis, Miles. "Squib." Cartoon.
      Daily Texan 15 Jan. 1986: 19.
```

34. Reference Work or Encyclopedia (Familiar)—MLA With familiar reference works, especially those revised regularly, identify the edition you are using by its date. You may omit the names of editors and most publishing information. No page number is given in the parenthetical note when a work is arranged alphabetically.

```
            Works Cited
Benedict, Roger William. "Northwest
      Passage." Encyclopaedia
      Britannica: Macropaedia. 1974
      ed.
```

Parenthetical note: `(Benedict)`

35. Reference Work (Less Familiar)—MLA
With less familiar reference tools, a full entry is required. (See model 34 for a comparison with familiar reference works.)

```
            Works Cited
Kovesi, Julius. "Hungarian
      Philosophy." The Encyclopedia
      of Philosophy. Ed. Paul
      Edwards. 8 vols. New York:
      Macmillan, 1967.
```

Parenthetical note: `(Kovesi)`

36. Bulletin or Pamphlet—MLA Treat pamphlets as if they were books.

```
            Works Cited
Computer Services for Students. The
      University of Texas at Austin.
      Austin: Computation Center,
      1994.
```

Parenthetical note: `(Computer Services 8-9)`

37. Government Document—MLA Give the name of the government (national, state, or local) and the agency issuing the report, the title of the document, and publishing information. If it is a congressional document other than the *Congressional Record,* identify the Congress and, when important, the session (for example, 99th Cong., 1st sess.) after the title of the document. Avoid a lengthy parenthetical note by naming the document in the body of your essay and placing only the relevant page numbers between parentheses, as in this sentence: "This information is from the *1985–86 Official Congressional Directory* (182–84)."

```
            Works Cited
United States. Cong. Joint Committee
      on Printing. 1985-86 Official
      Congressional Directory. 99th
      Cong., 1st sess. Washington:
      GPO, 1985.
```

To cite the *Congressional Record,* give only the date and page number:

> Cong. Rec. 8 Feb. 1974: 3942-43.

38. Computer Software—MLA Give the author if known, the version number if any (for example, *Microsoft Word.* Vers. 3.0), the manufacturer, the date, and (optionally) the system needed to run it. Name the software in your text rather than use an in-text note. For example, you could begin a sentence with something like this: "With software, such as Microsoft's *FoxPro.* . . ."

> Works Cited
>
> FoxPro. Vers. 2.5. Computer soft-
>   ware. Microsoft, 1993.
>   Macintosh, System 7, 68020
>   processor, 4 MB memory.

39. On-Line Database, Journal, or Conference—MLA On-line sources come to researchers via an electronic hookup—a modem, for example, or a direct link to the Internet. Some sources exist only online. For them, provide author, title of the on-line journal, date, number of pages (or *n. pag.* to indicate no pagination), title of the database (underlined), publication medium (*Online*), computer service or network, date you accessed the information, and address (optional). When page numbers or some other form of reference isn't available for an electronic text, avoid in-text parenthetical citations by naming the authors or identifying the site in your paper itself, with a sentence such as: "Nachman and Jenkins suggest that . . . ."

> Works Cited
>
> Nachman, Tony, and Kevin Jenkins.
>   "What's Wrong with Education
>   in America?" Trincoll Journal
>   1 Dec. 1994: n. pag. Online.
>   Internet. 22 Apr. 1995. Avail-
>   able WWW: http://www.trincoll.
>   edu/tj/trincolljournal.html.

If an electronic source you cite also has a printed version, begin the citation with information about that printed source, including the author's name, title, and date of publication. Provide page numbers if they are available through the on-line source, though they may not be. Then give all the information required of an electronic source: title of the database (underlined), publication medium (*Online*), computer service or network, date you accessed the information, and address (optional). If you have no page numbers, avoid a parenthetical note by citing the article in your paper itself, using a sentence such as: "Kim describes . . . ."

As with any citation, an electronic item should direct readers clearly to the original source. Be aware, however, that citation guidelines in this area are evolving.

Works Cited

Kim, Albert. "Frisco Tech."
     Entertainment Weekly 14 Apr.
     1995. _Pathfinder_. Online.
     Internet. 10 May 1995.
     Available WWW: http://www.
     pathfinder.com.

When citing material from on-line electronic conferences such as Listservs, user groups, or Usenet news groups, identify the author of the document or posting, the title of the document or posting, and the date on which the item was originally posted. Also, give the medium (_On-line posting_), the name of the conference or group, the network name, and the date of your access.

Because there is no page number to cite, avoid an in-text parenthetical citation by naming the author in the text of your paper, with a sentence such as: "Remner argues in favor of clipless pedals . . . ."

Works Cited

Remner, P. J. "Re: Toe Clips v.
     Clipless Pedals." 21 Apr. 1995.
     On-line posting. Newsgroup
     rec.bicycles.off-road. Usenet.
     24 Apr. 1995.

40. CD-ROM/Diskette Database or Publication—MLA To cite a CD-ROM or similar electronic database, provide basic information about the source itself—author, title, and publication information. Identify the publication medium (whether _CD-ROM, diskette,_ or _magnetic tape_) and the name of the vendor if available. (The vendor is the company publishing or distributing the database.) Conclude with the date of electronic publication.

Works Cited

Bevington, David. "Castles in the
     Air: The Morality Plays." _The
     Theater of Medieval Europe: New
     Research in Early Drama_. Ed.
     Simon Eckchard. Cambridge:
     Cambridge UP, 1993. _MLA
     Bibliography_. CD-ROM.
     SilverPlatter. Feb. 1995.

Parenthetical note: (Bevington 98)

For a CD-ROM database that is often updated (ProQuest, for example), you must provide publication dates for the item you are examining and for the data disk itself.

Works Cited

Alva, Sylvia Alatore. "Differential
     Patterns of Achievement Among
     Asian-American Adolescents."
     Journal of Youth & Adolescence
     22 (1993): 407-23. _ProQuest
     General Periodicals_. CD-ROM.
     UMI-ProQuest. June 1994.

Parenthetical note: (Alva 407-10)

Cite a book, encyclopedia, play, or other item published on CD-ROM or diskette just as if it were a printed source, adding the medium of publication (*diskette, CD-ROM,* for example). When page numbers aren't available, use the author's name in the text of the paper to avoid a parenthetical citation. For example, you might use a sentence that begins, "Bolter argues . . . ."

```
           Works Cited
   Bolter, Jay David. Writing Space: A
       Hypertext. Diskette. Erlbaum,
       1990.
```

41. Information Service or Database—MLA
After providing basic information about the source itself—author, title, and publication information—name the information service (in this case, ERIC) and give any order or reference numbers that would enable a reader to acquire the material. Your goal is to help readers find or order the information efficiently.

```
              Works Cited
   Croll, Valerie J., and Kathleen S.
       Shank. Teacher Training
       Resources: Preparing Teachers
       for Mainstreaming. A Selected
       Bibliography. Charleston, IL:
       Eastern Illinois U, 1983. ERIC
       ED 232 971.
```

Parenthetical note: (Croll and Shank 10-15)

42. Microfilm or Microfiche—MLA
Treat material on microfilm exactly as if you had seen its original hard-copy version.

```
            Works Cited
   "How Long Will the Chemise Last?"
       Consumer Reports. Aug. 1958:
       434-37.
```

Parenthetical note: ("How Long?" 434)

43. Biblical Citation—MLA
Note that titles of sacred works, including all versions of the Bible, are not underlined.

```
            Works Cited
   The Jerusalem Bible. Ed. Alexander
       Jones. Garden City: Doubleday,
       1966.
```

Parenthetical note: (John 18:37-38)

44. Videotape—MLA
Cite a video entry by title in most cases. You may include information about the producer, designer, performers, and so on. Identify the distributor, and provide a date. Avoid in-text parenthetical references to items on videocassette by naming the work in the body of your essay—for example, "In Oliveri's video *Dream Cars of the 50s & 60s* . . . ."

```
             Works Cited
   Dream Cars of the 50s & 60s.
       Videocassette. Compiled by
       Sandy Oliveri. Goodtimes Home
       Video, 1986.
```

45. Movie—MLA In most cases, list a movie by its title unless your emphasis is on the director, producer, or screenwriter. Provide information about actors, producers, cinematographers, set designers, and so on, to suit your readers. Identify the distributor, and give a date of production. Avoid in-text parenthetical references to films by naming the works in the body of your paper. You might use a reference such as: "In Lucas's film *American Graffiti* . . . ."

```
             Works Cited
American Graffiti. Dir. George
      Lucas. Perf. Richard Dreyfuss
      and Ronny Howard. Universal,
      1973.
```

46. Television Program—MLA List the TV program by episode or name of program. Avoid in-text parenthetical references to television shows by naming the programs in the body of your paper.

```
             Works Cited
"Mood Music." Prod. Peter Schindler.
      Dir. Matthew Diamond. With
      Jamie Lee Curtis and Richard
      Lewis. Anything but Love. ABC.
      KVUE, Austin. 25 Oct. 1989.
```

47. Radio Program—MLA Avoid in-text parenthetical references to radio shows by naming the programs in the body of your paper.

```
             Works Cited
Death Valley Days. Created by Ruth
      Cornwall Woodman. NBC Radio.
      WNBC, New York. 30 Sept. 1930.
```

48. Interview, Personal—MLA Refer to the interview in the body of your essay rather than in a parenthetical note, as suggested here: "In an interview, Ann Richards explained . . . ."

```
             Works Cited
Richards, Ann. Personal interview.
      4 Oct. 1993.
```

49. Musical Composition—MLA List the work on the Works Cited page by the name of the composer. If you have sheet music or a score, you can furnish complete publication information.

```
             Works Cited
Joplin, Scott. "The Strenuous Life:
      A Ragtime Two Step." St. Louis:
      Stark Sheet Music, 1902.
```

If you don't have a score or sheet music to refer to, provide a simpler entry. In either case, naming the music in the essay itself is preferable to a parenthetical reference.

```
             Works Cited
Porter, Cole. "Too Darn Hot." 1949.
```

50. Recording—MLA Naming the recording in the essay itself is preferable to a parenthetical reference.

Works Cited

Pavarotti, Luciano. <u>Pavarotti's
Greatest Hits</u>. London, 1980.

51. Speech—No Printed Text—MLA Give the location and date of the address. Naming the work in the essay itself is preferable to a parenthetical reference.

Works Cited

Reagan, Ronald. "The Geneva Summit
Meeting: A Measure of
Progress." U.S. Congress.
Washington, D.C., 21 Nov. 1985.

52. Speech—Printed Text—MLA

Works Cited

O'Rourke, P. J. "Brickbats and
Broomsticks." Capital Hilton.
Washington, D.C., 2 Dec. 1992.
Rpt. <u>The American Spectator</u>
Feb. 1993: 20 21.

Parenthetical note: (O'Rourke 20)

53. Lecture—MLA Naming the lecture in the essay itself is preferable to a parenthetical reference.

Works Cited

Cook, William W. "Writing in
the Spaces Left." Chair's
Address. CCCC Annual Meeting.
Cincinnati, 19 Mar. 1992.

54. Letter—Published—MLA

Works Cited

Eliot, George. "To Thomas Clifford
Allbutt." 1 Nov. 1873. In
<u>Selections from George Eliot's
Letters</u>. Ed. Gordon S. Haight.
New Haven: Yale UP, 1985: 427.

Parenthetical note: (Eliot 427)

55. Letter or E-mail—Unpublished—MLA Identifying the letter or e-mail communication in the essay itself is preferable to a parenthetical reference.

Works Cited

Newton, Albert. Letter to Agnes
Weinstein. 23 May 1917. Albert
Newton Papers. Woodhill
Library, Cleveland.
Pacheco, Miguel. E-mail to the
author. 14 Apr. 1995.

56. Artwork—MLA Naming the artwork in the essay itself is preferable to a parenthetical reference.

Works Cited

Fuseli, Henry. <u>Ariel</u>. The Folger
Shakespeare Library,
Washington, D.C.

57. Drama or Play—MLA Citing a printed text of a play, whether individual or collected, differs from citing an actual performance. For printed texts, provide the usual Works Cited information, taking special care when citing a collection in which various editors handle different plays. In parenthetical notes, give the act, scene, and line numbers when the work is so divided; give page numbers if it is not.

Works Cited

Stoppard, Tom. <u>Rosencrantz &</u>
    <u>Guildenstern Are Dead</u>. New
    York: Grove, 1967.

Parenthetical note: (Stoppard 11-15)

Works Cited

Shakespeare, William. <u>The Tragedy of</u>
    <u>Hamlet, Prince of Denmark</u>. Ed.
    Frank Kermode. <u>The Riverside</u>
    <u>Shakespeare</u>. Ed. G. Blakemore
    Evans. Boston: Houghton, 1974.
    1135-97.

Parenthetical note: (<u>Ham</u>. 5.2.219-24)

For actual performances of plays, give the title of the work, the author, and then any specific information that seems relevant—director, performers, producers, set designer, theater company, and so on. Conclude the entry with a theater, location, and date. Refer to the production directly in the body of your essay to avoid a parenthetical reference.

Works Cited

<u>Timon of Athens</u>. By William
    Shakespeare. Dir. Michael
    Benthall. Perf. Ralph
    Richardson, Paul Curran, and
    Margaret Whiting. Old Vic,
    London. 5 Sept. 1956.

24d MLA Sample Paper

The sample paper that follows is accompanied by checklists designed to help you set up a paper correctly in MLA style. When your work meets the specifications on the checklists, it should be in proper form.

• **Author's Note** I wrote "Mountain Bikes on Public Lands: Happy Trails?" (under the alias Curt Bessemer) to test how well on-line and Internet sources would support an undergraduate research topic. Electronic indexes proved particularly helpful in locating up-to-date magazine articles, while the Internet and WWW furnished three interesting references—and could have supplied many more. Unfortunately, the topic did not lend itself to articles in scholarly journals, so only one such source is included.

I was able to download several of the magazine articles used in the paper directly from the library's on-line catalog, which provides complete texts of recent articles from major publications. But there was a catch. Although it was possible to download and print the texts of these articles in my office, they arrived without page numbers. To cite these materials accurately, I still had to hotfoot it to the library to find the original articles. Like any new technology, on-line research still has its frustrations.

In the short time since the paper was composed, a great many more electronic sources have become available, thanks to the rapid expansion of the World Wide Web. Exploring the conflict between mountain bikers and environmentalists would be much richer now.

For example, typing "mountain biking" in the World Wide Web search engine AltaVista (http://www.altavista.digital.com/) produces between ten and twenty thousand hits, many of them individual biking home pages. Using a variety of keyword combinations, it should be possible to narrow likely sources to those focusing on political and environmental issues that relate to mountain biking.

Using another search engine called Yahoo (http://www.yahoo.com/), it's possible to find 160 mountain bike sites just by working through the search engine's categories from "Sports" to "Cycling" to "Mountain Biking." On Yahoo it doesn't take long to locate a group called TURF, which stands for Trails Users Rights Foundation, dedicated to maintaining bikers' access to paths, roads, and trails (http://members.aol.com/turfinfo/about.html). Following that link could lead to other sources on the topic.

Yet another way into the maze of mountain bike information would be simply to click on almost any of the numerous mountain biking home pages maintained by individuals. Most have links to their favorite sport sites.

JR

Checklist: *First Page—MLA*

MLA does not recommend a separate title page. The first page of your MLA paper should look like the facing page.

✔ Place your name, instructor's name, course title, and the date in the upper left-hand corner, beginning one inch from the top of the paper. Double-space the items.

✔ Identify your instructor by an appropriate title. When uncertain about academic rank, use *Mr.* or *Ms.*

Dr. James Duban	Professor Ferreira-Buckley
Mr. Sean Kinch	Ms. Christy Friend

✔ Center the title a double space below the date. Use the correct form for the title. Capitalize the first word and the last word. Capitalize all other words in the title *except* articles (*a, an, the*), prepositions, the *to* in infinitives, and coordinating conjunctions—unless they are the first or last words.

RIGHT: Mountain Bikes on Public Lands: Happy Trails?

Do not underline a title, capitalize every letter in it, place it between quotation marks, or terminate it with a period.

WRONG: <u>Mountain Bikes on Public Lands: Happy Trails?</u>
WRONG: MOUNTAIN BIKES ON PUBLIC LANDS: HAPPY TRAILS?
WRONG: "Mountain Bikes on Public Lands: Happy Trails?"
WRONG: Mountain Bikes on Public Lands: Happy Trails.

Titles may, however, include words or phrases that appear between quotation marks or are underlined. They may also end with question marks, as the sample title does.

RIGHT: Dylan's "Like a Rolling Stone" Reconsidered
RIGHT: Marriage in Shakespeare's <u>As You Like It</u>
RIGHT: Mountain Bikes on Public Lands: Happy Trails?

✔ Begin the body of the essay two lines (a double space) below the title. Double-space the entire body of the essay, including quotations.

✔ Use one-inch margins at the sides and bottom of this first page.

✔ Number this first page in the upper right-hand corner, one-half inch from the top and one inch from the right margin.

Professor Ruszkiewicz
English 306
6 May 1996

                    Mountain Bikes on Public Lands: Happy Trails?
¶1   Imagine that you have driven hundreds of miles to enjoy the
natural splendor and serenity of one of America's national parks.
Without a care in the world, you and your friends are hiking a
breathtaking trail up a scenic hillside or through a tranquil
canyon. Suddenly from around a bend comes a whooping gang of men and
women mounted on thick-framed, knobby-tired bicycles rushing toward
you on the trail in a flurry of dust and noise, climbing over logs,
leaping across boulders, scattering birds and wildlife in every
direction, pushing you into the underbrush as they whirl past in
gaudy shirts and spandex shorts, gouging ruts in the pathway,
laughing and screaming obscenities. Welcome to the sport of mountain
biking--at least the way angry hikers and environmentalists
sometimes portray it (Coello 148).
¶2   Imagine, now, that you are a rider on a lightweight, sturdy
machine designed to take you safely and comfortably across isolated
roads and trails miles from automobile traffic and madding crowds,
fat tires and maybe even shock absorbers softening the trail over
which you travel at a sober speed, savoring the scenery, expending no
energy but your own to enjoy the wilderness your tax dollars support.

Checklist: Body of the Essay—MLA

The body of an MLA research paper continues uninterrupted until the separate Notes page (if any) and the Works Cited page. Be sure to type or handwrite the essay on good-quality paper.

✔ Use margins of at least one inch all around. Try to keep the right-hand margin reasonably straight. Do not hyphenate words at the ends of lines.

✔ Place page numbers in the upper right-hand corner, one inch from the right edge of the page and half an inch from the top. Precede the page number with your last name.

✔ Indent the first line of each paragraph one half inch, or five spaces if you use a typewriter.

✔ Indent long quotations one inch, or ten spaces if you use a typewriter. In MLA documentation, long quotations are any that exceed four typed lines in the body of your essay. Double-space these indented quotations.

MLA documentation

You come up on a group of hikers or riders and courteously indicate
that you are passing on the left. But to your politeness, the hikers
reply with anger, curses, and maybe even a slap on the back, or a
board with nails (Drake 106). This too is mountain biking from the
point of view of its enthusiasts victimized by well-connected groups
eager to claim public lands for themselves.

¶3   Somewhere between these two portraits lies the truth about the
conflict currently raging between mountain bikers and trail hikers
(with equestrians caught somewhere in between) when it comes to access
to public land. Conservation groups, ecologists, and equestrians
would just as soon lump bikers with the drivers of motorized vehicles
already banned from many off-road areas, especially park trails.
These groups want to keep parks and wilderness areas in as natural a
state as possible and don't regard mechanical vehicles of any kind as
compatible with their goal. On the other hand, mountain bikers
consider these lands--especially the narrow hiking trails--as their
natural environment. While admitting that some bikers have been
irresponsible, they also believe that problems with mountain biking
have been greatly exaggerated. The Mountain Bike Book author Rob van
der Plas, for example, claims to have witnessed public officials and
hikers "manipulating or circumventing facts to find justification for
attempts to deny cyclists access" to trails (107). When all is said
and done, if mountain bikers wish to use trails in public lands and

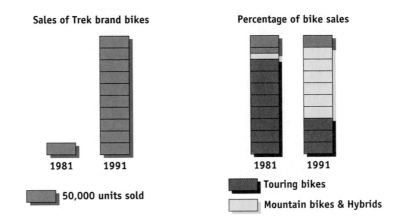

Fig. 1. Sales of mountain bikes in USA.

wilderness, they must behave responsibly in environmentally
sensitive areas and organize politically to defend their rights.
¶4   What some have characterized as a war between bikers and
environmental groups is due in part to the explosive popularity of
mountain bikes (see fig. 1). More comfortable and sturdy than the
drop-handled 10-speed racing bikes dominant just a generation ago,
mountain bikes now represent half the sales in what has become a
3.5-billion-dollar industry in the United States, with 25 million
Americans riding their bikes at least once a week (Castro 43).

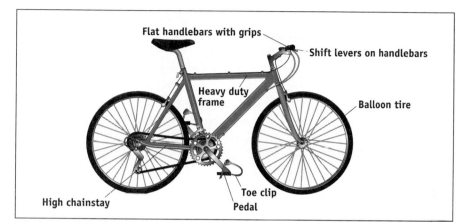

Fig. 2. Mountain bike.

¶5   Distinguishing mountain bikes from touring or racing bikes are
flat handlebars for upright posture, high chainstays for greater
road clearance, wide balloon tires for durability, and stout frames
for overall performance (see fig. 2). These features contribute to
the ruggedness of the vehicles as well as to rider comfort. The
sturdy structures and bulging tires that give trail bikes their
off-road capacity also make them strong and comfortable on-road
vehicles. This versatility probably accounts for the mountain bike's
current domination of the market. For if early mountain bikers

developed the sport for the thrill of ripping downhill as fast as possible, most bikers today take their rides for the same reason that hikers hoist a backpack and head for the hills--to enjoy the great outdoors. Rob van der Plas explains it well:

> What's nice about riding off road is not a function of the roughness, the dirt, or any of the other characteristics of the terrain. Instead what you'll relish most is the remoteness, the solitude, the experience of nature and the lack of traffic. (104)

In effect, the mountain bike has become the all-terrain, off-road, trail bike of choice, the most civilized, economical, and inexpensive machine for getting away from it all.

¶6   But how to get away from it all has now become the problem, especially in National Wilderness and Wilderness Study Areas, where the government controls access to thousands of potential recreational acres and where the 1964 Wilderness Act forbids "motor vehicles and other forms of mechanical transport" (van der Plas 108). In most other natural areas, service and fire roads provide the perfect routes for biking, though an important distinction is made between double-track and single-track trails. Double-track trails--which are usually just unpaved roads--are ordinarily open to bikers because they are wide and comfortably shared with other users. Single-track trails--the much narrower, more challenging, and more diverse paths

through wilderness areas--are both preferred by experienced trail
bikers and more likely to be closed to them. It is on these trails
that bikers compete with pedestrian or equestrian traffic and where
most conflicts occur.

¶7   Mountain bikes have been accused of damaging trails and causing
soil erosion, their thick and knobby tires eating away at the terrain,
especially after rains (Schwartz 75). Officials in natural areas
have shown increasing concern over such damage, going so far as to
consider banning even horses on park trails, let alone bikes
(O'Keefe 82). Yet horses at least remain on trails and move slowly
while aggressive bikers often do not (Coello 148). The editors of
Bicycling magazine acknowledge a problem: "We're tempted to take
shortcuts, arrogantly crushing vegetation. A second of convenience
wipes out years of growth" (36). So traditional environmental
coalitions have been eager to lobby against permitting bikers on
trails, and such groups have had considerable success in California,
where the mountain biking craze originated.

¶8   It isn't just environmental dangers that have made some people
angry at the bikers; it is their alien presence and sometimes
outrageous behavior. As David Schwartz puts it, "To traditional
trail users, the new breed of bicycle was alien and dangerous,
esthetically offensive and physically menacing" (75). Rob Buchanan
describes the situation in Marin County, California, this way:

> At first Marin's old guard, the equestrians and Sierra
> clubbers who'd always had the place to themselves,
> grudgingly put up with the new fad. Then the whole thing
> got out of hand. Weekends the hills were overrun with
> "wheeled locusts," as the San Francisco Chronicle put it,
> "driven by speed-crazed yuppies in Day-Glo Lycra." (80)

It probably doesn't help that many of the mountain bikers are
generally younger men and women, Generation Xers who seem to have
rejected the frail and sophisticated racing bikes of their parents
(Bails). The new bikers come from a generation that environmentalists
from the sixties and earlier don't understand or like. But that
impression isn't always true, as mountain biking activist and writer
Geoff Drake explains, complaining about attacks on him for defending
biking:

> You can't imagine how strange this is. A lifelong hiker
> and environmentalist, I find myself a renegade--an
> expatriate in the woods I love. What about my years of
> membership in Greenpeace and the Nature Conservancy? . . .
> Now, incredibly, I'm receiving the ire of environmentalists
> everywhere. (106)

¶9   Bicyclists have begun to respond to the threat the more
politically experienced environmentalists pose to their sport and
recreation. They point to the politically correct character of the

mountain bike as "an ideal vehicle for global ecological change" (Buchanan 82). They challenge unproven conclusions about trail erosion in the absence of hard evidence that bikes have actually caused it. In fact, they argue that the erosion of trails may be caused largely by runoff from rain and snow (van der Plas 108).

¶10   Just as important, bikers have begun to clean up their image and to organize in order to claim their rights to responsible use of the country's natural resources. Van der Plas, for example, suggests that bikers need to present themselves as "responsible, mature adults who eat lots of apple pie and watch fireworks" (108). An associate editor of Mountain Biking Magazine warns that "land access and liability problems . . . could ensue if the majority of the population thinks mountain biking as a whole is a gonzo activity for those with more muscle fibers than brain cells" (Fragnoli 13). To change that perception, groups such as the National Off-Road Bicycle Association (NORBA) have written codes to encourage members to behave responsibly, while the Women's Mountain Bike and Tea Society (WOMBATS) have, as Sara Corbett reports, moved aggressively to prove bikers can share trails with hikers. Biking groups and magazines have also been leaders in urging everyone to wear helmets while riding to prevent some of the almost 200,000 bike-related head injuries that occur each year (Goldsmith 308).

¶11   Trail riders, appreciating that all politics is local, have begun to take their civic responsibilities seriously. For example, in Austin, Texas, an off-road bicycle group called the Ridge Riders made allies in the local environmental community by helping to build trails in a state park and to clean and maintain trails in other local recreational areas (Skinner 8). Similar strategies are being pursued in Colorado, where the Boulder Off-road Alliance was established to lobby for enhanced trail access by offering various park agencies--including the U.S. Forest Service and Boulder County Parks--assistance with the construction and maintenance of trails. As a founder of the group, Rick Grubin, put it,

> We understood the concept of sweat equity very early on. . . . It's my hope that some day the land use agencies in our area have to compete for our resources. When we have reached this level, the sweat equity we have invested in will give mountain biking in Boulder County the political clout to affect [sic] real change.

¶12   As a result of such political action, biking groups that have demonstrated their willingness to protect the natural environment are beginning to have success in negotiating with environmental groups. In spring 1994, the International Mountain Bicycling Association (IMBA) and the powerful Sierra Club jointly endorsed the principle that "mountain biking is a legitimate form of recreation

MLA documentation

and transportation on trails, including singletrack, when and where it is practiced in an environmentally sound and socially responsible manner" (Stein 86). Several months later, the IMBA persuaded the U.S. Forest Service to acknowledge that bicycles, unlike motorized vehicles, have a legitimate place on trails, their agreement potentially opening up more tracks for mountain riders in the 191 million acres of land controlled by the Forest Service ("IMBA Breaks" 16). The agreements signed at Park City, Utah, and West Dover, Vermont, represent the kinds of compromises that we are likely to see more of in the future between people who wish to use our natural resources and those sworn to protect them. When such groups begin to realize their common interests and when groups such as mountain bikers earn their political clout through community action, we're likely to discover that there's room on the trail for everyone.

Works Cited

Bails, Richard James, Jr. "Survey Results." 20 Aug. 1994. Online
     posting. Newsgroup rec.bicylces.tech. Usenet. 3 Nov. 1994.
Bicycling Magazine, Editors of. Bicycling Magazine's Mountain Biking
     Skills. Emmaus: Rodale, 1990.
Buchanan, Rob. "Birth of the Gearhead Nation." Rolling Stone 9 July-
     23 Aug. 1992: 80+.
Castro, Janice. "Rock and Roll." Time 19 Aug. 1991: 42+.
Coello, Dennis. Touring on Two Wheels: The Bicycle Traveler's
     Handbook. New York: Lyons, 1988.
Corbett, Sara, "Ride with Pride." Outside Magazine. Mar. 1995.
     Online. Internet. 1 May 1995. Available WWW: http://
     web2starwave.com.
Drake, Geoff. "Trouble on the Mountain." Bicycling Aug. 1992: 106.
Fragnoli, Delaine. "Are We Extreme?" Mountain Biking Magazine Sept.
     1994: 13.
Goldsmith, Marsha F. "Campaigns Focus on Helmets as Safety Experts
     Warn Bicycle Riders to Use--and Preserve--Heads." JAMA 15 July
     1992: 308.
Grublin, Rick. "Mountain Biking Advocacy Group: Boulder Off-road
     Alliance (BOA)." 19 Aug. 1994. Online posting. Newsgroup
     rec.bicycle.soc. Usenet. 4 Nov. 1994.

"IMBA Breaks Through--Twice!" <u>Mountain Bike</u> Oct. 1994: 16.

O'Keefe, Eric. "Destabilized." <u>Texas Monthly</u> Sept. 1994: 82.

Schwartz, David M. "Toward Happy Trails: Bikers, Hikers and
    Olympians." <u>Smithsonian</u> June 1994: 74-87.

Skinner, Dawn. <u>Austin Cycling Notes</u> Aug. 1994: 8.

Stein, Theo. "The New MBA: Is It Finally in the Driver's Seat?" <u>MTB</u>
    Oct. 1994: 85-89.

van der Plas, Rob. <u>The Mountain Bike Book: Choosing, Riding and
    Maintaining the Off-Road Bicycle</u>. 3rd ed. San Francisco:
    Bicycle, 1993.

[25]

chapter

ACW Documentation

*I*n doing research, you may need to document some unconventional electronic sources—Web sites, MOOs, MUDs, Listservs, and Gophers. A style sheet developed by Janice R. Walker and endorsed by the Alliance for Computers and Writing (ACW) provides some guidelines. The ACW system should be used only with MLA documentation, since it follows MLA conventions in matters of capitalization, underlining, and most punctuation. Don't, for example, mix APA and ACW citations. The two basic steps of ACW documentation are outlined in Sections 25a-1 and 25a-2.

25a ACW In-Text Notes and Works Cited Page

•25a-1 [Step 1] In the text of your paper, place a note in parentheses to identify the source of every passage or idea you must document. Conventional in-text notes usually consist of authors' last names and page numbers.

```
(Goodfeld 210)
(Brooks and Heilman 24-26)
```

But electronic sources may not have conventional authors or page numbers. When such is the case, you may have to adapt the parenthetical note to fit the source, sometimes naming the site and date, for example, or the author and date.

```
(WorldMOO 5 Dec. 1994)
(Walker 1 May 1995)
```

Quite often, you can avoid an in-text note entirely by describing the source in the text of your paper itself. For example:

```
On the Resources page of the Smith-
sonian Institution Web Site, . . .
```

•25a-2 [Step 2] On a separate page at the end of your paper, list every source cited in a parenthetical note. This alphabetical list of sources is labeled "Works Cited." For the general arrangement of a Works Cited page, see page 223. For individual ACW Works Cited entries, use the following formula.

```
Author's Last Name, First Name.
    "Title of Work." Title of
    Complete Work. [protocol and
    address] [path] (date of
    access, visit, or message).
```

The formula will vary slightly, depending on the type of electronic source you need to document. Adapt these standards as needed to the sources you must document.

Be aware that electronic documentation is evolving. Check before using ACW documentation; your instructor may prefer that you stick with strict MLA formats.

25b ACW Form Directory

In this section are ACW Works Cited forms for the following items: FTP (File Transfer Protocol) items, WWW (World Wide Web), Telnet sites, synchronous communications (MOOs, MUDs, IRC), Gopher sites, Listserv and Newslist citations, and e-mail.

1. FTP (File Transfer Protocol)—ACW For the FTP site, give the full path needed to access the information.

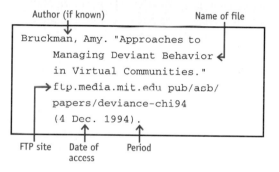

FTP is a system for downloading and uploading files on the Internet. If your access to the Internet is through the World Wide Web, you may have little need to document FTP sites.

2. WWW (World Wide Web)—ACW Many, if not most, of your electronic citations will be to WWW sites, accessed through "browser" software such as Netscape or Microsoft Internet Explorer. Web sites are usually formally titled on their home pages or opening screens: *CNN Interactive; Thomas: Legislative Information on the Internet.* Individual pages within larger sites may not have formal titles, but they will always be identified by a title bar at the top of the screen: "CNN—Feedback"; "Floor Activities This Week."

Be sure to record Web addresses accurately; even the smallest mistake may deny a reader access to the site you are documenting. When writing a paper on the same computer that gives you Web access, you can guarantee the accuracy of Web addresses by copying them directly off the browser and then pasting them into your Works Cited list.

Only a very few Web sites (such as the electronic magazine *Slate*) use actual page numbers. They aren't really necessary when you furnish an electronic address. Date of access to the WWW *is* important, since Web sites change quite frequently.

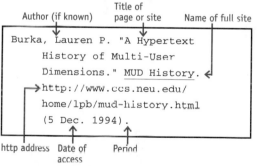

3. Telnet Site—ACW Give the Telnet address, as well as any directions for accessing the source.

227

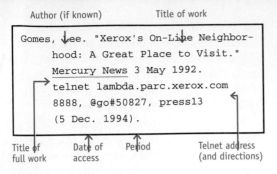

Author (if known) Title of work

```
Gomes, Lee. "Xerox's On-Line Neighbor-
     hood: A Great Place to Visit."
     Mercury News 3 May 1992.
     telnet lambda.parc.xerox.com
     8888, @go#50827, press13
     (5 Dec. 1994).
```

Title of   Date of   Period   Telnet address
full work   access   (and directions)

Author (if known) Publication information Title of work

```
Quittner, Joshua. "Far Out: Welcome
     to Their World Built of MUD."
     Published in Newsday, 7 Nov.
     1993. gopher/University of
     Koeln/About MUDs, MOOs and
     MUSEs in Education/Selected
     Papers/newsday (5 Dec. 1994).
```

Gopher search path   Date of   Period
                                  access

4. Synchronous Communications (MOOs, MUDs, IRC)—ACW

Provide an electronic address if applicable. MOOs and MUDs are electronic environments which allow users to converse in "real time," sometimes in imaginary settings (a writing lab, for example) or assumed roles.

Speaker(s)   Type of communication   Electronic address

```
Pine Guest. Personal interview.
     telnet world.sensemedia.net
     1234 (12 Dec. 1994).
```

Date of   Period
access

5. Gopher Site—ACW

Gopher sites contain directories of information that can be searched and accessed through the Internet. Gopher systems are used far less frequently now that Internet access is dominated by World Wide Web browsers.

6. Listserv and Newslist Citations—ACW

Provide the subject line of the posting and the address of the Listserv or Newslist.

Author   Subject line

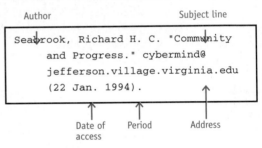

```
Seabrook, Richard H. C. "Community
     and Progress." cybermind@
     jefferson.village.virginia.edu
     (22 Jan. 1994).
```

Date of   Period   Address
access

7. E-Mail—ACW

Provide the subject line of the posting. An address is optional. You may wish to note that the item is personal e-mail.

Author (if known)   Subject   Address

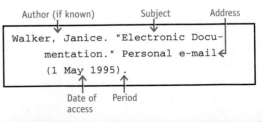

```
Walker, Janice. "Electronic Docu-
     mentation." Personal e-mail
     (1 May 1995).
```

Date of   Period
access

chapter

[26]

CMS Documentation

*W*riters who prefer full footnotes or endnotes rather than in-text notes often use the "humanities style" of documentation recommended in *The Chicago Manual of Style* (fourteenth ed., 1993). Basic procedures for this documentation system, known here as CMS, are spelled out in the following sections. If you encounter documentation problems not discussed below or prefer the author-date style of CMS documentation, refer to the full manual or to *A Manual for Writers of Term Papers, Theses, and Dissertations* (sixth ed., 1996). Because notes in CMS humanities style include full publishing information, separate bibliographies are optional. However, both notes and bibliographies are covered in Sections 26a and 26b.

26a CMS Notes

• 26a-1 In the text of your paper, place a raised number after any sentence or clause you need to document.

These note numbers follow any punctuation marks, except for dashes, and run consecutively throughout a paper. For example, a direct quote from Brian Urquhart's *Ralph Bunche: An American Life* is here followed by a raised note number.

```
Ralph Bunche never wavered in his
belief that the races in America had
to learn to live together: "In all
of his experience of racial discrim-
ination Bunche never allowed himself
to become bitter or to feel racial
hatred."1
```

The number is keyed to the first note (see Section 26a-2). To create such a raised, or superscript, number on a typewriter, roll down the carriage slightly and type the figure, or select "superscript" in your word-processing character menu or ruler.

• 26a-2 Link every note number to a footnote or endnote.

The basic CMS note itself consists of a note number, the author's name (in normal order), the title of the work, full publication information within parentheses, and appropriate page numbers. The first line of the note is indented approximately three spaces.

```
1. Brian Urquhart, Ralph Bunche:
An American Life (New York: Norton,
1993), 435.
```

To document particular types of sources, including books, articles, magazines, and electronic sources, see Section 26c, CMS Form Directory.

CMS style allows you to choose whether to place your notes at the bottom of each page (footnotes) or in a single list titled "Notes" at the end of your paper (endnotes). Endnotes are more common now than footnotes and easier to manage—though some word processors can arrange footnotes at the bottom of pages automatically. Individual footnotes are single-spaced, with double spaces between them. Endnotes are double-spaced throughout the list.

Following are some guidelines to use when preparing notes.

1. When two or more sources are cited within a single sentence, the note numbers appear right after the statements they support.

> While some in the humanities fear that electronic technologies may make the "notion of wisdom" obsolete,[2] others suggest that technology must be the subject of serious study even in elementary and secondary school.[3]

The notes for this sentence would appear as follows.

> 2. Sven Birkerts, The Gutenberg Elegies: The Fate of Reading in an Electronic Age (Boston: Faber and Faber, 1994), 139.
> 3. Neil Postman, "The Word Weavers/the World Makers," in The End of Education: Redefining the Value of School (New York: Alfred A. Knopf, 1995), 172-93.

Notice that note 2 documents a particular quotation, while note 3 refers to a full book chapter.

2. When you cite a work several times in a paper, the first note provides full information about the author(s), title, and publication.

> 1. Helen Wilkinson, "It's Just a Matter of Time," Utne Reader (May/June 1995): 66-67.

In short papers, any subsequent citations require only the last name of the author(s) and page number(s).

> 3. Wilkinson, 66.

In longer papers, the entry may also include a shortened title to make references from page to page clearer.

> 3. Wilkinson, "Matter of Time," 66.

If you cite the same work successively, you may use the Latin abbreviation *Ibid.* (meaning "in the same place"), followed by the page number(s) of the citation.

> 4. Newt Gingrich, "America and the Third Wave Information Age," in To Renew America (New York, HarperCollins, 1995), 51.
> 5. Ibid., 55.

To avoid using *Ibid.* when documenting the same source in succession, simply use a page reference—for example, (55)—within the text itself.

> Gingrich points out that many people take relatively new conveniences for granted today[4] and suggests that changes in the future will be even more dramatic (55).

When successive citations are to exactly the same page, *Ibid.* alone can be used.

```
     4. Newt Gingrich, "America and
the Third Wave Information Age," in
To Renew America (New York,
HarperCollins, 1995), 51.
     5. Ibid.
```

Here's how a set of notes using several different sources and subsequent short references might look.

```
               Notes
     1. Helen Wilkinson, "It's Just a
Matter of Time," Utne Reader
(May/June 1995): 66-67.
     2. Paul Osterman, "Getting
Started," Wilson Quarterly (autumn
1994): 46-55.
     3. Newt Gingrich, "America and
the Third Wave Information Age,"
in To Renew America (New York:
HarperCollins, 1995), 51-61.
     4. Ibid., 54.
     5. Wilkinson, 66.
     6. Ibid.
     7. Ibid., 67.
     8. Osterman, 48-49.
     9. Gingrich, 60.
    10. Ibid., 53.
```

Notice that notes 4 and 10 refer to the Gingrich chapter and notes 6 and 7 refer to Wilkinson's article.

26b CMS Bibliographies

· **At the end of your paper, list alphabetically every source cited or used in the paper.** This list is usually titled "Works Cited" if it includes only works actually mentioned in the essay; it is titled "Bibliography" if it also includes works consulted in preparing the paper but not actually cited. Because CMS notes are quite thorough, a Works Cited or Bibliography page may be optional, depending on the assignment. Check with your instructor or editor.

A typical **CMS Works Cited/Bibliography entry for a book** includes the following basic information.

• Name of author(s), last name first, followed by a period and one space.
• Title of work, underlined or italicized, followed by a period and one space.
• Place of publication, followed by a colon and one space.
• Publisher, followed by a comma and one space.
• Date of publication, followed by a period.

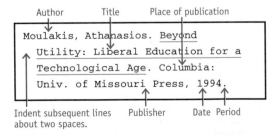

Author   Title   Place of publication

```
Moulakis, Athanasios. Beyond
   Utility: Liberal Education for a
   Technological Age. Columbia:
   Univ. of Missouri Press, 1994.
```

Indent subsequent lines   Publisher   Date   Period
about two spaces.

A typical **CMS Works Cited/Bibliography entry for an article in a scholarly journal** (where the pagination is continuous throughout a year) includes the following basic information.

- Author, last name first, followed by a period and one space.
- Title of article, followed by a period (or other final punctuation mark) and enclosed between quotation marks.
- Name of the periodical, underlined or italicized, followed by one space.
- Volume number, followed by one space.
- Date of publication in parentheses, followed by a colon and one space.
- Page or location, followed by a period. Page numbers should be inclusive, from the first page of the article to the last, including notes and bibliography.

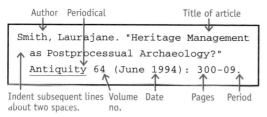

A typical **CMS Works Cited/Bibliography entry for an article in a popular magazine** includes the following basic information.

- Author, last name first, followed by a period and one space.
- Title of article, followed by a period and enclosed between quotation marks.

- Name of the periodical, underlined or italicized, followed by a comma and one space.
- Date of publication, followed by a comma and one space. Do not abbreviate months.
- Page and/or location, followed by a period. Pages should be inclusive.

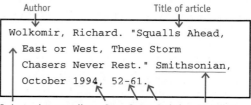

There are so many variations to these general entries, however, that you should check the CMS Form Directory in Section 26c for the correct format of any unusual entry.

When an author has more than one work on the list, those works are listed alphabetically under the author's name using this form.

> Altick, Richard D. The Shows of London. Cambridge: Belknap-Harvard University Press, 1978.
>
> ---. Victorian People and Ideas. New York: Norton, 1973.
>
> ---. Victorian Studies in Scarlet. New York: Norton, 1977.
>
> ---. Writers, Readers, and Occasions Columbus: Ohio State UP, 1989.

26c CMS Form Directory

In this section are CMS notes and bibliography forms for more than a dozen types of sources. The numbered items are the note forms, often showing specific page numbers as would be common with notes; the matching bibliography entries appear immediately after. Sources are listed in the following order.

Books
Articles and magazines
Reference works and electronic sources

You will find a detailed index to these entries on pages ii and iii at the front of this book.

1. Book, One Author—CMS

1. Steven Weinberg, Dreams of a Final Theory (New York: Pantheon Books, 1992), 38.

Weinberg, Steven. Dreams of a Final Theory. New York: Pantheon Books, 1992.

2. Book, Two or Three Authors or Editors—CMS

2. Peter Collier and David Horowitz, Destructive Generation: Second Thoughts about the '60s (New York: Summit, 1989), 24.

Collier, Peter, and David Horowitz. Destructive Generation: Second Thoughts about the '60s. New York: Summit, 1989.

3. Book, Four or More Authors or Editors—CMS

Use *et al.* or *and others* after the first author in the notes, but list all authors in the bibliography when that is convenient.

3. Philip Curtin and others, eds., African History (Boston: Little, Brown, 1978), 77.

Curtin, Philip, Steve Feierman, Leonard Thompson, and Jan Vansina, eds. African History. Boston: Little, Brown, 1978.

4. Book, Edited—Focus on the Editor—CMS

If you cite an edited work by the editor's name, identify the original author after the title of the work.

4. Scott Elledge, ed., Paradise Lost, by John Milton (New York: Norton, 1975).

Elledge, Scott, ed. Paradise Lost, by John Milton. New York: Norton, 1975.

5. Book, Edited—Focus on the Original Author—CMS

5. William Shakespeare, The Complete Works of Shakespeare, 4th ed., ed. David Bevington (New York: HarperCollins, 1992).

Shakespeare, William. The Complete Works of Shakespeare. 4th ed. Edited by David Bevington. New York: HarperCollins, 1992.

6. Book Written by a Group—CMS

6. Council of Biology Editors, Scientific Style and Format: The CBE Manual for Authors, Editors, and Publishers, 6th ed. (Cambridge: Cambridge University Press, 1994).

Council of Biology Editors. Scientific Style and Format: The CBE Manual for Authors, Editors, and Publishers. 6th ed. Cambridge: Cambridge University Press, 1994.

7. Book, No Author—CMS List it by its title, alphabetized by the first major word (excluding *The, A,* or *An*).

7. Webster's Collegiate Thesaurus (Springfield, Mass.: G. & C. Merriam, 1976).

Webster's Collegiate Thesaurus. Springfield, Mass.: G. & C. Merriam, 1976.

8. Work of More Than One Volume—CMS Use the form below when referring to specific pages.

8. Karlheinz Spindler, Abstract Algebra with Applications (New York: Dekker, 1994), 1:17-18.

Spindler, Karlheinz. Abstract Algebra with Applications. Vol. 1. New York: Dekker, 1994.

9. Work in a Series—CMS Do not underline or italicize a series name.

9. Grayson Kirk and Nils H. Wessell, eds., The Soviet Threat: Myths and Realities, Proceedings of the Academy of Political Science, no. 33 (New York: Academy of Political Science, 1978), 62.

Kirk, Grayson, and Nils H. Wessell, eds. The Soviet Threat: Myths and Realities. Proceedings of the Academy of Political Science, no. 33. New York: Academy of Political Science, 1978.

10. Chapter of a Book—CMS

10. Delia Owens and Mark Owens, "Home to the Dunes," in The Eye of the Elephant: An Epic Adventure in the African Wilderness (Boston: Houghton Mifflin, 1992), 11-27.

Owens, Delia, and Mark Owens. "Home to the Dunes." In The Eye of the Elephant: An Epic Adventure in the African Wilderness. Boston: Houghton Mifflin 1992.

11. Article in a Scholarly Journal—CMS Scholarly journals are usually identified by volume number or season (rather than day, week, or month of publication). Such journals are usually

paginated year by year, with a year's work treated as a volume.

> 11. Karl P. Wentersdorf, "Hamlet's Encounter with the Pirates," Shakespeare Quarterly 34 (1983): 434-40.

> Wentersdorf, Karl P. "Hamlet's Encounter with the Pirates." Shakespeare Quarterly 34 (1983): 434-40.

12. Article in a Popular Magazine—CMS

Magazines are paginated issue by issue and identified by monthly or weekly dates of publication (instead of by volume number). When an article does not appear on consecutive pages (as in the following example), omit page numbers in the bibliography entry.

> 12. Robert Sabbag, "Fear & Reloading in Gun Valley," Men's Journal, October 1994, 64.

> Sabbag, Robert. "Fear & Reloading in Gun Valley." Men's Journal, October 1994.

13. Article or Selection from a Reader or Anthology—CMS

> 13. Camille Paglia, "Madonna--Finally, a Real Feminist," in The Presence of Others, ed. Andrea Lunsford and John Ruszkiewicz (New York: St. Martin's Press, 1994), 486-89.

> Paglia, Camille. "Madonna--Finally, a Real Feminist." In The Presence of Others, edited by Andrea Lunsford and John Ruszkiewicz. New York: St. Martin's Press, 1994.

14. Article in a Newspaper—CMS

Identify the edition of the paper cited (for example, final edition, home edition, or Western edition), except when citing editorials or features that appear in all editions. Since an individual story may move in location from edition to edition, page numbers are not ordinarily provided. Section numbers are given for papers that use them. Individual news stories are usually not listed in a bibliography.

> 14. Celestine Bohlen, "A Stunned Venice Surveys the Ruins of a Beloved Hall," New York Times, 31 January 1995, national edition, sec. B.

15. Encyclopedia—CMS

When a reference work (encyclopedia, dictionary, thesaurus) is familiar, omit the names of authors, editors, and most publishing information. No page number is given either when a work is arranged alphabetically; instead the item referenced is named, following the abbreviation *s.v.* (*sub verbo,* meaning "under the word"). Familiar reference works are not listed in the bibliography.

> 15. The Oxford Companion to English Literature, 4th ed., s.v. "Locke, John."

16. Computer Software—CMS

> 16. FoxPro Vers. 2.5, Microsoft, Seattle, Wash.

> FoxPro Vers. 2.5. Microsoft,
>   Seattle, Wash.

17. Computer Sources and Services—CMS
These standards are in flux. CMS follows the recommendations for electronic documentation of
the International Standards Organization (ISO).
However, many issues remain unresolved as new
sources and formats evolve. Entries for electronic
entries generally include three features: a description of the computer source in brackets, such
as [electronic bulletin board] or [database on-
line]; the date the material was accessed, updated, or cited [cited 28 May 1996]; and an electronic address, following the words *Available
from*.

> 17. Tony Nachman and Kevin
> Jenkins, "What's Wrong with
> Education in America?" in Trincoll
> Journal [online journal] 1 December
> 1994 [cited 22 April 1995]; avail-
> able from WWW: http://www.trincoll.
> edu/tj/trincolljournal.html.

> Nachman, Tony, and Kevin Jenkins.
>   "What's Wrong with Education in
>   America?" In Trincoll Journal [on-
>   line journal] 1 December 1994
>   [cited 22 Apr. 1995]. Available
>   from WWW: http://www.trincoll.
>   edu/tj/trincolljournal.html.

18. Biblical Citation—CMS Biblical citations ap-
pear in notes, but not in the bibliography. If important, you may mention the version of the Bible cited.

> 18. John 18.37-38 Jerusalem Bible.

chapter

[27]

APA Documentation

In many college courses (anthropology, astronomy, business, education, home economics, linguistics, political science, psychology, sociology), you will be expected to follow the conventions of documentation recommended by the American Psychological Association (APA). A full explanation of APA procedures is provided by the *Publication Manual of the American Psychological Association,* fourth edition (1994), which is available in most college libraries. The two basic steps of APA are outlined in Sections 27a and 27b.

27a APA In-Text Notes

· [Step 1] In the text of your paper, place a note in parentheses to identify the source of every passage or idea you must document. For example, here is a sentence derived from information in an article by E. Tebeaux titled "Ramus, Visual Rhetoric, and the Emergence of Page Design in Medical Writing of the English Renaissance."

> Technical writing developed in important ways during the English Renaissance (Tebeaux, 1991).

As you can see, the basic form of the APA parenthetical note consists of an author's last name and a date. A comma follows the author's name.

> (Tebeaux, 1991)

Quite often in APA notes, a research article is identified by the author's last name mentioned in the body of the essay, followed immediately by the year of publication in parentheses.

> According to Grunman (1984), children fed a diet . . .

Such a note is perhaps the most common form of APA citation.

A page number may be given for indirect citations and *must* be given for direct quotations. A comma follows the date if page numbers are given. Page numbers are preceded by *p.* or *pp.*

> During the English Renaissance, writers began to employ "various page design strategies to enhance visual access" (Tebeaux, 1991, p. 413).

When appropriate, the documentation may be distributed throughout a passage.

> Tebeaux (1991) observes that, for writers in the late sixteenth century, the philosophical ideas of Peter Ramus "provided a significant impetus to major changes in page design" (p. 413).

APA parenthetical notes should be as brief and inconspicuous as possible.

Following are some guidelines to use when preparing in-text notes.

1. When two or more sources are used in a single sentence, the notes are inserted as needed after the statements they support.

> While Porter (1981) suggests that
> the ecology of the aquifer might be
> hardier than suspected "given the
> size of the drainage area and the
> nature of the subsurface rock"
> (p. 62), there is no reason to
> believe that the county needs
> another shopping mall in a vicinity
> described as "one of the last out-
> posts of undisturbed nature in the
> county" (Martinez, 1982, p. 28).

Notice that a parenthetical note is placed outside of quotation marks but before the period ending the sentence.

2. When you cite more than one work written by an author in a single year, assign a small letter after the date to distinguish between the author's two works.

> (Rosner, 1991a)
>
> (Rosner, 1991b)
>
> The charge is raised by Rosner
> (1991a), quickly answered by
> Anderson (1991), and then raised
> again by Rosner (1991b).

3. When you need to cite more than a single work in a note, separate the citations with a semicolon and list them in alphabetical order.

> (Searle, 1993; Yamibe, 1995)

27b APA References Page

· *[Step 2] On a separate page at the end of your paper, list every source cited in a parenthetical note.* This alphabetical list of sources is labeled "References." A References page entry for an article on Renaissance medical writing by E. Tebeaux would appear as follows if it were in a college paper submitted to an instructor.

> Tebeaux, E. (1991). Ramus, visual
> rhetoric, and the emergence of
> page design in medical writing
> of the English Renaissance.
> Written Communication, 8, 411-
> 445.

For a full sample References page, see page 259.

A typical **APA References entry for a book** includes the following basic information.

- Author(s), last name first, followed by a period and one space. Initials are used instead of first and middle names unless two authors mentioned in the paper have identical last names and initials.
- Date in parentheses, followed by a period and one space.
- Title of work, underlined, followed by a period, also underlined (unless some other information separates

the name of the title from the period), and one space. Only the first word of the title, the first word of a subtitle, and proper nouns and adjectives are capitalized.
- Place of publication, followed by a colon and one space.
- Publisher, followed by a period.

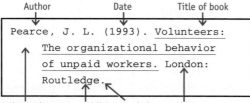

Author — Date — Title of book

Pearce, J. L. (1993). Volunteers: The organizational behavior of unpaid workers. London: Routledge.

Indent subsequent lines five spaces. — Publisher — Period — Place

A typical **APA References entry for an article in a scholarly journal or magazine** includes the following basic information.

- Author(s), last name first, followed by a period and one space.
- Date in parentheses, followed by a period and one space.
- Title of the article, followed by a period and one space. Only the first word of the title, the first word of a subtitle, and proper nouns and adjectives are capitalized. The title does not appear between quotation marks.
- Name of the periodical, underlined, followed by a comma and space, also underlined. All major words are capitalized.
- Volume number, underlined, followed by a comma, also underlined, and one space.
- Page numbers, followed by a period.

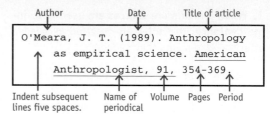

Author — Date — Title of article

O'Meara, J. T. (1989). Anthropology as empirical science. American Anthropologist, 91, 354-369.

Indent subsequent lines five spaces. — Name of periodical — Volume — Pages — Period

A typical **APA References entry for an article in a popular magazine or newspaper** includes the following basic information.

- Author(s), last name first, followed by a period and one space.
- Date in parentheses, followed by a period and one space. Give the year first, followed by the month (do not abbreviate it) and day, if necessary.
- Title of work, followed by a period and one space. Only the first word and proper nouns and adjectives are capitalized. The title does not appear between quotation marks.
- Name of the periodical, underlined, followed by a comma, also underlined. All major words are capitalized.
- Page or location indicated by the abbreviation *p.* or *pp.*, followed by a period.

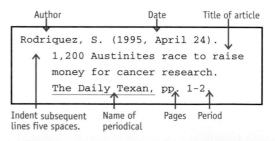

Author — Date — Title of article

Rodriquez, S. (1995, April 24). 1,200 Austinites race to raise money for cancer research. The Daily Texan, pp. 1-2.

Indent subsequent lines five spaces. — Name of periodical — Pages — Period

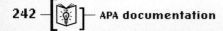

A typical **APA References entry for an on-line document** includes the following basic information.

- Author(s), last name first, followed by a period and one space.
- Date in parentheses, followed by a period and one space. Give the year first, followed by the month (do not abbreviate it) and the day, if necessary.
- Title of work, followed by a period and one space.
- Publication information with the medium (for example, *on-line*, *CD-ROM*, *computer software*) in square brackets, followed by a period and one space.
- Path statement or electronic address, preceded by the word *Available*. Include the protocol/directory/file name or document number for retrieval. No period follows the path statement.

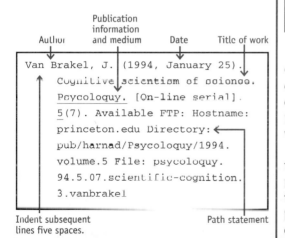

Author · Publication information and medium · Date · Title of work

```
Van Brakel, J. (1994, January 25).
    Cognitive scientism of science.
    Psycoloquy. [On-line serial].
    5(7). Available FTP: Hostname:
    princeton.edu Directory:
    pub/harnad/Psycoloquy/1994.
    volume.5 File: psycoloquy.
    94.5.07.scientific-cognition.
    3.vanbrakel
```

Indent subsequent lines five spaces.

Path statement

There are so many variations to these generic entries, however, that you should check the *Publication Manual of the American Psychological Association* (1994) when you do a major APA-style paper. When writing a student paper, you may want to consult pages 330–40 of the APA manual.

The References page itself appears separately following the body of the essay (and a footnote page, if there is one). It lists bibliographical information on all the materials you used in composing the essay. Here's a checklist for a References page.

27c APA Form Directory

In this section are APA References page and parenthetical note forms for a variety of sources. A detailed index of these items is available on pages ii and iii at the front of this book.

1. Book, One Author—APA

References
Pearson, G. (1949). <u>Emotional disor-</u>
<u>ders of children.</u> Annapolis,
MD: Naval Institute Press.

Parenthetical notes:
Pearson (1949) found . . .
(Pearson, 1949)
(Pearson, 1949, p. 49)

2. Book, Two Authors—APA Notice the ampersand (&) between authors' names in the References list item and parenthetical notes. Note, also, that *and* is used when the authors are identified in the text itself.

References
Lasswell, H. D., & Kaplan, A.
(1950). <u>Power and society:</u>
<u>A framework for political</u>
<u>inquiry.</u> New York: Yale
University Press.

Parenthetical notes:
Lasswell and Kaplan (1950)
found . . .
(Lasswell & Kaplan, 1950)
(Lasswell & Kaplan, 1950, pp.
210-213)

3. Book, Three or More Authors—APA

References
Rosenberg, B., Gerver, I., & Howton,
F. W. (1971). <u>Mass society in</u>
<u>crisis: Social problems and</u>
<u>social pathology</u> (2nd ed.).
New York: Macmillan.

Parenthetical notes:
First note. Rosenberg, Gerver, and
Howton (1971) found . . .
Subsequent notes. Rosenberg et al.
(1971) found . . .
First note. (Rosenberg, Gerver, &
Howton, 1971)
Subsequent notes. (Rosenberg et
al., 1971)

If a work has six or more authors, use the first author's name followed by *et al.* for all parenthetical references, including the first. In the References list, however, identify all the authors.

4. Book, Revised—APA

References
Edelmann, A. T. (1969). <u>Latin</u>
<u>American government and</u>
<u>politics</u> (Rev. ed.).
Homewood, IL: Dorsey.

Parenthetical notes:

> Edelmann (1969) found . . .
>
> (Edelmann, 1969)
>
> (Edelmann, 1969, p. 62)

5. Book, Edited—APA Notice that APA uses an ampersand (&) to join the names of two editors or authors.

> References
>
> Journet, D., & Kling, J. (Eds.).
> (1984). Readings for technical
> writers. Glenview, IL: Scott,
> Foresman.

Parenthetical notes:

> Journet and Kling (1984) ob-
> serve . . .
>
> (Journet & Kling, 1984)

6. Book, No Author—APA

> References
>
> Illustrated atlas of the world.
> (1985). Chicago: Rand, McNally.

Parenthetical notes:

> in Illustrated Atlas (1985) . . .
>
> (Illustrated Atlas, 1985, pp.
> 88-89)

When the author is listed as "Anonymous," cite the work that way in the References list.

> (Anonymous, 1995)

7. Book, a Collection or Anthology—APA

> References
>
> Feinstein. C. H. (Ed.). (1967).
> Socialism, capitalism, and
> economic growth. Cambridge,
> England: Cambridge University
> Press.

Parenthetical notes:

> Feinstein (1967) found . . .
>
> (Feinstein, 1967)

8. Work within a Collection, Anthology, or Reader—APA List the item on the References page by the author of the piece you are actually citing, not the editor(s) of the collection. Then provide the title of the particular selection, its date, the editor(s) of the collection, the title of the collection, pages on which the selection appears, and publication information.

> References
>
> Patel, S. (1967). World economy in
> transition (1850-2060). In C.
> H. Feinstein (Ed.), Socialism,
> capitalism, and economic growth
> (pp. 255-270). Cambridge,
> England: Cambridge University
> Press.

Parenthetical notes:

> Patel (1967) found . . .
>
> (Patel, 1967)

9. Chapter in a Book—APA

References

Clark, K. (1969). Heroic material-
   ism. In Civilisation (pp. 321-
   347). New York: HarperCollins.

Parenthetical notes:

Clark (1969) observes . . .
(Clark, 1969)

10. Article in a Scholarly Journal—APA Schol-
arly journals are usually identified by volume
number or season (rather than day, week, or
month of publication) and are paginated year by
year, with a full year's work gathered together and
treated as a volume. Cite articles from such scholarly journals by providing author, date, title of article, journal, volume, and page numbers.

References

Tebeaux, E. (1991). Ramus, visual
   rhetoric, and the emergence of
   page design in medical writing of
   the English Renaissance. Written
   Communication, 8, 411-445.

Parenthetical notes:

Tebeaux (1991) observes . . .
(Tebeaux, 1991, p. 411)

11. Article in a Monthly Magazine—APA To cite
a magazine published monthly, give the author's
name, date (including month), title of the article,
name of the magazine and volume number if
available (underlined), and page numbers.

References

Bass, R. (1995, May/June). The perfect day. Sierra, 80, 68-78.

Parenthetical notes:

Bass (1995) notes . . .
(Bass, 1995)

12. Article in a Weekly or Biweekly Maga-
zine—APA To cite a weekly or biweekly periodical
or magazine, give the author's name, date (including month and day), title of the article, name
of the magazine and volume number if available
(underlined), and page numbers.

References

Moody, J. (1993, December 20). A
   vision of judgment. Time, 142,
   58-61.

Parenthetical notes:

Moody (1993) observes . . .
(Moody, 1993)
(Moody, 1993, p. 60)

13. Article in a Newsletter—APA To cite a
newsletter, give the author's name, date, title of
the article, name of the magazine and volume
number if available (underlined), and page numbers. If no volume number is given, provide as
full a date as possible.

References

Busiel, C. (1995, Spring).

Shakespeare and hypertext.

Virtu(re)al.news@cwrl, 7.

Parenthetical notes:

Busiel (1995) explains . . .

(Busiel, 1995)

14. Article in a Periodical, No Author Named—APA Note that quotation marks are used around shortened titles in the parenthetical notes.

References

Aladdin releases desktop tools. (1993, October). Macworld, 10, 35.

Parenthetical notes:

In the article "Aladdin releases" (1993) . . .

("Aladdin releases," 1993)

15. Newspaper Article, Author Named—APA If the newspaper article does not appear on consecutive pages, give all the page numbers, separated by a comma. Note that abbreviations for page (*p.*) and pages (*pp.*) are used with newspaper entries.

References

Bragg, R. (1994, October 15).

Weather gurus going high-tech. San Antonio Express-News, pp. 1A, 7A.

Parenthetical notes:

Bragg (1994) reports . . .

(Bragg, 1994, p. 7A)

16. Newspaper Article, No Author Named—APA

References

Scientists find new dinosaur species in Africa. (1994, October 14). The Daily Texan, p. 3.

Parenthetical notes:

In the article "Scientists find" (1994) . . .

("Scientists find," 1994)

17. Computer Software—APA

References

Crawford, C. (1985). Balance of power [Computer software]. Northbrook, IL: Mindscape, SFN.

Parenthetical notes:

Crawford (1985) includes . . .

(Crawford, 1985)

18. On-line Information—APA Standards for documenting on-line materials are still developing. In most cases, you should identify any material you find online and provide a path for others to locate it. To do that, provide the basic information you give for printed sources. After the title of a periodical or work seen online, insert "[Online]." Conclude the on-line source entry by giving a path statement, information that will enable readers to find the material. Path statements vary, but they typically consist of the protocol, directory, and file name of the source.

                    References
Dubrowski, J. (1994, October 18).
        Mixed signals from Washington
        leave automakers puzzled [On-
        line]. Available: C-reuters@
        clarinet.com. Directory:
        biz/industry/automotive

Parenthetical note:

        Dubrowski (1994) reports . . .
        (Dubrowski, 1994)

                    References
Willett, E. F., Jr. (1989, November
        20). How our laws are made [On-
        line]. Available WWW:http://
        thomas.loc.gov/home/lawsmade.
        toc.html

Parenthetical note:

        Willett (1989) explains . . .
        (Willett, 1989)

19. Electronic Correspondence, E-mail, Bulletin Boards—APA APA style treats such information as personal communication. Because personal communications are not available to other researchers, no mention is made of them in the References list. Electronic communications such as e-mail or bulletin boards that are not stored or archived have limited reference use for researchers too. You must use your judgment about listing them as references. Personal communications, however, should be acknowledged in the body of the essay in parenthetical notes.

Parenthetical note:

        According to Rice (personal
        communication, October 14, 1994) . . .

20. Movie/Videotape—APA This is also the basic form for films, audiotapes, slides, charts, and other nonprint sources. The specific type of media is described between square brackets, as shown here for a film. In most cases, APA references will be listed by identifying the writer, though that varies, as the example shows.

                    References
Zeffirelli, F. (Director). (1968).
        Romeo and Juliet [Film].
        Hollywood, CA: Paramount.

Parenthetical notes:

        Zeffirelli (1968) features . . .
        (Zeffirelli, 1968)

21. Musical Recording—APA Music is ordinarily listed by the writer.

References

Dylan, B. (1989). What was it you
       wanted? [Recorded by Willie
       Nelson]. On Across the border-
       line [CD]. New York: Columbia.

Parenthetical note:

> In the song "What Was It
> You Wanted?" (Dylan, 1989, track
> 10) . . .

22. Book Review—APA Notice that brackets surround the description of the article, which in this case has no title. If the review had a title, that title would precede the bracketed description, which would still be included in the entry.

References

Farquhar, J. (1987). [Review of the
       book Medical power and social
       knowledge]. American Journal of
       Psychology, 94, 256.

Parenthetical notes:

> Farquhar (1987) observes . . .
> (Farquhar, 1987)

27d APA Sample Paper

This final version of an essay by Lori S. McWilliams has been revised to enhance its usefulness as a model. As a result of these changes, some material has been dropped and a few paragraphs reshaped. The language has been sharpened, mechanical errors have been edited, and an electronic source added. Yet the bulk of the essay remains just as Lori McWilliams wrote it in her first year in college.

Were Lori writing this paper today on the subject of acupuncture, she would enjoy a wealth of new on-line sources. Typing the keyword "acupuncture" in the World Wide Web search engine AltaVista (http://www.altavista.digital.com/) produces approximately 8,000 hits. Combining the keywords "acupuncture" and "history" provides more focused access to sites such as "The History of Acupuncture in China" and "The History of Acupuncture in the West," both of which might provide useful information for this research project.

Following the topic categories in Yahoo (http://www.yahoo.com/Health/), another WWW search engine, leads from "Health" to "Alternative Medicine" to "Acupuncture," a relatively small site, but one which contains a link to "Acupuncture.com" (http://www.Acupuncture.com/). This site offers links to other topics as varied as "Acupuncture Laws, by State" and "Chinese Nutrition."

Indeed, you may find that on-line research is particularly valuable as a tool for stimulating ideas. The sites you explore may offer new perspectives on your topic even when the information they provide proves thin.

Checklist: *Title Page for a Paper—APA*

APA style requires a separate title page; use the facing page as a model and review the following checklist.

- ✔ Arrange and center the title of your paper, your name, and your school.
- ✔ Use the correct form for the title, capitalizing all important words and all words of four letters or more. Articles, conjunctions, and prepositions are not capitalized unless they are four letters or more. Do not underline the title or use all-capital letters.
- ✔ Number the cover sheet and all subsequent pages in the upper right-hand corner. Place a short title for the paper on the same line as the page number as shown; the short title consists of the first two or three words of the title.

Acupuncture: Energy or Nerves?

Lori S. McWilliams

The University of Texas at Austin

The body of the APA paper runs uninterrupted until the separate References page. Be sure to keyboard or handwrite the essay on good-quality paper. The first page of an APA paper should look like the facing page.

✔ On the first page of the body of the paper, include the short title of the essay and the page number (2) in the upper right-hand corner. Number all subsequent pages the same way.

✔ Repeat the title of your paper, exactly as it appears on the title page, on the first page of the research essay itself.

✔ Be sure the title is centered and properly capitalized.

✔ Begin the body of the essay two lines (a double space) below the title.

✔ Double-space the body of the essay.

✔ Use $1\frac{1}{2}$ inch margins at the sides, top, and bottom of this and all subsequent pages.

✔ Indent the first lines of paragraphs five spaces.

✔ Indent long quotations (more than forty words) five spaces. In student papers, APA permits long quotations to be single-spaced.

✔ Do not hyphenate words at the right-hand margin.

Acupuncture: Energy or Nerves?

¶1   Pain plagues many people. Western science has continually manipulated chemistry to produce analgesics; science has also tried relieving pain through surgery. Despite advances, Holzman (1986) notes that "there is still no satisfactory set of treatments to consistently and permanently alleviate all sources of pain" (p. 2). One technique effective in up to 65% of all cases of chronic pain is the ancient Chinese technique of acupuncture (Langone, 1984). Physicians and scientists in the United States, however, have long been suspicious of acupuncture, in part because of doubts about how it works. Eastern practitioners believe acupuncture relieves pain by adjusting the innate energy within the body; western scientists believe that acupuncture must work through the nervous system. In fact, both of these views--eastern and western--can contribute to an understanding of how acupuncture works.

¶2   According to Langone, acupuncture involves "the insertion of hair-thin needles, singly or in combination, into the strategic points on the body to ease pain and treat a myriad of ailments" (p. 70). Needles used for insertion vary in length, anywhere from 1/2 inch to 3 inches. In the past, acupuncture needles have been made of gold, silver, copper, brass, bone, flint, and stone (Duke, 1972). Rose-Neil (1979) notes that the earliest acupuncture needles were made of stone and called "stone piercers" or "stone borers" (p. 65).

The material used for the needles today is 26-32 gauge stainless steel (Komarov, 1995). Acupuncture needles are inserted into the body at approximately 360 different locations from head to toe and manipulated by manual or electrical rotation to relieve pain.

¶3   Time and tradition have proven the effectiveness of acupuncture. Chang (1976) traces the origins of acupuncture back 6,000 years, but Langone (1984) believes that the Chinese have been using acupuncture medicinally for only about 2,000 years. Rose-Neil (1979) gives this account of acupuncture's development in China:

> It was noted that soldiers wounded by arrows sometimes recovered from illnesses which had afflicted them for many years. The idea evolved that, by penetrating the skin at certain points, diseases were, apparently, cured. It was observed that the size of the wound did not matter, but only its location and depth. The Chinese began to copy the effects of the arrow, puncturing the skin with needles. (p. 65)

Though the East believes in acupuncture, western doctors tended to dismiss acupuncture as almost whimsical. McGarey (1974) attributes this attitude to a western focus on the process of disease rather than on the body itself. Not until Richard Nixon's historic trip to China in 1970, however, did the West take a serious interest in the mechanisms of acupuncture. It was obvious that acupuncture worked, but the two cultures did not agree on how. Belkin (1992) notes only slow acceptance of the procedures in the United States.

APA documentation

¶4   To the Chinese, health is maintained by the flow of energy in the body. Chang (1976) cites this passage from the Nei Ching, an ancient collection of writings on acupuncture, to illustrate the principle:

> The root of the way of life, of birth and change is Qi (energy); the myriad things of heaven and earth all obey this law. Thus Qi in the periphery envelopes heaven and earth, Qi in the interior activates them. The source wherefrom the sun, moon, and stars derive their light, the thunder, rain, wind, and cloud their being, the four seasons and the myriad things their birth, growth, gathering and storing: all this is brought about by Qi. Man's possession of life is completely dependent upon this Qi. (p. 17)

To maintain health, the energy must be transported through the body by means of lines called meridians that conduct energy. Twelve acupuncture meridians in the body join the 360 acupuncture points. Each meridian has a point of entry and a point of exit. The energy enters the meridian, flows through its entire length, and then exits. Upon exit, the energy promptly enters another meridian and repeats its course (Chang, 1976). If the continuous flow is disrupted, pain and disease will occur. Since the body expends much of its energy coping with the pain of an ailment, acupuncture intervenes by restoring energy so that the body may heal.

¶5   Western scientists, dismissing this concept of energy, prefer to explain acupuncture by reference to the nervous system. One early explanation--called the gate theory--suggested that pain is controlled by gates located in the brain and the spinal cord. Needles stimulating the body produce large impulses that flood the gates, thus preventing them from transmitting additional impulses and blocking pain. This theory was gradually refined. Benson (1979) suggests, for example, that acupuncture relieves pain by "either altering the capacity of the nerves which carry impulses . . . or by changing the programming of the central nervous system itself" (p. 128). Stimulating a nerve close to an acupoint inhibits pain impulses to the brain.

¶6   More recently, western scientists have proposed that the pain relief achieved by acupuncture may be caused by endorphins. Endorphins are naturally occurring substances produced by the body that kill pain as effectively as morphine; hence the name endorphin, which means "the morphine within" (Olshan, 1980, p. 6). Bruce Pomerantz of the University of Toronto has conducted experiments based on endorphins and their relationship to acupuncture. Using anesthetized animals, Pomerantz "located cells that fire rapidly [within the brain] when the animal's toe was pricked with a pin. Acupuncture slowed down those cells' firing, and within about 90 minutes after acupuncture they recovered their normal response to pain" ("Neural," p. 234).

APA documentation

¶7   The East believes that acupuncture relieves pain and sickness by restoring an energy balance in the body and continues to develop new medical techniques (Baocheng, 1991). The West attributes its effects to the normal workings of the nervous system. Both explanations have merit. In trying to understand the folk medicine of the East, western scientists have finally come to understand a pain-suppression mechanism not previously understood. Langone (1984) quotes a New York doctor who now asserts that "for pain, [acupuncture] is probably the safest treatment, with the fewest side effects and the greatest benefit. It should be the first line of defense, not the last" (p. 72).

Checklist: *References Page—APA*

Sources contributing directly to the paper are listed alphabetically on a separate sheet immediately after the body of the essay. For more information about the purpose and form of this list, see pages 241–49.

✔ Center the title "References" at the top of the page.
✔ All sources mentioned in the text of the paper must appear in the References list; similarly, every source listed in the References list must be mentioned in the paper.
✔ Arrange the items in the References list alphabetically by the last name of the author. Give initials only for first and middle names. If no author is given for a work, list and alphabetize it by title, excluding articles (*The, A, An*).
✔ The first line of each entry is flush with the left-hand margin. Subsequent lines are indented five spaces.
✔ The list is ordinarily double-spaced. In student papers, APA style does permit single spacing of individual entries, but double spacing is preserved between the single-spaced items.
✔ Punctuate items in the list carefully. Do not forget the period at the end of each entry.
✔ In the References list, capitalize only the first word and any proper nouns and adjectives in the title of a book or article. Within a title, capitalize the first word after a colon.
✔ If you have two or more entries by the same author, list them by year of publication, from earliest to latest. If an author publishes two works in the same year, list them alphabetically by title.

References

Baocheng, H. (1991, June 17). Pizhen--A new acupuncture therapy. Beijing Review, 34, 44-45.

Belkin, L. (1992, January 28). Practicing acupuncture made easy. The New York Times, p. B1.

Benson, H. (1979). The mind/body effect. New York: Simon.

Chang, S. T. (1976). The complete book of acupuncture. Millbrae, CA: Celestial Arts.

Duke, M. (1972). Acupuncture. New York: Jove.

Holzman, A. D. (1986). Pain management: A handbook of psychological treatment approaches. New York: Pergamon.

Komarov, E. W. (1995). Traditional acupuncture [On-line web site]. Available WWW:http://www.dbls.inssys.com/hom/elaine/index.html.

Langone, J. (1984, August). Acupuncture: A new respect for an ancient remedy. Discover, 5, 70-73.

McGarey, W. A. (1974). Acupuncture and body energies. Phoenix: Gabriel Press.

A neural mechanism for acupuncture. (1976, November 20). Science News, 110, 334.

Olshan, N. H. (1980). Power over your pain without drugs. New York: Rawson, Wade.

Rose-Neil, S. (1979). Acupuncture. In Ann Hill (Ed.), A visual encyclopedia of unconventional medicine (pp. 64-65). New York: Crown.

27 APA

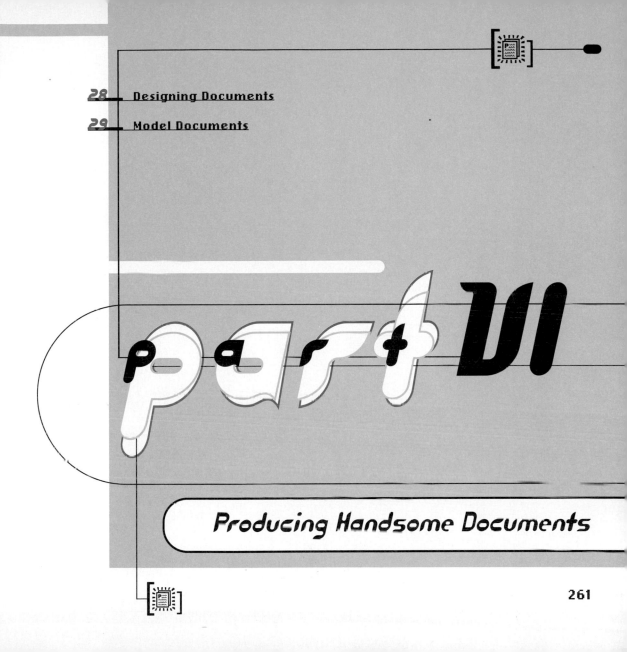

part VI

Producing Handsome Documents

chapter

A — Planning
B — Choosing Type
C — Building Your Design

Designing Documents

> *Effective graphic design favorably predisposes people to accept your product, service, or point of view.*
> —*Roger Parker*, **Looking Good in Print**

*D*ocument design, desktop publishing, visual presentation—whatever you call the systems our information society uses to present its messages attractively—writers today need to learn about them so they can make their work look good in print. This chapter gives an overview of the principles and strategies of document design. Chapter 29 offers some model documents that may be useful.

Don't think that you need an elaborate desktop publishing program to produce good-looking documents. As the desktop publishing expert Roger Parker says, "The power is in the user, not the software."

28a Planning

In document design, success begins with planning. Since you're going to combine several elements—different kinds and sizes of type, graphics, boxes or borders, and possibly illustrations—you have to think ahead about how each element will affect the whole. Keep all decisions tentative until you do a mock-up to see how everything fits together.

• 28a-1 Analyze your audience and purpose. Document design is about audience and purpose; it's as simple as that. When you plan your document, you should make every decision about layout and print with one question in mind: How can I appeal to my audience to achieve the effect I want? Ask yourself the following questions.

- Who is in my audience? (See the Audience Analysis Checklist on page 7.)
  - What do they expect from this document?
  - What tone is appropriate for this audience?
  - What strategies can I use to engage their interest?
- What is my purpose? (See the Purpose Analysis Checklist on page 7.)
  - What effect do I want to achieve with this document?
  - What tools do I have for achieving that effect?

• 28a-2 Analyze the components of the document and the constraints under which you must work. Ask yourself the following questions.

- What components will I be working with?
  - How much printed text will I have?
  - What graphics or illustrations would be appropriate?
  - How can I combine them for the best effect?
- What constraints will I be working under?
  - What tools do I have and know how to use?
  - How much time can I invest?
  - What are my cost limitations?

You'll do well to write out the answers to these questions before you draft your document.

• 28a-3 Sketch out a preliminary plan, choosing type and layout that suit the character of your document. For example,
if you're writing a serious brochure about a historical exhibit, use modest-sized print and simple graphics. For a jazzy poster announcing a blues concert, use different sizes of type and choose dramatic graphics. Plan where you might place the graphics. See Section 28b to learn more about type sizes and fonts (faces).

Use 10- or 12-point type and simple headings for an academic paper, and choose a conventional two- or three-column layout for a church or company newsletter. Use large, dramatic type to create impact and employ eye-catching layouts for flyers or news releases.

Simple reports and academic papers may not require much design planning. However, if you are working on a brochure, newsletter, or computer presentation, make pencil sketches beforehand to try out your options. For example:

Remember that for brochures and some other documents, you need to plan layouts that show two pages at a time.

28b Choosing Type

Writers working on a computer today have available a dazzling variety of fonts (or type faces), type sizes, and styles. The type choices you make from this cornucopia may be your most important design decision because type can influence the appearance of a document more than any other visual element.

In the space available here, it's impossible to do justice to the craft of typography, a rich field that has been growing and changing since the days of Johannes Gutenberg. What follows touches only the basics. If you want to learn more, check out some of the many books on desktop publishing.

• 28b-1 Know the font families. Learn to distinguish among these categories of fonts.

265

Serif Fonts Serifs are the little curves or "feet" at the bottom of letter strokes that pull the eye along from one word to the next. Among the most commonly used serif fonts are these.

Bookman
Courier (resembles typewriter print)
New Century Schoolbook
Palatino
Times

Serif fonts are the workhorses of the print world, used for passages of extended print in most magazines, newspapers, and reports. Choose serif fonts for most print in your routine documents.

Sans Serif Fonts These fonts without serifs give your print a cleaner, more modern look. They don't, however, read quite as smoothly in long passages of print. Some favorite sans serif fonts are these.

Chicago
Futura
Geneva
Helvetica
Lucida Sans

Use sans serif fonts for most of your display type—headings and subheadings, headlines, and announcement type. You can also use sans serif for succinct memos that you want to have an impact.

Decorative or Ornamental Fonts These range from graceful to dramatic to jazzy. Here are examples of some of the fancier ones.

Brickhouse
Democratica Bold
Linoscript
LUSHUS
Out West
RAMIZ

And there are many others, wild and wonderful. Use them to catch attention and to create special effects, but do so sparingly. They're too splashy for routine documents.

Symbol Fonts These special characters, often called dingbats, have given everyday writers a new graphic capacity. To find out what you have available, look under *Zapf Dingbats, Monotype Sorts,* and *Wingdings* in your font menu. Just a few of the things you'll find are decorative symbols such as these.

✳ ❦ ♣ ☙ ✖ ✳ ❀ or these ✓ ■ ◆ ➔ ➚

You'll also find useful icons such as these.

☎ 🖳 ☏ ⏰ 💡 👤 👤 🌐 ✎ ✈ ☞ ✂

There's also an assortment of arrows and mathematical symbols.

You can use dingbats as borders, as icons, as page dividers, or just as lines that set off text.

• 28b-2 Combine fonts with care. Typography experts recommend that you use only two, or at the most three, fonts in a document—otherwise your document can look jumbled. Printers typically choose a serif font for the main body of print and sans serif fonts for headlines, headings, and other display type. To see good examples of how fonts can be skillfully combined, look at the front page of a major paper such as *The New York Times* or *The Wall Street Journal* or at the front pages of a magazine such as *People* or *Newsweek*.

You can use decorative fonts for the masthead of newsletters, for some elements in brochures, for attention-getting lines on posters or announcements, and for programs or flyers. As a rule, don't combine more than two decorative fonts. But there are no firm guidelines to go by. Just experiment to see what looks good. It's so easy to change fonts that you have nothing to lose by trying different combinations.

• 28b-3 Choose appropriate type styles. These type styles are available in most up-to-date word-processing programs.

Boldface	SMALL CAPS	**Shadow**
Italic	ALL CAPS	Outline

You can also condense or expand the letters of a word. For example:

HALLOWEEN
HALLOWEEN
HALLOWEEN

Here's a quick rundown on what different type styles do.

Summary

Type style	Uses	Effect
Boldface	Titles, headings	Strong emphasis
Italic	Special words, titles (see Section 19b)	Highlighting
Small caps	Captions, labels	Emphasis, space savers
All caps	Headlines, display	Strong emphasis
Shadow	Posters, captions	Artistic, dramatic
Outline	Mastheads, titles, special effects	Artistic, dramatic

As word processing takes over from typing, underlining is fading from the print picture. Use other means of emphasis, usually italics, unless you are writing a paper that must conform strictly to a specific format. In that case, inquire before you submit your final draft.

> **CAUTION** Boldfaced type takes up more space than regular type. When you put a line in boldface, it will expand on the page. If you use too much boldfaced type, you lessen its impact.

> **CAUTION** Type sizes aren't uniform among fonts. For example, *Linoscript* and *Ovt West* in 10-point type are so small they're unreadable while Courier, Bookman, and Helvetica look fine in 10 point.

• 28b-4 Choose appropriate type sizes.

Make the size of your type proportionate to its importance. Display type—headlines, headings, mastheads—should usually be larger than your text; how much larger depends on how strongly you want to emphasize the content of the heading and on how much space you have.

Use 10- or 12-point type for academic papers and most reports. Headings and titles for such papers can be a size larger, and subheadings the same size as text, but in boldface. But be sure to ask whether your instructor or supervisor has specific guidelines and follow those.

Headlines for newsletters, flyers, announcements, and so on warrant special attention because if the readers skip them, they're likely to skip the rest of your material too.

- Make headlines three to four times as large as type in the body of the article.
- If you use all capitals for a headline, keep it to only a few words. Even when you use mostly lowercase letters, keep headlines to two lines.

[
Graphic design should provide a road map that steers your readers from point to point.

—Roger Parker, Looking Good in Print
]

- Think of headlines as sentences to be read quickly, and arrange them in segments that make sense by themselves.

C A U T I O N Keep charts and graphs simple. If you include too much data in a pie chart or bar graph, you will confuse your reader.

28c Building Your Design

• 28c-1 Think about how you can make the body language of your document inviting.

Arrange the layout to help your reader move through the document as easily as possible. Take these elements into account.

Direction Native English readers approach text from upper left to lower right, so you should arrange text and graphics accordingly. Put your most important points at the top. The upper right-hand corner is a good place for a featured photograph or announcement. Put routine information such as phone numbers or credits in the lower right-hand corner.

Organization Readers absorb information more easily if it's broken into units. You can create these units by breaking your text into "chunks" with headings, lists, boxes, borders, columns, and screens. Notice that this book makes frequent use of this strategy. For other examples, see the models on pages 273, 277, and 279 in Chapter 29.

White Space Incorporate white space (or blank space—it doesn't have to be white) as a design element by leaving areas around headlines open and by providing wide space between columns.

Leave ample margins, use double or triple spacing between items, and set illustrations or graphics off with a border of space. Above all, your page should look spacious and uncrowded. See the examples in Chapter 29.

Charts, Graphs, and Tables Use these graphics to make statistical information accessible and effective, keeping them close to the data they illustrate. With a little practice, you can create such visual aids with up-to-date software programs. You'll find two examples on the next page.

Photographs and Artwork When you can, use photographs and artwork to enhance your written text. Readers like to see things, just as they like to hear stories, so take advantage of the capacity that computers now give you to illustrate points you're making. If you have access to a scanner, you can copy a picture from a book or article or you can "cut and paste" an image from an electronic encyclopedia such as Encarta. (See the cave painting illustration on p. 18 in Section 3b-6.) Remember to use restraint, however. Artwork and photographs should relate directly to the written text and never be used just for decoration.

269

28c-2 Remember that document design has no hard and fast rules—that's what gives it such possibilities. You can try anything. Play around with the tools your computer offers, always keeping in mind that your goal is to engage your readers. But be careful not to get carried away. The design elements of any document should never distract from the message itself.

And be patient! Working out the details of your design can be time-consuming and frustrating if you're not a computer expert. But you'll know it's worth the effort when you see how good your work can look in print.

28c-3 Use ingenuity to get around technical limitations. Even if you don't have the opportunity or skill to use an up-to-date computer program with graphics and color, you can still enhance your documents in several ways.

- Highlight information by printing it in larger type and drawing a line above and below it.
- If you're limited to black printing, print your document on colored paper.
- Create charts and graphs by hand and paste them into your document. Make a photocopy of an illustration or photo and paste it in.
- Find strategies for breaking up extended passages of print: use bulleted lists, indent a whole passage and draw a box around it, or insert lines of asterisks or other symbols between sections.

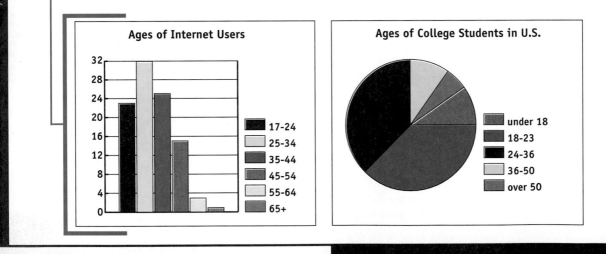

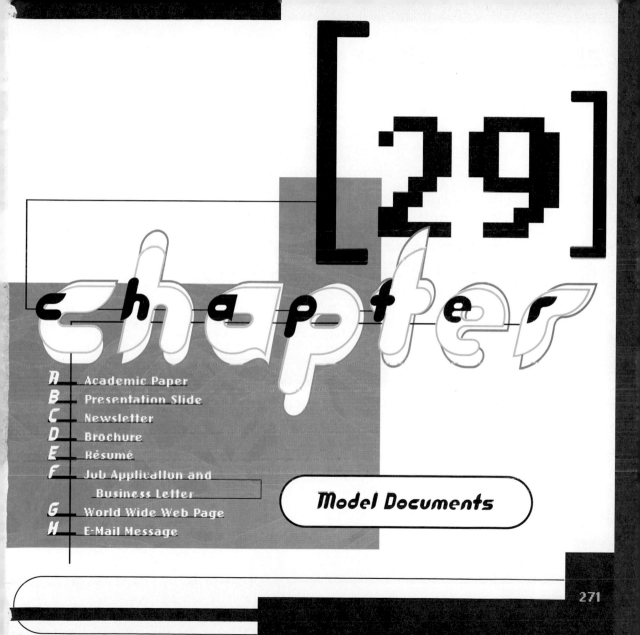

[29]

chapter

A Academic Paper
B Presentation Slide
C Newsletter
D Brochure
E Résumé
F Job Application and
    Business Letter
G World Wide Web Page
H E-Mail Message

Model Documents

Checklist

✔ Find out what format and documentation style the instructor prefers, and follow those conventions. Find the appropriate guide in Part V.

✔ If the instructor permits an informal style, consider how to use graphics, illustrations, headings, and subheadings to make the paper attractive and readable.

✔ Write your name and other relevant information on the top of the first page; continue with a running head and page numbers on the following pages. The running head (typically your last name) ordinarily is placed in the upper right-hand corner.

✔ Choose a traditional serif font in 10- or 12-point type for the body of the paper; choose a simple sans serif font for title, headings, and subheadings. Such headings can be boldfaced.

✔ Double-space the paper.

✔ Leave margins of one inch at the top, bottom, and sides of pages.

✔ Use graphics, especially charts and graphs, to clarify and reinforce statistical information. (See pp. 269–270.)

✔ Type or print out the paper, proofread it carefully, and clip the pages together.

Top and bottom margins, one inch

Author, course information, and date

No indentation for first paragraph after title and heading

Title in boldface, sans serif display type

Double spacing

First heading in boldface display type

Body of paper in traditional serif type

Illustration

Right and left margins, one inch

Italicized caption for illustration

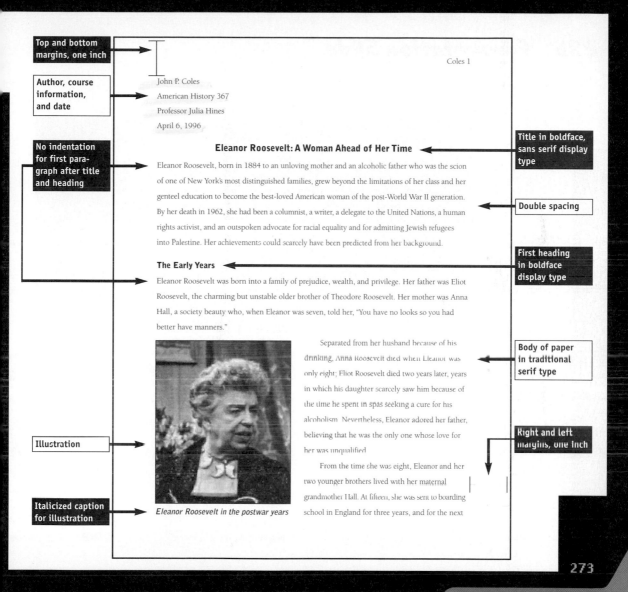

John P. Coles

American History 367

Professor Julia Hines

April 6, 1996

Eleanor Roosevelt: A Woman Ahead of Her Time

Eleanor Roosevelt, born in 1884 to an unloving mother and an alcoholic father who was the scion of one of New York's most distinguished families, grew beyond the limitations of her class and her genteel education to become the best-loved American woman of the post-World War II generation. By her death in 1962, she had been a columnist, a writer, a delegate to the United Nations, a human rights activist, and an outspoken advocate for racial equality and for admitting Jewish refugees into Palestine. Her achievements could scarcely have been predicted from her background.

The Early Years

Eleanor Roosevelt was born into a family of prejudice, wealth, and privilege. Her father was Eliot Roosevelt, the charming but unstable older brother of Theodore Roosevelt. Her mother was Anna Hall, a society beauty who, when Eleanor was seven, told her, "You have no looks so you had better have manners."

Separated from her husband because of his drinking, Anna Roosevelt died when Eleanor was only eight; Eliot Roosevelt died two years later, years in which his daughter scarcely saw him because of the time he spent in spas seeking a cure for his alcoholism. Nevertheless, Eleanor adored her father, believing that he was the only one whose love for her was unqualified.

From the time she was eight, Eleanor and her two younger brothers lived with her maternal grandmother Hall. At fifteen, she was sent to boarding school in England for three years, and for the next

Eleanor Roosevelt in the postwar years

273

29b Presentation Slide

Checklist

✔ Organize your presentation tightly with a clear beginning and ending.
✔ Prepare note cards or an outline from which to work.
✔ Prepare visual slides, charts, or illustrations to reinforce points. Use presentation software, if available, to create professional-looking panels.
✔ Prepare slides in large, easy-to-read print. Test them ahead of time.
✔ Be sure slides are clearly marked and in sequence.
✔ Test your audiovisual equipment ahead of time.
✔ Use information on slides only as cues and reinforcement; don't walk your audience through your text.
✔ Maintain eye contact with your audience; don't hide in your notes.
✔ Stick precisely to your allotted time; practice to be sure.
✔ Speak slowly. Cut material rather than rush through your presentation.

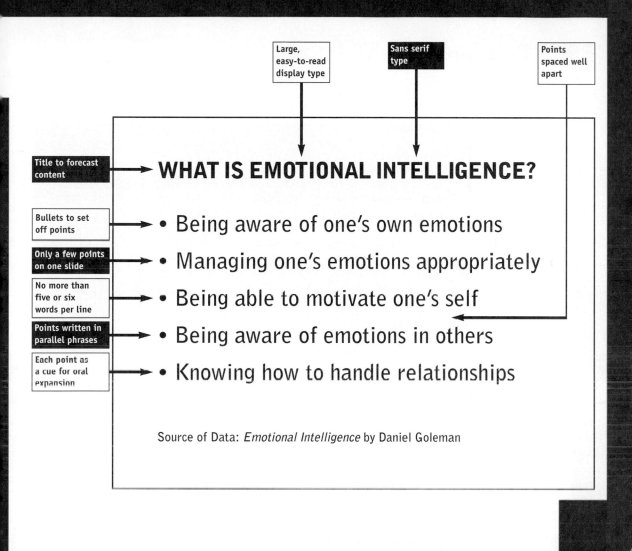

Large,
easy-to-read
display type

Sans serif
type

Points
spaced well
apart

Title to forecast
content

Bullets to set
off points

Only a few points
on one slide

No more than
five or six
words per line

Points written in
parallel phrases

Each point as
a cue for oral
expansion

WHAT IS EMOTIONAL INTELLIGENCE?

- Being aware of one's own emotions
- Managing one's emotions appropriately
- Being able to motivate one's self
- Being aware of emotions in others
- Knowing how to handle relationships

Source of Data: *Emotional Intelligence* by Daniel Goleman

Checklist

✔ Decide what the components of your newsletter will be.
✔ Choose a two- or three-column format.
✔ Sketch layout with pencil and paper ahead of time, trying various arrangements.
✔ If newsletter will run more than one page, plan all pages ahead.
✔ Create a distinctive title that highlights the organization's name.
✔ Leave plenty of space around the title.
✔ Use borders, boxes, lines, and white space to separate items.
✔ Create short paragraphs in order to avoid long stretches of print.
✔ Use a sans serif font for most headlines and other display type.
✔ Use a traditional serif font for extended passages of print.
✔ Use relevant graphics and photographs when possible, but don't use too many.
✔ Position graphics and photographs near the top of the page.
✔ Use color if the budget allows; use colored paper if it does not.

FRIENDS OF THE LIBRARY

Newsletter

Volume 2, Number 5 — March 1996

PARENTS AS READERS

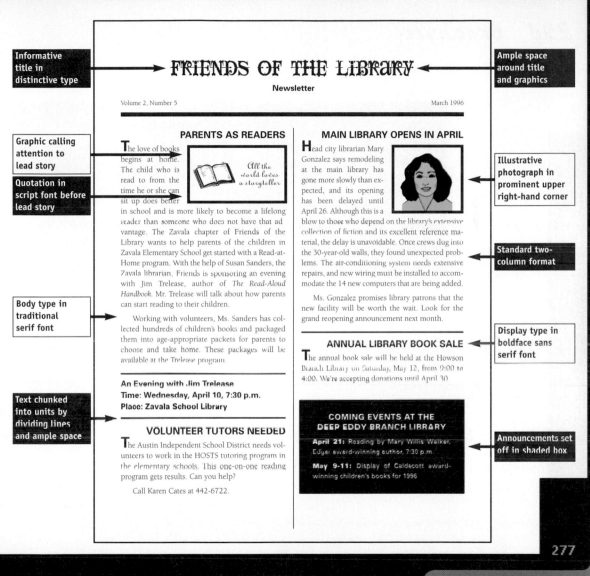

The love of books begins at home. The child who is read to from the time he or she can sit up does better in school and is more likely to become a lifelong reader than someone who does not have that advantage. The Zavala chapter of Friends of the Library wants to help parents of the children in Zavala Elementary School get started with a Read-at-Home program. With the help of Susan Sanders, the Zavala librarian, Friends is sponsoring an evening with Jim Trelease, author of *The Read-Aloud Handbook*. Mr. Trelease will talk about how parents can start reading to their children.

Working with volunteers, Ms. Sanders has collected hundreds of children's books and packaged them into age-appropriate packets for parents to choose and take home. These packages will be available at the Trelease program.

All the world loves a storyteller

An Evening with Jim Trelease
Time: Wednesday, April 10, 7:30 p.m.
Place: Zavala School Library

VOLUNTEER TUTORS NEEDED

The Austin Independent School District needs volunteers to work in the HOSTS tutoring program in the elementary schools. This one-on-one reading program gets results. Can you help?

Call Karen Cates at 442-6722.

MAIN LIBRARY OPENS IN APRIL

Head city librarian Mary Gonzalez says remodeling at the main library has gone more slowly than expected, and its opening has been delayed until April 26. Although this is a blow to those who depend on the library's extensive collection of fiction and its excellent reference material, the delay is unavoidable. Once crews dug into the 30-year-old walls, they found unexpected problems. The air-conditioning system needs extensive repairs, and new wiring must be installed to accommodate the 14 new computers that are being added.

Ms. Gonzalez promises library patrons that the new facility will be worth the wait. Look for the grand reopening announcement next month.

ANNUAL LIBRARY BOOK SALE

The annual book sale will be held at the Howson Branch Library on Saturday, May 12, from 9:00 to 4:00. We're accepting donations until April 30.

COMING EVENTS AT THE DEEP EDDY BRANCH LIBRARY

April 21: Reading by Mary Willis Walker, Edgar award-winning author, 7:30 p.m.

May 9-11: Display of Caldecott award-winning children's books for 1996

29d Brochure

Checklist

✔ Sketch out all panels beforehand, and put them in proper sequence.
✔ Keep presentation simple, but tell where to get more information.
✔ Leave plenty of space around headings and graphics.
✔ Use illustrations and graphics when possible.
✔ Break information into chunks by using lists and dividing lines.
✔ Use easy-to-read serif type fonts for body of print and simple sans serif fonts for headings and titles.
✔ If possible, make each panel self-contained.
✔ Use color if the budget permits; use colored paper if it doesn't.

- Ample space around heading
- Illustration in prominent place
- Ample space around illustration
- Text chunked into units by dividing lines and ample space

- Repetition of design and color, creating unity
- Information chunked in short paragraphs
- Key information presented in lists
- Points set off with bullets

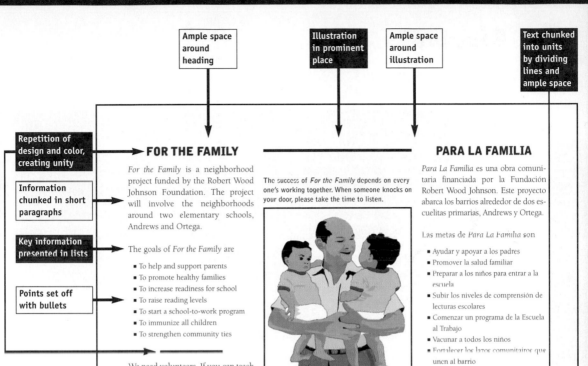

FOR THE FAMILY

For the Family is a neighborhood project funded by the Robert Wood Johnson Foundation. The project will involve the neighborhoods around two elementary schools, Andrews and Ortega.

The goals of *For the Family* are

- To help and support parents
- To promote healthy families
- To increase readiness for school
- To raise reading levels
- To start a school-to-work program
- To immunize all children
- To strengthen community ties

We need volunteers. If you can teach English or crafts, or are a health care professional, give us a call.

Roberto Cantu: 442-8060

The success of *For the Family* depends on every one's working together. When someone knocks on your door, please take the time to listen.

El éxito de *Para La Familia* depende de que todos trabajemos juntos. Cuando alguien toque su puerta, por favor ponga de su parte y bríndele su atención.

PARA LA FAMILIA

Para La Familia es una obra comunitaria financiada por la Fundación Robert Wood Johnson. Este proyecto abarca los barrios alrededor de dos escuelitas primarias, Andrews y Ortega.

Las metas de *Para La Familia* son

- Ayudar y apoyar a los padres
- Promover la salud familiar
- Preparar a los niños para entrar a la escuela
- Subir los niveles de comprensión de lecturas escolares
- Comenzar un programa de la Escuela al Trabajo
- Vacunar a todos los niños
- Fortalecer los lazos comunitarios que unen al barrio

Necesitamos voluntarios. Si Usted puede enseñar inglés, trabajos manuales o artesanales o es un profesional del campo de la salud, por favor llámenos.

29e Résumé

Sean M. O'Brian

Permanent Address
302 S. Reynolds
Toledo, OH 43615
(419) 112-6060

Current Address
1617 Briarcrest, #201
Latrobe, PA 15650
(412) 881-5213

Specific position →

OBJECTIVE Beginning position as cinematographer, film editor, writer

Information that reflects special expertise and distinction ←

EDUCATION Seminar Participant: "The American Cinema," American Film Institute, Los Angeles, CA, June-July 1995
Worked with Francis Ford Coppola and Sydney Pollock.
Won "Outstanding Film Student" citation.

Relevant educational information; professional credentials →

B.A. in Radio, Television, Film, 1994, St. Vincent College, Latrobe, PA
Senior thesis: "The Art of Paddy Chayevsky."
Courses in film production; screen writing; history of the film I, II, & III; editing.

President: St. Vincent College Film Club, 1992-93
Founded college film journal: *Frame and Shoot*, 1992.
Coordinated Allegheny Film Festival, 1993.

Relevant extra-curricular activities ←

Manager: St. Vincent Photography Lab, 1992-94
Managed campus photo lab. Held informal classes on photography, lab work.
Maintained and repaired cameras and equipment.

Relevant student work experience ←

Specific achievement in field →

AWARDS Best Animated Film: *Bayou By You*, 16 mm., 7 min., Midwestern Film Conference (1994).
Best Student Film: *Treed*, 35 mm., 13 min., Allegheny Film Festival (1992).

Actual work experience in related areas →

EXPERIENCE 1993-94. Production Assistant, University Films, Inc., Greensburg, PA
Gained experience with casting, script writing and revision, crew management, development, editing.

Summer 1993. Intern, KYUU-TV, Cleveland, OH
Worked as editor, guest coordinator, news writer.

Summer 1990. Gofer, Heliotrope Studios, Los Angeles, CA

References →

REFERENCES Available upon request.

29F Job Application and Business Letter

Checklist

✔ Choose one format—for example, modified-block form or block form—and be consistent in the letter.

✔ Leave margins of at least one inch, and double-space between paragraphs.

✔ Include a heading—return address and date—and a full inside address.

✔ Include a salutation, using the person's full name and title when you know it. If you're unsure, use a title: Dear Director of Personnel.

✔ Get to the point quickly in the first paragraph. In subsequent paragraphs, answer *who, what, where when,* and *why* questions that your reader might have.

✔ Remember that your letter may become part of a permanent record on the topic on which you're writing. Be sure your information is accurate.

✔ Maintain a consistent tone, polite but personal.

✔ Choose an appropriate closing (*Yours truly* or *Sincerely*), and sign the letter. Type your name beneath the signature.

✔ Proofread with great care, and get a second person to check your letter. Don't depend on a spelling checker to catch spelling errors.

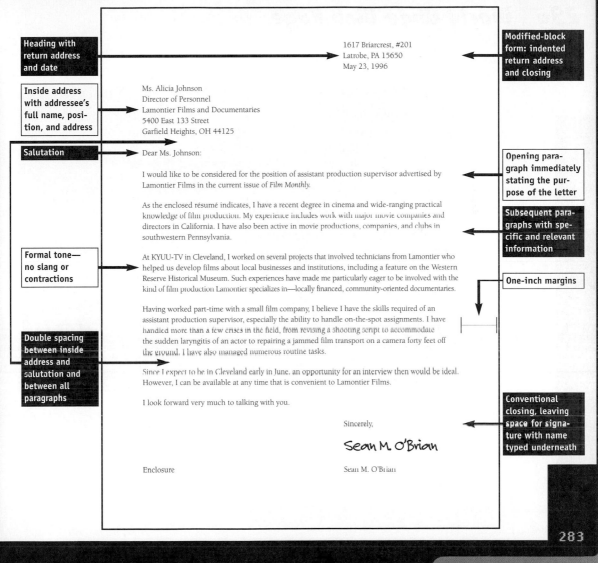

Heading with return address and date

Inside address with addressee's full name, position, and address

Salutation

Formal tone—no slang or contractions

Double spacing between inside address and salutation and between all paragraphs

1617 Briarcrest, #201
Latrobe, PA 15650
May 23, 1996

Modified-block form: indented return address and closing

Ms. Alicia Johnson
Director of Personnel
Lamontier Films and Documentaries
5400 East 133 Street
Garfield Heights, OH 44125

Dear Ms. Johnson:

I would like to be considered for the position of assistant production supervisor advertised by Lamontier Films in the current issue of *Film Monthly*.

Opening paragraph immediately stating the purpose of the letter

As the enclosed résumé indicates, I have a recent degree in cinema and wide-ranging practical knowledge of film production. My experience includes work with major movie companies and directors in California. I have also been active in movie productions, companies, and clubs in southwestern Pennsylvania.

Subsequent paragraphs with specific and relevant information

At KYUU-TV in Cleveland, I worked on several projects that involved technicians from Lamontier who helped us develop films about local businesses and institutions, including a feature on the Western Reserve Historical Museum. Such experiences have made me particularly eager to be involved with the kind of film production Lamontier specializes in—locally financed, community-oriented documentaries.

One-inch margins

Having worked part-time with a small film company, I believe I have the skills required of an assistant production supervisor, especially the ability to handle on-the-spot assignments. I have handled more than a few crises in the field, from revising a shooting script to accommodate the sudden laryngitis of an actor to repairing a jammed film transport on a camera forty feet off the ground. I have also managed numerous routine tasks.

Since I expect to be in Cleveland early in June, an opportunity for an interview then would be ideal. However, I can be available at any time that is convenient to Lamontier Films.

I look forward very much to talking with you.

Sincerely,

Sean M. O'Brian

Sean M. O'Brian

Conventional closing, leaving space for signature with name typed underneath

Enclosure

29g World Wide Web Page

Checklist

✔ Design your home page and linking secondary pages so they are small and can be loaded quickly. Many Internet users may be using slow modems; for users in nonprofit organizations, especially in developing countries, access to the Internet and time on the Internet may be very expensive.

✔ Preview your main points on your home page so browsers can quickly tell if your site will give them what they need.

✔ Use only images that have high information content, and keep them to a minimum. Elaborate color images gobble up RAM memory, are slow to materialize and to download, and often trigger "You don't have enough memory" messages.

✔ Make sure all graphics and photos relate directly to your topic; avoid "chart junk" that distracts the reader.

✔ Warn your readers ahead of time when clicking on a link will lead to a large amount of information that could be time-consuming and expensive to read and download.

✔ Keep your text succinct, clear, and easy to read quickly.

Note: Many of these suggestions come from an Internet site created by Philip Bogdonoff of the World Bank Electronic Media Center. For more information and discussion, see his site at http://www.worldbank.org/html/emc/documents/zippywww.html

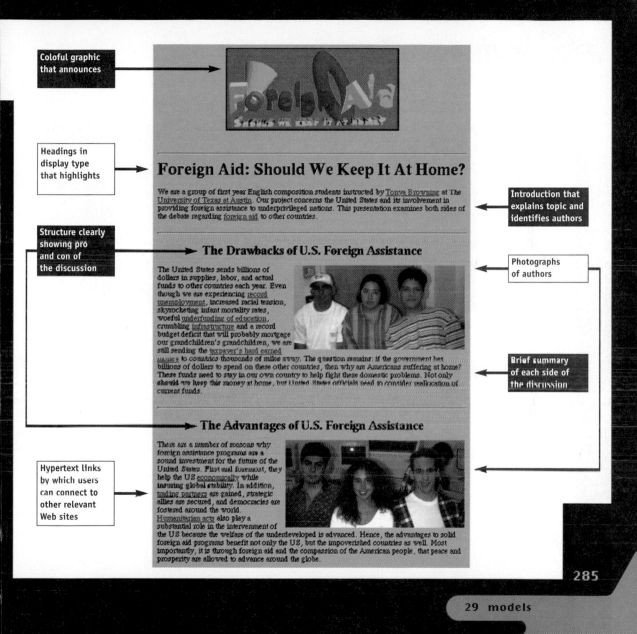

Coloful graphic that announces

Headings in display type that highlights

Structure clearly showing pro and con of the discussion

Hypertext links by which users can connect to other relevant Web sites

Foreign Aid: Should We Keep It At Home?

We are a group of first year English composition students instructed by Tonya Browning at The University of Texas at Austin. Our project concerns the United States and its involvement in providing foreign assistance to underprivileged nations. This presentation examines both sides of the debate regarding foreign aid to other countries.

The Drawbacks of U.S. Foreign Assistance

The United States sends billions of dollars in supplies, labor, and actual funds to other countries each year. Even though we are experiencing record unemployment, increased racial tension, skyrocketing infant mortality rates, voeful underfunding of education, crumbling infrastructure and a record budget deficit that will probably mortgage our grandchildren's grandchildren, we are still sending the taxpayer's hard earned money to countries thousands of miles away. The question remains: if the government has billions of dollars to spend on these other countries, then why are Americans suffering at home? These funds need to stay in our own country to help fight these domestic problems. Not only should we keep this money at home, but United States officials need to consider reallocation of current funds.

The Advantages of U.S. Foreign Assistance

There are a number of reasons why foreign assistance programs are a sound investment for the future of the United States. First and foremost, they help the US economically while insuring global stability. In addition, trading partners are gained, strategic allies are secured, and democracies are fostered around the world. Humanitarian acts also play a substantial role in the intervention of the US because the welfare of the underdeveloped is advanced. Hence, the advantages to solid foreign aid programs benefit not only the US, but the impoverished countries as well. Most importantly, it is through foreign aid and the compassion of the American people, that peace and prosperity are allowed to advance around the globe.

Introduction that explains topic and identifies authors

Photographs of authors

Brief summary of each side of the discussion

285

29 models

29-h E-Mail Message

Checklist

✔ Verify *exact* addresses. The slightest error will abort the mail.

✔ Remember that e-mail may be stored or printed out and filed. It doesn't necessarily disappear when the computer shuts down.

✔ Send brief messages, easily readable on screen.

✔ Keep paragraphs short, and double-space between them.

✔ Adapt your style to your audience. Although e-mail tends to be less formal than regular business letters, keep a respectful tone in business and professional communications.

✔ When helpful, include additional information such as your mailing address and FAX number.

model documents

Date and time printed

Exact e-mail address for each recipient

Short message

Brief, informative paragraphs

Conversational tone

Additional useful information

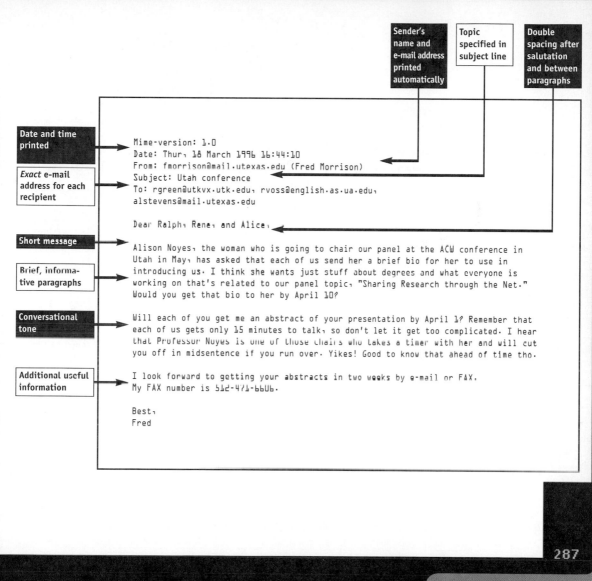

Mime-version: 1.0
Date: Thur, 18 March 1996 16:44:10
From: fmorrison@mail.utexas.edu (Fred Morrison)
Subject: Utah conference
To: rgreen@utkvx.utk.edu, rvoss@english.as.ua.edu,
alstevens@mail.utexas.edu

Dear Ralph, Rene, and Alice,

Alison Noyes, the woman who is going to chair our panel at the ACW conference in
Utah in May, has asked that each of us send her a brief bio for her to use in
introducing us. I think she wants just stuff about degrees and what everyone is
working on that's related to our panel topic, "Sharing Research through the Net."
Would you get that bio to her by April 10?

Will each of you get me an abstract of your presentation by April 1? Remember that
each of us gets only 15 minutes to talk, so don't let it get too complicated. I hear
that Professor Noyes is one of those chairs who takes a timer with her and will cut
you off in midsentence if you run over. Yikes! Good to know that ahead of time tho.

I look forward to getting your abstracts in two weeks by e-mail or FAX.
My FAX number is 512-471-6606.

Best,
Fred

glossary of usage

a, an. Indefinite articles. **A** and **an** are indefinite articles because they point to objects in a general way (**a** book, **a** church), while the definite article **the** refers to specific things (**the** book, **the** church). **A** is used when the word following it begins with a consonant sound: **a** *house*, **a** *year*, **a** *boat*, **a** *unique* experience. **An** is used when the word following it begins with a vowel sound: **an** *hour*, **an** *interest*, **an** *annoyance*, **an** *illusory* image.

Notice that you choose the article by the *sound* of the word following it. Not all words that begin with vowels actually begin with vowel sounds, and not all words that begin with consonants have initial consonant sounds.

accept/except. Very commonly confused. **Accept** means "to take, receive, or approve of something." **Except** means "excluding, or not including."

I **accepted** all the apologies **except** George's.

accidently/accidentally. **Accidently** is a misspelling. The correct spelling is **accidentally.**

adverse/averse. Often confused. **Adverse** describes something hostile, unfavorable, or difficult.

Averse indicates the opposition someone has to something; it is ordinarily followed by *to.*

Travis was **averse** to playing soccer under **adverse** field conditions.

advice/advise. These words aren't interchangeable. **Advice** is a noun meaning "an opinion" or "counsel." **Advise** is a verb meaning "to give counsel or advice."

I'd **advise** you not to give Maggie **advice** about running her business.

affect/effect. A troublesome pair! Each word can be either a noun or a verb, although **affect** is ordinarily a verb and **effect** a noun. In its usual sense, **affect** is a verb meaning "to influence" or "to give the appearance of."

How will the stormy weather **affect** the plans for the outdoor concert?

The meteorologist **affected** ignorance when we asked her for a forecast.

Only rarely is **affect** a noun, as a term in psychology meaning "feeling" or "emotion." On the other hand, **effect** is usually a noun, meaning "consequence" or "result."

> The **effect** of the weather may be serious.

Effect may, however, also be a verb, meaning "to cause" or "to bring about."

> The funnel cloud **effected** a change in our plans.
> Compare with: The funnel cloud **affected** our plans.

African American. The term now preferred by many Americans of African ancestry, replacing *black* and *Negro*.

aggravate/irritate. Many people use both of these verbs to mean "to annoy" or "to make angry." However, formal English preserves a fine—and useful— distinction between them. **Irritate** means "to annoy," while **aggravate** means "to make something worse."

> It **irritated** Greta when her husband **aggravated** his allergies by smoking.

ain't. It may be in the dictionary, but **ain't** isn't acceptable in academic or professional writing. Avoid it.

all ready/already. Tricky, but not difficult. **All ready,** an adjective phrase, means "prepared and set to go."

> Rita signaled that the camera was **all ready** for shooting.

Already, an adverb, means "before" or "previously."

> Rita had **already** loaded the film.

all right. All right is the only acceptable spelling. **Alright** is not acceptable in standard English.

allude/elude. Commonly confused. **Allude** means "to refer to" or "to mention something indirectly." **Elude** means "to escape."

> Kyle's joke **alluded** to the fact that it was easy to **elude** the portly security guard.

allude/refer. Allude means "to refer to" or "to mention something indirectly"; **refer** means "to mention something directly."

> Carter **alluded** to rituals the new students didn't understand.
> Carter did, however, **refer** to ancient undergraduate traditions and the honor of the college.

allusion/illusion. These terms are often misused. An **allusion** is an indirect reference to something. An **illusion** is a false impression or a misleading appearance.

> The entire class missed Professor Sweno's **allusion** to the ghost in *Hamlet*.
> Professor Sweno entertained the **illusion** that everyone read Shakespeare as often as he did.

a lot. Often misspelled as one word. It is two. Many readers consider **a lot** inappropriate in academic writing, preferring **many, much,** or some comparable expression.

already. See **all ready/already.**

alright. See **all right.**

American. Though often used to describe citizens of the United States of America, the term can also refer to any citizen of the Americas, North or South. Be careful how you use this term when writing to audiences that may include Americans not from the United States.

among/between. Use **between** with two objects and **among** with three or more.

> Francie had to choose **between** Richard and Kyle.
>
> Francie had to choose from **among** a dozen actors.

amount/number. Use **amount** for quantities that can be measured, but not counted. Use **number** for things that can be counted, not measured: the **amount** of water in the ocean; the **number** of fish in the sea. The distinction between these words is being lost, but it is worth preserving. Remember that **amount of** is followed by a singular noun, while **number of** is followed by a plural noun.

amount of *money*	**number of** *dimes*
amount of *paint*	**number of** *colors*
amount of *support*	**number of** *voters*

an. See **a, an.**

and etc. A redundant expression. Use **etc.** alone or **and so on.** See **etc.**

and/or. A useful form in some situations, especially in business and technical writing, but some readers regard it as clumsy. Work around it if you can, especially in academic writing. **And/or** is typed with no space before and after the slash.

Anglo. A common term in some areas of North America for designating white or nonminority people. The term is inaccurate in that many people considered white are not, in fact, *Anglo-Saxon* in origin.

angry/mad. The distinction between these words is rarely observed, but, strictly speaking, one should use **angry** to describe displeasure and **mad** to describe insanity.

anyone/any one. These expressions have different meanings. Notice the difference highlighted in these sentences.

> **Any one** of those problems could develop into a crisis.
>
> I doubt that **anyone** will be able to find a solution to **any one** of the equations.

anyways. A nonstandard form. Use **anyway.**

> **Incorrect:** It didn't matter **anyways.**
>
> **Correct:** It didn't matter **anyway.**

as being. A wordy expression. You can usually delete **being.**

> In most cases, telephone solicitors are regarded **as (being)** a nuisance.

Asian American. The term now preferred by many Americans of Asian ancestry, replacing *Oriental.*

averse/adverse. See **adverse/averse.**

awful. **Awful** is inappropriate as a synonym for **very.**

> **Inappropriate:** The findings of the two research teams were **awful** close.
>
> **Revised:** The findings of the two research teams were **very** close.

awhile/a while. The expressions are not interchangeable. **Awhile** is an adverb; **a while** is a noun phrase. After prepositions, always use **a while.**

> Bud stood **awhile** looking at the grass.
>
> Bud decided that the lawn would not have to be cut for **a while.**

bad/badly. These words are troublesome. Remember that **bad** is an adjective describing what something is like; **badly** is an adverb explaining how something is done.

> Stanley's taste in music wasn't **bad.**
>
> Unfortunately, he treated his musicians **badly.**

Problems usually crop up with verbs that explain how something feels, tastes, smells, or looks. In such cases, use **bad.**

> The physicists felt **bad** about the disappearance of their satellite.
>
> The situation looked **bad.**

basically. **Basically** is an adverb that means "fundamentally" or "essentially."

> The proposal was **basically** sound.
>
> Throughout a long career, Arlo worked **basically** as a folk singer, though he occasionally played the blues.

Many writers abuse the term, however, employing it as filler. When cutting the term doesn't change the meaning of a sentence, delete "basically."

> **Wordy:** It was a holiday, but **basically** we had no plans for a picnic.
>
> **Revised:** It was a holiday, but we had no plans for a picnic.

because of/due to. Careful writers usually prefer **because of** to **due to** in many situations.

> **Awkward:** The investigation into Bud's disappearance stalled **due to** Officer Bricker's sudden concern for correct procedure.
>
> **Revised:** The investigation into Bud's disappearance stalled **because of** Officer Bricker's sudden concern for correct procedure.

However, *due to* is often the better choice when it serves as a **subject complement** after a **linking verb.** The examples illustrate the point.

> subj.   l. v.   subj. comp.
> Bricker's discretion *seemed* **due to** *cowardice.*

> subj.   l. v.   subj. comp.
> His discretion *was* **due to** *the political and social prominence of the Huttons.*

being as/being that. Both of these expressions sound wordy and awkward when used in place of **because** or **since**. Use **because** and **since** in formal and academic writing.

> **Wordy: Being that** her major was astronomy, Jenny was looking forward to the eclipse.

> **Revised: Since** her major was astronomy, Jenny was looking forward to the eclipse.

beside/besides. **Beside** is a preposition meaning "next to" or "alongside"; **besides** is a preposition meaning "in addition to" or "other than."

> **Besides** a sworn confession, the detectives also had the suspect's fingerprints on a gun found **beside** the body.

Besides can also be an adverb meaning "in addition" or "moreover."

> Professor Bellona didn't mind assisting the athletic department, and **besides,** she actually liked coaching volleyball.

between. See **among/between.**

black. A term falling somewhat out of favor to describe people of African descent. Many American blacks now prefer the term **African American.**

British. The term refers to the people of Scotland and Wales in addition to those of England. *English* refers chiefly to those people of the British Isles who come from within the borders of England itself.

but what. In most writing, **that** alone is preferable to the colloquial **but that** or **but what.**

> **Colloquial:** There was little doubt **but what** he'd learned a few things.

> **Revised:** There was little doubt **that** he'd learned a few things.

can/may. Understand the difference between the auxiliary verbs **can** and **may**. Use **can** to express an ability to do something.

> Charnelle **can** work differential equations.

> According to the *Handbook of College Policies,* Dean Rack **can** lift the suspension.

Use **may** to express either permission or possibility.

> You **may** want to compare my solution to the problem to Charnelle's.

> Dean Rack **may** lift the suspension, but I wouldn't count on that happening.

cannot. **Cannot** is ordinarily written as one word, not two.

can't. Writers sometimes forget the apostrophe in this and other contractions: **don't, won't.**

can't hardly. A colloquial expression that is, technically, a double negative. Use **can hardly** instead when you write.

> **Colloquial:** I **can't hardly** see the road.

> **Revised:** I **can hardly** see the road.

censor/censure. These words have different meanings. As verbs, **censor** means "to cut," "to repress," or "to remove"; **censure** means "to disapprove" and "to condemn."

The student editorial board voted to **censor** the four-letter words from Connie Lim's editorial and to **censure** her for attempting to publish the controversial piece.

conscience/conscious. Don't confuse these words. **Conscience** is a noun referring to an inner ethical sense; **conscious** is an adjective describing a state of awareness or wakefulness.

The linebacker felt a twinge of **conscience** after knocking the quarterback **unconscious.**

consensus. This expression is redundant if followed by **of opinion; consensus** by itself implies an opinion. Use **consensus** alone.

Redundant: The student senate reached a **consensus of opinion** on the issue of censorship.

Revised: The student senate reached a **consensus** on the issue of censorship.

contact. Some people object to using **contact** as a verb meaning "to get in touch with" or "to call." The usage is common, but you might want to avoid it in formal or academic writing.

could of/would of/should of. Nonstandard forms when used instead of **could have, would have,** or **should have.**

Incorrect: Coach Rhoades imagined that his team **could of** been a contender.

Correct: Coach Rhoades imagined that his team **could have** been a contender.

couple of. Casual. Avoid it in formal or academic writing.

Casual: The article accused the admissions office of a **couple of** major blunders.

Revised: The article accused the admissions office of **several** major blunders.

credible/credulous. Credible means "believable"; **credulous** means "willing to believe on slim evidence." See also **incredible/incredulous.**

Officer Bricker found Mr. Hutton's excuse for his speeding **credible.** However, Bricker was known to be a **credulous** police officer, always wishing to give someone a second chance.

criteria, criterion. Criteria, the plural form, is more familiar, but the word does have a singular form, **criterion.**

John Maynard, aged sixty-four, complained that he was often judged according to a single **criterion,** age.

Other **criteria** ought to matter in hiring.

curriculum, curricula. Curriculum is the singular form; **curricula** is the plural.

Dean Perez believed that the **curriculum** in history had to be strengthened.

Indeed, she believed that the **curricula** in all the liberal arts departments needed rethinking.

data/datum. Data has a singular form, **datum.** In speech and informal writing, **data** is commonly treated as both singular and plural. In academic writing, use **datum** when the singular is needed. If **datum** seems awkward, try to rewrite the sentence to avoid the singular.

> **Singular:** The most intriguing **datum** in the study was the percentage of population decline.

> **Plural:** In all the **data,** no figure was more intriguing than the percentage of population decline.

different from/different than. In formal writing, **different from** is usually preferred to **different than.**

> **Formal:** Ike's account of his marriage proposal was **different from** Bernice's.

> **Informal:** Ike's account of his marriage proposal was **different than** Bernice's.

discreet/discrete. Discreet means "tactful" or "sensitive to appearances" (**discreet** behavior); **discrete** means "individual" or "separate" (**discrete** objects).

> Joel was **discreet** about the money spent on his project.

> He had several **discrete** funds at his disposal.

disinterested/uninterested. These two words don't mean the same thing. **Disinterested** means "neutral" or "uninvolved"; **uninterested** means "not interested" or "bored."

> Alyce and Richard sought a **disinterested** party to arbitrate their dispute.

> Stanley was **uninterested** in the club's management.

don't. Writers sometimes forget the apostrophe in this and other contractions: **can't, won't.**

due to/because of. See **because of/due to.**

due to the fact that. Wordy. Replace it with **because** whenever you can.

> **Wordy:** Coach Meyer was fired **due to the fact that** his team lost every game.

> **Revised:** Coach Meyer was fired **because** his team lost every game.

effect/affect. See **affect/effect.**

elicit/illicit. These words have vastly different meanings. **Elicit** means to "draw out" or "bring forth"; **illicit** describes something illegal or prohibited.

> The detective tried to **elicit** an admission of **illicit** behavior from Bud.

elude/allude. See **allude/elude.**

eminent/imminent. These words are sometimes confused. **Eminent** means "distinguished" and "prominent"; **imminent** describes something about to happen.

> The arrival of the **eminent** scholar is **imminent.**

enthused. A colloquial expression that should not appear in academic or professional writing. Use **enthusiastic** instead.

> **Colloquial:** Francie was **enthused** about U-2's latest album.
>
> **Revised:** Francie was **enthusiastic** about U-2's latest album.

Never use **enthused** as a verb.

equally as. Redundant. Use either **equally** or **as** to express a comparison, whichever works in a particular sentence.

> **Redundant:** Sue Ellen is **equally as** concerned as Hector about bilingual education.
>
> **Revised:** Sue Ellen is **as** concerned as Hector about bilingual education.
>
> **Revised:** Sue Ellen and Hector are **equally** concerned about bilingual education.

Eskimo. Falling out of favor as a term to describe the native peoples of northern Canada and Alaska. Many now prefer *Inuit.*

etc. This common abbreviation for *et cetera* should be avoided in most academic and formal writing. Instead, use **and so on** or **and so forth.** Never use **and etc.**

even though. **Even though** is two words, not one.

everyone/every one. These similar expressions mean different things. **Everyone** describes a group collectively. **Every one** focuses on the individual elements within a group or collective term. Notice the difference highlighted in these sentences.

> **Every one** of those problems could develop into an international crisis **everyone** would regret.
>
> I doubt that **everyone** will be able to attend **every one** of the sessions.

except/accept. See **accept/except.**

fact that, the. Wordy. You can usually replace the entire expression with **that.**

> **Wordy:** Bud was aware of **the fact that** he was in a strange room.
>
> **Revised:** Bud was aware **that** he was in a strange room.

faith/fate. A surprising number of writers confuse these words and their variations: **faithful, fateful, faithless. Faith** refers to confidence, trust, or a religious belief; **fate** means "destiny" or "outcome."

farther/further. Although the distinction between these words is not always observed, it is useful. Use **farther** to refer to distances that can be measured.

> It is **farther** from El Paso to Houston than from New York to Detroit.

Use **further,** meaning "more" or "additional," when physical distance or separation is not involved.

The detective decided that the crime warranted **further** investigation.

fate/faith. See **faith/fate.**

fewer than/less than. Use **fewer than** with things you can count; use **less than** with quantities that must be measured or can be considered as a whole.

> The express lane was reserved for customers buying **fewer than** ten items.
>
> Matthew had **less than** half a gallon of gasoline.
>
> He also had **less than** ten dollars.

flaunt/flout. These words are confused surprisingly often. **Flaunt** means "to show off"; **flout** means "to disregard" or "to show contempt for."

> To **flaunt** his wealth, Mr. Lin bought a Van Gogh.
>
> **Flouting** a gag order, the newspaper published its exposé of corruption in the city council.

fun, funner, funnest. Used as an adjective, **fun** is usually not appropriate in academic writing; replace it with a more formal expression.

> **Informal:** Skiing is a **fun** sport.
>
> **Formal:** Skiing is an **enjoyable** sport.

The comparative and superlative forms, **funner** and **funnest**, while increasingly common in spoken English, are inappropriate in written English. In writing, use **more fun** or **most fun.**

Informal: Albert found tennis **funner** than squash.

Formal: Albert found tennis **more fun** than squash.

Spoken: He thought racquetball the **funnest** of the three sports.

Written: He thought racquetball the **most fun** of the three sports.

gay. A term now widely used to mean "homosexual." Less formal than *homosexual,* **gay** is still appropriate in most writing. While **gay** is often used without regard to gender, some prefer it as a term that refers mainly to homosexual men, with **lesbian** the appropriate term for homosexual women.

get. The principal parts of this verb are as follows:

Present	Past	Past Participle
get	got	got, gotten

Gotten usually sounds more polished than **got** as the past participle in American English, but both forms are acceptable.

> Aretha **has gotten** an A average in microbiology.
>
> Aretha **has got** an A average in microbiology.

Many expressions, formal and informal, rely on **get.** Use the less formal ones, such as these, only with appropriate audiences.

> get it together
>
> get straight
>
> get real

good and. Informal. Avoid it in academic writing.

> **Informal:** The lake was **good and** cold when the sailors threw Sean in.
> **Formal:** The lake was **icy** cold when the sailors threw Sean in.

good/well. These words cause many problems. As a modifier, **good** is an adjective only; **well** can be either an adjective or an adverb. Consider the difference between these sentences, in which each word functions as an adjective.

> Katy is **good.**
> Katy is **well.**

Good is often mistakenly used as an adverb.

> **Incorrect:** Juin conducts the orchestra **good.**
> **Correct:** Juin conducts the orchestra **well.**

> **Incorrect:** The bureaucracy at NASA runs **good.**
> **Correct:** The bureaucracy at NASA runs **well.**

Complications occur when writers and speakers—eager to avoid using **good** incorrectly—substitute **well** as an adjective where **good** used as an adjective may be more accurate.

> **Incorrect:** After a shower, Coach Rhoades smells **well.**
> **Correct:** After a shower, Coach Rhoades smells **good.**

> **Correct:** I feel **good.** [Usually describes a state of mind]
> **Also correct:** I feel **well.** [Describes a physical state: not ill]

handicapped. Falling out of favor as a term to describe people with physical disabilities. However, euphemistic alternatives such as *differently abled* and *physically challenged* have been roundly criticized. *Disabled* is usually appropriate.

hanged, hung. Hanged has been the past participle conventionally reserved for executions; **hung** is used for other meanings. The distinction is a nice one that is probably worth observing.

> Connie was miffed when her disgruntled editorial staff decided she should be **hanged** in effigy.
> Portraits of the faculty were **hung** in the student union.

he/she. Using **he/she** (or *his/her* or *s/he*) is a way to avoid a sexist pronoun reference. However, many readers find expressions with slashes clumsy and prefer *he or she* and *his or her.*

Hispanic. A term falling somewhat out of favor among some groups, in part because of its imprecision. Groups that have fallen under the Hispanic label now often prefer to be identified more precisely: *Chicano/Chicana, Cuban American, Latin American, Mexican American, Puerto Rican.*

hisself. A nonstandard form. Don't use it.

hopefully. As a sentence modifier, **hopefully** upsets some readers' sensitivities. In most situations, you will do well to avoid using **hopefully** when you mean "I hope" or "it is hoped."

> **Not: Hopefully,** the weather will improve.

> **Revised: I hope** the weather will improve.

Use *hopefully* only when you mean "with hope."

> Geraldo watched **hopefully** as Al Capone's safe was pried open.

illicit/elicit. See **elicit/illicit.**

illusion/allusion. See **allusion/illusion.**

imminent/eminent. See **eminent/imminent.**

imply/infer. Think of these words as opposite sides of the same coin. **Imply** means "to suggest" or "to convey an idea without stating it." **Infer** is what you might do to figure out what someone else has implied: you examine evidence and draw conclusions from it.

> By joking calmly, the pilot sought to **imply** that the aircraft was out of danger. However, from the hole that had opened in the wing, the passengers **inferred** that the landing would not be routine.

incredible/incredulous. Incredible means "unbelievable"; **incredulous** means "unwilling to believe" and "doubting." See also **credible/credulous.**

> The press found the governor's explanation for his wealth **incredible.** You could hardly blame them for being **incredulous** when he attributed his vast holdings to coupon savings.

infer/imply. See **imply/infer.**

into. Avoid using this word in its faddish sense of meaning "interested in" or "involved with."

> **Informal:** The college was finally **into** computers.

> **Formal:** The college was finally **involved with** computers.

irregardless. A nonstandard form. Use **regardless** instead.

irritate/aggravate. See **aggravate/irritate.**

its/it's. Don't confuse these terms. **Its** is a possessive pronoun meaning "belonging to it." **It's** is a contraction for *it is.*

judgment/judgement. The British spell this word with two *e*'s. Americans spell it with just one: **judgment.**

kind of. This expression is colloquial when used to mean "rather." Avoid **kind of** in formal writing.

> **Colloquial:** The college trustees were **kind of** upset by the bad publicity.

> **Revised:** The college trustees were **rather** upset by the bad publicity.

less than. See **fewer than/less than.**

lie/lay. These two verbs cause much trouble and confusion. Here are their principal parts.

Present	Past	Present Participle	Past Participle
lie (to recline)	lay	lying	lain
lay (to place)	laid	laying	laid

Notice that the past tense of **lie** is the same as the present tense of **lay.** It may help you to remember that **to lie** (meaning "to recline") is *intransitive*—that is, it doesn't take an object. You can't lie *something*.

> Travis **lies** under the cottonwood tree.
>
> He **lay** there all afternoon.
>
> He was **lying** in the hammock yesterday.
>
> He had **lain** there for weeks.

To lay (meaning "to place" or "to put") is *transitive*—it takes an object.

> Jenny **lays** a *book* on Travis's desk.
>
> Yesterday, she **laid** a *memo* on his desk.
>
> Jenny was **laying** the *memo* on Travis's desk when he returned.
>
> Travis had **laid** almost three *yards* of concrete that afternoon.

like/as. Many readers object to **like** used to introduce clauses of comparison. **As, as if,** or **as though** are preferred when a comparison involves a subject and a verb.

> **Not:** Mr. Butcher is self-disciplined, **like** you would expect a champion weightlifter to be.
>
> **Revised:** Mr. Butcher is self-disciplined, **as** you would expect a champion weightlifter to be.
>
> **Not:** It looks **like** he will win the local competition again this year.
>
> **Revised:** It looks **as if** he will win the local competition again this year.

Like is acceptable when it introduces a prepositional phrase, not a clause.

> Yvonne looks **like** her mother.
>
> The sculpture on the mall looks **like** a rusted Edsel.

literally. When you write that something is **literally** true, you mean that it is exactly as you have stated. The following sentence means that Bernice emitted heated water vapor, an unlikely event no matter how angry she was.

> Bernice **literally** steamed when Ike ordered her to marry him.

If you want to keep the image (*steamed*), omit **literally.**

> Bernice steamed when Ike ordered her to marry him.

lose/loose. Be careful not to confuse these words. **Lose** is a verb, meaning "to misplace," "to be deprived of," or "to be defeated." **Loose** can be either an adjective or a verb. As an adjective, **loose** means "not tight"; as a verb, **loose** means "to let go" or "to untighten."

> Without Martin as quarterback, the team might **lose** its first game of the season.
>
> The strap on Martin's helmet had worked **loose.**
>
> It **loosened** so much that Martin **lost** his helmet.

mad, angry. See **angry/mad.**

majority/plurality. There is a useful difference in meaning between these two words. A **majority** is more than half of a group; a **plurality** is the largest part of a group when there is *less than* a *majority*. In an election, for example, a candidate who wins 50.1 percent of the vote can claim a **majority.** One who wins a race with 40 percent of the vote may claim a **plurality,** but not a majority.

man, mankind. These terms are considered sexist by many readers since they implicitly exclude women from the human family.

> **Man** has begun to conquer space.

Look for alternatives, such as *humanity, people, men and women, the human race,* or *humankind.*

> **Men and women** have begun to conquer space.

many times. Wordy. Use **often** instead.

may/can. See **can/may.**

media/medium. Medium is the singular of **media.**

> Connie believed that the press could be as powerful a **medium** as television.

> The visual **media** are discussed in the textbook.

The term **media** is commonly used to refer to newspapers and magazines, as well as television and radio.

> President Xiony declined to speak to the **media** about the fiscal problems facing the college.

Mexican American. A preferred term for describing Americans of Mexican ancestry.

midst/mist. Some people write **mist** when they mean **midst,** but the words are unrelated. **Midst** means "between" or "in the middle of." A **mist** is a mass of fine particles suspended in the air.

might of. A nonstandard form. Use **might have** instead.

> **Incorrect:** Ms. Rajala **might of** never admitted the truth.

> **Correct:** Ms. Rajala **might have** never admitted the truth.

mist/midst. See **midst/mist.**

moral, morale. Don't confuse these words. As a noun, **moral** is a lesson. **Morale** is a state of mind.

> The **moral** of the fable was to avoid temptation.

> The **morale** of the team was destroyed by the accident.

must of. Nonstandard. Use **must have** instead.

> **Incorrect:** Someone **must of** read the book.

> **Correct:** Someone **must have** read the book.

Native American. The term now preferred by many people formerly described as American Indian.

nice. This adjective has little impact when used to mean "pleasant": It was a **nice** day; Sally is a **nice** person. In many cases, **nice** is damning with faint praise. Find a more specific word or expression. **Nice** can be used effectively to mean "precise" or "fine."

> There was a **nice** distinction between the two positions.

nohow. Nonstandard for **not at all** and **under any conditions.**

> **Incorrect:** Mrs. Mahajan wouldn't talk **nohow.**
>
> **Correct:** Mrs. Mahajan wouldn't talk **at all.**

nowheres. Nonstandard version of **nowhere** or **anywhere.**

> **Incorrect:** The chemist couldn't locate the test tube **nowheres.** It was **nowheres** to be found.
>
> **Correct:** The chemist couldn't locate the test tube **anywhere.** It was **nowhere** to be found.

number/amount. See **amount/number.**

off of. A wordy expression. **Off** is sufficient.

> Arthur drove his Jeep **off** the road.

O.K., OK, okay. Not the best choice for formal writing, but give the expression respect. It's an internationally recognized expression of approval. OK?

Oriental. A term falling out of favor as a description of the people or cultures of East Asia. Terms preferred are *Asian* or *East Asian*.

passed/past. Be careful not to confuse these words. **Passed** is a verb form; **past** can function as a noun, adjective, adverb, or preposition. The words are not interchangeable. Study the differences in the following sentences.

> *Passed* **as Verb, Past Tense:** Tina **passed** her economics examination.
>
> *Passed* **as Verb, Past Participle:** Earlier in the day she had **passed** an English quiz.

> *Past* **as Noun:** In the **past,** she did well.
>
> *Past* **as Adjective:** In the **past** semester, she got straight *A*'s.
>
> *Past* **as Adverb:** Smiling, Tina walked **past** the teacher.
>
> *Past* **as Preposition:** Although it was **past** midnight, Tina was still celebrating.

persecute/prosecute. Persecute means "to oppress" or "to torment"; **prosecute** is a legal term, meaning "to bring charges or legal proceedings" against someone or something.

> Connie Lim felt **persecuted** by criticisms of her political activism.
>
> She threatened to **prosecute** anyone who interfered with her First Amendment rights.

personal/personnel. Notice the difference between these words. **Personal** refers to what is private, belonging to an individual. **Personnel** refers to the people staffing an office or institution.

> Drug testing all airline **personnel** would infringe upon **personal** freedom.

phenomena/phenomenon. You can win friends and influence people by spelling these words correctly and using **phenomenon** as the singular form.

> The astral **phenomenon** of meteor showers is common in August.
>
> Many other astral **phenomena** are linked to particular seasons.

plurality/majority. See **majority/plurality.**

plus. Don't use **plus** as a conjunction or conjunctive adverb meaning "and," "moreover," "besides," or "in addition to."

> **Not:** Mr. Burton admitted to cheating on his income taxes this year. **Plus** he acknowledged that he had filed false returns for the last three years.

> **Revised:** Mr. Burton admitted to cheating on his income taxes this year. **Moreover,** he acknowledged that he had filed false returns for the last three years.

prejudice/prejudiced. Many writers and speakers use **prejudice** when they need **prejudiced.** **Prejudice** is a noun; **prejudiced** is a verb form.

> **Incorrect:** Joe Kamakura is **prejudice** against liberals.

> **Correct:** Joe Kamakura is **prejudiced** against liberals.

> **Incorrect: Prejudice** people are found in every walk of life.

> **Correct: Prejudiced** people are found in every walk of life.

> **Correct: Prejudice** is found in every walk of life.

principal/principle. Two terms commonly confused because of their multiple meanings. **Principal** means "chief" or "most important." It also names the head of an elementary or secondary school. (Remember, the **principal** is your pal.). Finally, it can refer to a sum of money lent or borrowed.

> Ike intended to be the **principal** breadwinner of the household.

> Bernice accused Ike of acting like a power-mad high school **principal.**

> She argued that they would need two incomes just to meet their mortgage payments—both interest and **principal.**

A **principle,** on the other hand, is a guiding rule or fundamental truth.

> Ike declared it was against his **principles** to have his wife work.

prioritize. Many readers object to this word, regarding it as less appropriate than its equivalents: **rank** or **list in order of priority.**

proceed to. A wordy and redundant construction when it merely delays the real action of a sentence.

> **Wordy:** We **proceeded to** open the strongbox.

> **Tight:** We **opened** the strongbox.

quote. Some people do not accept **quote** used as a noun. To be safe, use **quotation** in formal writing.

real. Often used as a colloquial version of **very,** as in this sentence: "I was **real** scared." This usage is inappropriate in academic writing.

really. An adverb too vague to make much of an impression in many sentences: It was **really** hot; I am **really** sorry. Replace **really** with a more precise expression, or delete it.

reason is . . . because. The expression is redundant. Use one of the two parts of the expression—not both.

> **Redundant:** The **reason** the cat is ferocious is **because** she is protecting her kittens.
>
> **Revised:** The **reason** the cat is ferocious is **that** she is protecting her kittens.
>
> **Revised:** The cat is ferocious **because** she is protecting her kittens.

refer/allude. See **allude/refer.**

relate to. A colloquial expression used vaguely and too often to mean "to identify with" or "to appreciate."

> **Colloquial:** Bud could **relate to** being a campus football hero.
>
> **Revised:** Bud could **identify with** being a campus football hero.

set/sit. These two verbs can cause problems. Here are their principal parts.

Present	Past	Present Participle	Past Participle
set (put down)	set	setting	set
sit (take a seat)	sat	sitting	sat

It may help you to remember that **to sit** (meaning "to take a seat") is *intransitive*—that is, it doesn't take an object. You can't sit *something*.

> Haskell **sits** under the cottonwood tree.
>
> He **sat** there all afternoon.
>
> He was **sitting** in the hammock yesterday.

He had **sat** there for several weeks.

To set (meaning "to place" or "to put") is *transitive*—it takes an object.

> Jenny **set** a *plate* on the table.
>
> At Christmas, we **set** a *star* atop the tree.
>
> Alex was **setting** the *music* on the stand when it collapsed.
>
> Connie discovered that Travis **had set** a *subpoena* on her desk.

s/he. Most readers object to this construction which, like *he/she* and *she/he,* is an alternative to the nonsexist but clumsy *he or she.* Avoid **s/he.**

should of. Mistaken form of **should have.** Also incorrect are **could of** and **would of.**

sit/set. See **set/sit.**

so. Vague when used as an intensifier, especially when no explanation follows, as in this sentence: Sue Ellen was **so** sad. **So** used this way can sound trite (How sad is **so** sad?) or juvenile (Professor Sweno's play was **so** bad.) If you use **so,** complete your statement.

> Sue Ellen was **so** sad she cried for an hour.
>
> Professor Sweno's play was **so** bad that the audience cheered for the villains.

stationary/stationery. **Stationary**, an adjective, means "immovable, fixed in place." **Stationery** is a noun meaning "writing material." The words are not interchangeable.

supposed to. Many writers forget the **d** at the end of **suppose** when the word is used with auxiliary verbs.

> **Incorrect:** Calina was **suppose to** check her inventory.
>
> **Correct:** Calina was **suppose̲d to** check her inventory.

than/then. These words are occasionally confused. **Than** is a conjunction expressing difference or comparison; **then** is an adverb expressing time.

> If the film is playing tomorrow, Shannon would rather go **then than** today.

theirselves. A nonstandard form. Use **themselves** instead.

> **Incorrect:** All the strikers placed **theirselves** in jeopardy.
>
> **Correct:** All the strikers placed **themselves** in jeopardy.

then/than. See **than/then.**

this. As a pronoun, **this** is sometimes vague and in need of clarification.

> **Vague:** We could fix the car if you had more time or I owned the proper tools. Of course, **this** is always a problem.
>
> **Clear:** We could fix the car if you had more time or I owned the proper tools. Of course, **my lack of proper tools** is always a problem.

This (and **these**) may be inappropriate when used informally as demonstrative adjectives that refer to objects not previously mentioned.

> **Inappropriate *This*:** Jim owns **this** huge Harley motorcycle.
>
> **Inappropriate *These*:** After she moved out, we found **these** really ugly roaches in her apartment.

Such forms are common in speech but should not appear in writing.

> **Revised:** Jim owns **a** huge Harley motorcycle.
>
> **Revised:** After she moved out, we found ugly roaches in her apartment.

throne/thrown. A surprising number of writers use **thrown** when they mean **throne.**

> Charles I was **thrown** from his **throne** by an angry army of Puritans.

thusly. A fussy, nonstandard form. Don't use it. **Thus** is stuffy enough without the *-ly.*

till/until. Until is used more often than **till** in school and business writing, though the words are usually interchangeable. No apostrophe is used with **till.** You may occasionally see the poetic form **'til,** but don't use it in academic or business writing.

to/too. Most people know the difference between these words. However, a writer in a hurry can easily put down the preposition **to** when the adverb **too** is intended. If you make this error often, check for it when you edit.

Incorrect: Coach Rhoades was **to** surprised to speak after his team won its first game in four years.

Correct: Coach Rhoades was **too** surprised to speak after his team won its first game in four years.

toward/towards. Toward is preferred, though either form is fine.

try and. An informal expression. In writing, use **try to** instead.

Informal: After its defeat, the soccer team decided to **try and** drown its sorrows.

Formal: After its defeat, the soccer team decided to **try to** drown its sorrows.

TV. This abbreviation for *television* is common, but in most writing it is still preferable to write out the entire word. The abbreviation is usually capitalized.

type. You can usually delete this word.

Wordy: Hector was a polite **type** of guy.

Revised: Hector was polite.

uninterested/disinterested. See **disinterested/uninterested.**

unique. Something **unique** is one of a kind. It can't be compared with anything else, so expressions such as *most* unique, *more* unique, or very unique don't make sense. The word **unique**, when used properly, should stand alone.

Incorrect: Joe Rhoades's coaching methods were **very unique.**

Correct: Joe Rhoades's coaching methods were **unique.**

Quite often **unique** appears when another, more specific adjective is appropriate.

Incorrect: The **most unique** merchant on the block was Tong-chai.

Correct: The **most inventive** merchant on the block was Tong-chai.

until/till. See **till/until.**

used to. Many writers forget the **d** at the end of **use.**

Incorrect: Leroy was **use to** studying after soccer practice.

Correct: Leroy was **used to** studying after soccer practice.

utilize. Many readers prefer the simpler term **use.**

Pretentious: Mr. Ringling **utilized** his gavel to regain the crowd's attention.

Revised: Mr. Ringling **used** his gavel to regain the crowd's attention.

very. Many teachers and editors will delete **very** almost every time it appears. Overuse has deadened the impact of the word. Whenever possible, use a more specific term or expression.

Weak: I was **very angry.**

Revised: I was **furious.**

well/good. See **good/well.**

who/whom. Use **who** when the pronoun is a subject; use **whom** when it is an object.

Who wrote the ticket?

To whom was the ticket given?

-wise. Don't add **-wise** to the end of a word to mean "with respect to." Many people object to word coinages such as *sportswise, weatherwise,* and *healthwise.* However, a number of common and acceptable English expressions do end in **-wise:** *clockwise, lengthwise, otherwise.* When in doubt about an expression, check a dictionary.

with regards to. Drop the **s** in **regards.** The correct expression is **with regard to.**

won't. Writers sometimes forget the apostrophe in this and other contractions: **can't, don't.**

would of. Mistaken form of **would have.** Also incorrect are **could of** and **should of.**

you all. Southern expression for *you,* singular or plural. It is not used in academic writing.

you're/your. Homonyms that often get switched. **You're** is the contraction for *you are;* **your** is a possessive form.

You're certain Maxine has been to Java?

Your certainty on this matter may be important.

index

Books
in APA style documentation: in-text
citations, 240–241, 244–245;
references page, 240–241, 244–245
in CMS style documentation: bibliographies, 232, 234–235; in-text
citations, 231–232, 234–235
library catalogs and, 163–164,
165–166, 170, 171
in MLA style documentation, 195–199;
in-text notes, 190–192; Works
Cited lists, 193
Brackets ([ ]), 141, 180
Brainstorming, 10
British, 292
Brochure, model document, 278–279
Bulletins, in MLA style documentation, 202
Business letter, model document, 282–283
but
comma with, 124, 126
as coordinating conjunction, 57–58,
77, 124, 126
but what, 292

can, may, 292
cannot, 292
can't, 292
can't hardly, 292
Capitalization, 144–146, 148
Cards
bibliography, 172–173
note, 173–174
Cartoons, in MLA style documentation,
201–202
Case, pronoun, 103–106
Causation adverbs, in transitions, 26
cause, 113
Cause and effect structure, in paragraphs,
24
CD-ROM/diskette databases, in MLA style
documentation, 204–205
censor/censure, 293
challenge, 113

Charts, 65
"chartjunk" and, 186–187
in design process, 269, 270
identifying sources for, 178
for presenting information, 65
models of, 270
Chicago Manual of Style documentation.
See CMS style documentation
Choice, slashes to indicate, 142
"Chunking," writing, 65
Civil language, 40–41, 42–43, 51–54
Claim-and-support arguments, 42, 43
Claims and illustrations, paragraph unity
and, 22–23
Clarity in writing, 64–65, 137
Class distinctions, 54, 145
Classification for development, 25
Clauses. *See also* Independent clauses;
Subordinate (dependent) clauses
commas with, 122–123, 128
nonrestrictive, 106
relative, 74–75
restrictive, 106
Closing paragraphs, 30–31
CMS style documentation, 230–237
bibliographies, 232–237
footnotes and endnotes, 230–232, 234–237
form directory, 234–237
Collaboration, 19–20, 38, 181
Collective nouns
pronouns referring to, 101–102
subject-verb agreement with, 88
College papers, guidelines for, 44
Colloquial language, 49
Colon (:), 130–131
capitalization following, 144
preceding a list, 130
with quotation marks, 135
Comma (,), 122–126
with absolute modifiers, 123
after conjunctive adverbs, 122
after exclamations in middle of
sentence, 119–120

after introductory clauses, 122
conventional uses of, 126
with coordinating conjunctions, 124
in dates, 126, 150
with ellipses, 138
enclosing function, 123–124
with independent clauses, 124–126, 128
linking function, 124–125
with nonrestrictive modifiers 123
in numbers, 126, 150
with quotation marks, 134, 135
separation function, 122–123
unnecessary, 125–126
Commands, 118, 119
Comma splices, 76–77, 128
Common knowledge, 178
Comparatives, 84
Comparison(s)
analogies as, 25, 70
parallelism and, 59–60
pronoun case in, 105
Comparison and contrast for development,
in paragraphs, 26
Complex sentences, 67, 68
Compound-complex sentences, 67, 68
Compound nouns, 139
Compound sentences, 67, 68, 124
Compound words
apostrophes to show possession in,
146–147
hyphens in, 139
Computers. *See also* Electronic media;
E-mail; Internet; World Wide Web
drafting on, 16
on-line catalogs, 163–164, 165–166, 170
paragraphs and, 31–32
spelling checker, 155
in topic selection, 11
tracking new ideas on, 17
Computer software
in APA style documentation, 247
in CMS style documentation, 237
in MLA style documentation, 203

Conclusion of paper
   in drafting process, 37–38
   strong, 18
   testing introduction against, 185
Congressional Record, 202–203
   Conjunctions. *See* Coordinating
      conjunctions; Subordinating
      conjunctions
Conjunctive adverbs
   commas after, 122–123
   frequently used, 129
   semicolons with, 128
Connotative language, 50–51, 156
conscience/conscious, 293
consensus, 293
consequently, 26, 128, 129
contact, 293
Contractions, apostrophes in, 146–147
Contrasts
   commas and, 122, 123
   similarity and contrast terms, 26
convince, 113
Coordinate adjectives, commas with, 125
Coordinating conjunctions
   capitalizing, in titles, 144
   commas before, 124, 126
   comma splices and, 77
   with independent clauses, 57–58
   semicolons and, 128
Coordination, 57–58
could of/would of/should of, 293
Count nouns, 113
couple of, 293
credible/credulous, 293
crippled, 53
criteria, criterion, 293
Critical thinking, 40–44
curriculum, curricula, 293–294

Dangling modifiers, 83–84
Dash (—), 131, 138–139
Databases, in MLA style documentation,
   204–205

data/datum, 294
Data-to-conclusion arguments, 41–42
Dates
   commas in, 126, 150
   question marks with uncertain, 118
Decimals, 118
Definite articles, 113
Definitions for development, 24–25
Degrees
   abbreviating, 148
   commas with, 126
Deletions. *See* Omissions
Demonstrative pronouns, 26
Denotative language, 50–51, 156
Dependent clauses. *See* Subordinate
   (dependent) clauses
Derision, quotation marks to show, 135
Designing documents, 264–270
Desktop publishing, 264–270
Details, specific, 64
Diagrams, identifying sources for, 178
Dialogue. *See also* Quotations, direct
   colons to introduce, 130
   dashes to highlight interruptions in, 138
   quotation marks to mark, 134
Dictionaries, 152–153, 155–156, 167
different from/different than, 294
Direct objects, with transitive verbs, 111
Disability, bias and, 53
Discovery drafts, 17
discreet/discrete, 294
disinterested/uninterested, 294
Dissertations, in MLA style documentation,
   199
Document design. *See* Designing documents
Dollar sign ($), 149
don't, 294
Double negatives, 82–83
Downshifting, 64
Drafting a paper, 16–20
   audience in, 35
   developing points in, 36
   editing in, 18–20, 36–38

proofreading in, 20, 38
   revision in, 19–20, 34–36
Drafts
   evaluating, 18–19
   responding to, 19–20
   revising, 34–36
Drama, in MLA style documentation, 208
due to/because of. See because of/due to
due to the fact that, 294

each, 102
Economic groups, 54, 145
Economy in writing, 65–67
Edited works
   in APA style documentation, 245
   in MLA style documentation, 195, 196
Editing
   for adverb placement, 82
   for bias in language, 54
   in drafting process, 18–20, 36–38
   of introductory modifying phrases, 83
   premature, 16
   for subject/verb agreement, 88
Editorials, in MLA style documentation, 201
effect/affect. See affect/effect
either, 102
either . . . or
   pronoun agreement and, 103
   subject-verb agreement and, 87
elderly, 53
Electronic media. *See also* Computers;
      E-mail; Internet; World Wide Web
   addresses, 118, 142
   paragraphs in, 31–32
   punctuation in, 118, 142
   as source for research, 162, 163–166,
      169–172; ACW style documenta-
      tion, 226–228; APA style documen-
      tation, 243, 247–248; CMS style
      documentation, 237; MLA style
      documentation, 194, 203–205
Electronic style, 31–32, 284–287
elicit/illicit, 294

Introduction/body/conclusion structure for development, 13
Introduction of paper
  in drafting process, 37–38
  opening paragraphs in, 16, 28–30
  testing conclusion against, 185
Introductory phrases and clauses, commas after, 122
Inverted sentence order, 89–90
invite, 113
Irony, quotation marks to show, 135
irregardless, 298
Irregular verbs, 94–95
irritate/aggravate. See aggravate/irritate
it
  reference of, 100–101
  without antecedent, 101
Italics, 135, 136–137
it is, 66
its/it's, 147, 298

Job application, model document, 282–283
Joint ownership, apostrophes to show, 147
Journal articles. *See* Articles, in works
Journalist's questions, 17
judgment/judgement, 298

Key facts, in opening paragraph, 30
Keyword searches, 164, 166, 169, 170
kind of, 298

Language
  bias in. *See* Bias in language
  civil, 40–41, 42–43, 51–54
  connotative, 50–51, 156
  denotative, 50–51, 156
  foreign, 136–137, 197–198
  levels of, 48–49
later, in transitions, 26
Lectures, in MLA style documentation, 207
lesbian, 53
less than. See fewer than/less than

Letters
  in MLA style documentation, 207
  model document, 282–283
  salutation, commas in, 126
Libraries
  bibliographical indexes, 12
  browsing, in topic selection, 11
  catalogs, 163–164, 165–166, 170, 171
  periodical indexes, 164–166, 168, 169, 171
lie/lay, 298–299
like/as, 299
likewise, in transitions, 26
Linking pronouns, for development, 27
Linking verbs, 110–111
  colons with, 130
  predicate adjectives and, 80
  pronoun case after, 105
  subject-verb agreement and, 89
Lists
  bibliographic/Works Cited. *See* Works Cited lists
  colons to introduce, 130
  in electronic communications, 32
  as independent sentences, 75
  parentheses with, 140
  semicolons to introduce, 129
  working, 13
Listserv discussion groups, 172, 204, 228
literally, 299
little, 114
look, as linking verb, 89, 111
lose/loose, 299
-ly
  as adverb ending, 80, 81, 150
  hyphens with, 139

mad, angry. See angry/mad
Magazine articles. *See* Articles, in works
majority/plurality, 299–300
man, as catchall term, 52
man, mankind, 300

many
  as indefinite pronoun, 102
  as quantifier, 114
many times, 300
may, can. See can, may
meanwhile, 129
media/medium, 300
Metaphors, 40–41, 69–70
  mixed metaphor, 69
Mexican American, 300
Microfilm/microfiche, in MLA style documentation, 205
midst/mist, 300
might of, 300
Misplaced modifiers, 83–84
mist/midst. See midst/mist
Mixed metaphor. *See* Metaphors
MLA style documentation, 190–208
  form directory, 195–208
  in-text references, 177, 190–193, 195–208
  Works Cited lists, 182–183, 193–208, 222–224
MLA style papers
  headings in, 185
  quotations in, 181, 191
  sample, 208–224
  tables and figures in, 187
  titles in, 185
Modals, 92–93, 111–112
Model documents, 271–287
Modern Language Association (MLA). *See* MLA style documentation; MLA style papers
Modifiers, 80–84. *See also* Adjective(s); Adverb(s)
  absolute, 81, 83–84, 123
  comparatives, 84
  dangling, 83–84
  double negatives, 82–83
  misplaced, 83–84
  nonrestrictive, 124
  restrictive, 124
  superlatives, 84
  unit, hyphens with, 139

313

tables and figures in, 186–187.
See also Patterns of development
of work area, 16
Oriental, 301
otherwise, 129
our, 147
Outlining, 12
formal sentence outlines in, 13, 14
scratch outlines in, 13, 177
working lists in, 13
Overloaded sentences, 57, 61

p., pp., 240
Pamphlets, in MLA style documentation, 202
Paragraph(s), 22–32
appearance of, 27–28
audience and, 28
closing, 30–31
development of, 24–26
in drafting process, 37
in electronic media, 31–32
long, 28, 29
new, starting, 28
opening, 16, 28–30, 31
short, 28, 29
topic sentences, 22–23
unity of, 22–24
Paragraph sprawl, controlling, 22–24
Parallel construction, 59–60
Parallelism for development, 27
Paraphrasing information, 184
Parentheses ( ), 140–141. *See also* ACW
style documentation; APA style
documentation
passed/past, 301
Passive voice, 95–96
Past perfect tense, 92
Past progressive tense, 92, 109–110
Past tense, 92, 108–110
Patterns of development
analogy, 25, 70
for arguments, 41–42, 43

cause and effect, 24
classification, 25
comparison and contrast, 26
definition, 24–25
evidence to conclusion, 13
introduction/body/conclusion, 13
narration/process, 25–26, 29–30
for paragraphs, 24–26
Pauses, ellipses to indicate, 137
Peer editing. *See* Collaboration
Perfect tenses, 92, 93, 108–110
Period (.), 118
in abbreviations, 118, 147–149
for comma splices, 76–77
with ellipses, 138
with quotation marks, 135
run-on sentences and, 77
Periodical indexes, 164–166, 168, 169, 171
persecute/prosecute, 301
personal/personnel, 301
Personal pronouns, 147
persuade, 113
Persuasive writing, 40–44
phenomena/phenomenon, 301
Photographs, in design process, 269
Phrases. *See also* Prepositional phrases
condensing dependent clauses to, 67
condensing verb, 66
foreign, italics with, 136–137
introductory, commas with, 122
lead in, correcting sprawling, 65
noun, 59
Plagiarism, 181, 184
Planning stage of writing, 17
in document design, 264–265
Plays, in MLA style documentation, 208
plenty of, 114
Plural form
apostrophes to mark, 147
spelling and, 154–155
plurality/majority, 302
Poetry
capitalizing first word in, 144

deletions from, 138
slashes to divide lines of, 141
Political groups, capitalizing, 145
Positive statements, 65
Possessive case, 103–104
apostrophes to indicate, 105–106, 146–147
pronoun, 100, 103–104, 105–106, 147
and pronoun-antecedent agreement, 100
Post hoc, ergo propter hoc, 44
Predicate adjectives, 80
Predication, faulty, 60–61
Prefixes, hyphens with, 139
prejudice/prejudiced, 302
Preparation for writing, 10–11
Prepositional phrases
colons with, 130
reducing number of, 66–67
semicolons between independent
clauses in, 129
Prepositions, capitalizing, in titles, 144
Presentation slide, model document, 274–275
Present perfect progressive tense, 109–110
Present perfect tense, 92, 108–110
Present progressive tense, 92, 109–110
Present tense, 92, 93, 109–110
principal/principle, 302
prioritize, 302
proceed to, 302
Process of writing, 4–5
Procrastination, 16, 18
Professional organizations, 168
Professions
derisive attitudes toward, 54
gender bias and, 52
Pronoun(s), 100–106
agreement and, 100–103
case of, 103–106
demonstrative, 26
indefinite, 87–88, 89, 102–103, 106
linking, 27
negative, 82
personal, 147

verbals versus, 75
voice, 92, 95–96
Verbals
definition of, 75
sentence fragments caused by, 75
very, 139, 305
Videotapes
in APA style documentation, 248
in MLA style documentation, 205
Voice, 92, 95–96

warn, 113
well/good. *See good/well*
when, 58
where
as subordinating conjunction, 58
in transitions, 26
which
introducing modifying clauses with, 106
in modifying human subject, 106
reference of, 100–101
as subordinating conjunction, 58
in transitions, 26
while, 58
White space in documents, 269, 275
who
in modifying human subject, 106
as subordinating conjunction, 58
in transitions, 26
whom, in transitions, 26
who/whom, 104–105, 305–306

-wise, 306
with regards to, 306
won't, 306
Wordiness
in drafting process, 37
eliminating, 65–67
Words
choice of, 36–37
compound, 139, 146–147
condensing dependent clauses to, 67
first, in sentences: capitalizing, 144;
dates as, 150; *here, there*, 89; *it is,
there are*, 66; numerals as, 150
foreign, italics for, 136–137
Working lists, 13
Works Cited lists
in ACW style documentation, 226–228
in APA style documentation, 241–249,
258–259
in CMS style documentation, 232–237
data needed for, 172–173, 174
in MLA style documentation, 182–183,
193–208, 222–224
World Wide Web (WWW), 170–172,
284–285. *See also* Internet
ACW style documentation, 227
addresses: in bibliographic information, 174, 227; slashes to indicate,
142
establishing site on, 32, 181, 284–285
model web page, 284–285

paragraphs on, 32
search tools, 171, 172, 249
would of, 306
Writer's Workshop, 11
Writing process, 4
breaks in, 18
drafting in, 16–20, 35–38
editing in. *See* Editing
myths about writing, 4, 5
procrastination in, 16, 18
proofreading in, 20, 38, 152–153, 155
revision in, 19–20, 34–36, 100
stages of, 5
starting, 16
Writing situation, 4–7
audience, 6–7
connotative versus denotative language
and, 51
purpose, 6, 7, 34
topic selection, 6
WWW. *See* World Wide Web

Yahoo, 171, 249
yet
comma with, 124, 126
as coordinating conjunction, 57–58,
77, 124, 126
in transitions, 26
you all, 306
your, 147
your/you're, 306

319

index